HOW TO TEACH

MJP
PUBLISHERS

HOW TO TEACH

George Drayton Strayer

&

Naomi Norsworthy

Chennai   New Delhi   Tirunelveli

Honour Copyright
&
Exclude Piracy

This book is protected by copyright. Reproduction of any part in any form including photocopying shall not be done except with authorization from the publisher.

ISBN 978-93-87488-43-4   **MJP Publishers**

All rights reserved   No. 44, Nallathambi Street,
Printed and bound in India   Triplicane, Chennai 600 005

MJP 404   © Publishers, 2018

Publisher : C. Janarthanan

Project Editor : C. Ambica

PUBLISHER'S NOTE

The legacy of a country is in its varied cultural heritage, historical literature, developments in the field of economy and science. The top nations in the world are competing in the field of science, economy and literature. This vast legacy has to be conserved and documented so that it can be bestowed to the future generation. The knowledge of this legacy is slowly getting perished in the present generation due to lack of documentation.

Keeping this in mind, the concern with retrospective acquiring of rare books has been accented recently by the burgconing reprint industry. MJP Publishers is gratified to retrieve the rare collections with a view to bring back those books that were landmarks in their time.

In this effort, a series of rare books would be republished under the banner, "MJP Publishers". The books in the reprint series have been carefully selected for their contemporary usefulness as well as their historical importance within the intellectual. We reconstruct the book with slight enhancements made for better presentation, without affecting the contents of the original edition.

Most of the works selected for republishing covers a huge range of subjects, from history to anthropology. We believe this reprint edition will be a service to the numerous researchers and practitioners active in this fascinating field. We allow readers to experience the wonder of peering into a scholarly work of the highest order and seminal significance.

MJP Publishers

PREFACE

The art of teaching is based primarily upon the science of psychology. In this book the authors have sought to make clear the principles of psychology which are involved in teaching, and to show definitely their application in the work of the classroom. The book has been written in language as free from technical terms as is possible.

In a discussion of the methods of teaching it is necessary to consider the ends or aims involved, as well as the process. The authors have, on this account, included a chapter on the work of the teacher, in which is discussed the aims of education. The success or failure of the work of a teacher is determined by the changes which are brought to pass in the children who are being taught. This book, therefore, includes a chapter on the measurement of the achievements of children. Throughout the book the discussion of the art of teaching is always modified by an acceptance upon the part of the writers of the social purpose of education. The treatment of each topic will be found to be based -upon investigations and researches in the fields of psychology and education which involve the measurement of the achievements of children and of adults under varying conditions. Wherever possible, the relation between the principle of teaching laid down and the scientific inquiry upon which it is based is indicated.

Any careful study of the mental life and development of children reveals at the same time the unity and the diversity of the process involved. For the sake of definiteness and clearness, the authors have differentiated between types of mental activity and the corresponding types of classroom exercises. They have, at the same time, sought to make clear the interdependence of the various aspects of teaching method and the unity involved in mental development.

George Drayton Strayer

Naomi Norsworthy

November 15, 1916

Contents

I

The Work of the Teacher

Education is a group enterprise. We establish schools in which we seek to develop whatever capacities or abilities the individual may possess in order that he may become intelligently active for the common good. Schools do not exist primarily for the individual, but, rather, for the group of which he is a member. Individual growth and development are significant in terms of their meaning for the welfare of the whole group. We believe that the greatest opportunity for the individual, as well as his greatest satisfaction, are secured only when he works with others for the common welfare. In the discussions which follow we are concerned not simply with the individual's development, but also with the necessity for inhibitions. There are traits or activities which develop normally, but which are from the social point of view undesirable. It is quite as much the work of the teacher to know how to provide for the inhibition of the type of activity which is socially undesirable, or how to substitute for such reactions other forms of expression which are worthy, as it is to stimulate those types of activity which promise a contribution to the common good. It is assumed that the aim of education can be expressed most satisfactorily in terms of social efficiency.

An acceptance of the aim of education stated in terms of social efficiency leads us to discard other statements of aim which have been more or less current. Chief among these aims, or statements of aim, are the following:

(1)   culture;

(2)   the harmonious development of the capacities or abilities of the individual;

(3)   preparing an individual to make a living;

(4)   knowledge.

We will examine these aims briefly before discussing at length the implications of the social aim.

Those who declare that it is the aim of education to develop men and women of culture vary in the content which they give to the term culture. It is conceivable that the person of culture is one who, by virtue of his education, has come to understand and appreciate the many aspects of the social environment in which he lives; that he is a man of intelligence, essentially reasonable; and that he is willing and able to devote himself to the common good. It is to be feared, however, that the term culture, as commonly used, is interpreted much more narrowly. For many people culture is synonymous with knowledge or information, and is not interpreted to involve preparation for active participation in the work of the world. Still others think of the person of culture as one who has a type or kind of training which separates him from the ordinary man. A more or less popular notion of the man of culture pictures him as one living apart from those who think through present-day problems and who devote themselves to their solution. It seems best, on account of this variation in interpretation, as well as on account of the unfortunate meaning sometimes attached to the term, to discard this statement of the aim of education.

The difficulty with a statement of aim in terms of the harmonious development of the abilities or capacities possessed by the individual is found in the lack of any criterion by which we may determine the desirability of any particular kind of development or action. We may well ask for what purpose are the capacities or abilities of the individual to be developed. It is possible to develop an ability or capacity for lying, for stealing, or for fighting without a just cause. What society has a right to expect and to demand of our schools is that they develop or nourish certain tendencies to behave, and that they strive earnestly to eliminate or to have inhibited other tendencies just as marked. Another difficulty with the statement of aim in terms of the harmonious development of the capacities is found in the difficulty of interpreting what is meant by harmonious development. Do we mean equal development of each and every capacity, or do we seek to develop each capacity to the maximum of the individual's possibility of training? Are we to try to secure equal development in all directions? Of one thing we can be certain. We cannot secure equality in achievement among individuals who vary in capacity. One boy may make a good mechanic, another a successful business man, and still another a musician. It is only as we read into the statement of harmonious development meanings which do not appear upon the surface, that we can accept this statement as a satisfactory wording of the aim of education.

The narrow utilitarian statement of aim that asserts that the purpose of education is to enable people to make a living neglects to take account of the necessity for social coöperation. The difficulty with this statement of aim is that it is too narrow. We do hope by means of education to help people to make a living, but we ought also to be concerned with the kind of a life they lead. They ought not to make a living by injuring or exploiting others. They ought to be able to enjoy the nobler pleasures as well as to make enough money to buy food, clothing, shelter, and the like. The bread-and-butter aim breaks down as does the all-around development aim because it fails to consider the individual in relation to the social group of which he is a member.

To declare that knowledge is the aim of education is to ignore the issue of the relative worth of that which we call knowledge. No one may know all. What, then, from among all of the facts or principles which are available are we to select and what are we to reject? The knowledge aim gives us no satisfactory answer. We are again thrown back upon the question of purpose. Knowledge we must have, but for the individual who is to live in our modern, industrial, democratic society some knowledges are more important than others. Society cannot afford to permit the school to do anything less than provide that equipment in knowledge, in skill, in ideal, or in appreciation which promises to develop an individual who will contribute to social progress, one who will find his own greatest satisfaction in working for the common good.

In seeking to relate the aim of education to the school activities of boys and girls, it is necessary to inquire concerning the ideals or purposes which actuate

them in their regular school work. *Ideals of service* may be gradually developed, and may eventually come to control in some measure the activities of boys and girls, but these ideals do not normally develop in a school situation in which competition is the dominating factor. We may discuss at great length the desirability of working for others, and we may teach many precepts which look in the direction of service, and still fail to achieve the purpose for which our schools exist. An overemphasis upon marks and distinctions, and a lack of attention to the opportunities which the school offers for helpfulness and coöperation, have often resulted in the development of an individualistic attitude almost entirely opposed to the purpose or aim of education as we commonly accept it.

There is need for much reorganization in our schools in the light of our professed aim. There are only two places in our whole school system where children are commonly so seated that it is easy for them to work in coöperation with each other. In the kindergarten, in the circle, or at the tables, children normally discuss the problems in which they are interested, and help each other in their work. In the seminar room for graduate students in a university, it is not uncommon to find men working together for the solution of problems in which they have a common interest. In most classrooms in elementary and in high schools, and even in colleges, boys and girls are seated in rows, the one back of the other, with little or no opportunity for communication or coöperation. Indeed, helping one's neighbor has often been declared against the rule by teachers. It is true that pupils must in many cases work as individuals for the sake of the attainment of skill, the acquirement of knowledge, or of methods of work, but a school which professes to develop ideals of

service must provide on every possible occasion situations in which children work in coöperation with each other, and in which they measure their success in terms of the contribution which they make toward the achievement of a common end.

The socially efficient individual must not only be actuated by ideals of service, but must in the responses which he makes to social demands be governed by his own careful thinking, or by his ability to distinguish from among those who would influence him one whose solution of the problem presented is based upon careful investigation or inquiry. Especially is it true in a democratic society that the measure of the success of our education is found in the degree to which we develop the scientific attitude. Even those who are actuated by noble motives may, if they trust to their emotions, to their prejudices, or to those superstitions which are commonly accepted, engage in activities which are positively harmful to the social group of which they are members. Our schools should strive to encourage the spirit of inquiry and investigation.

A large part of the work in most elementary schools and high schools consists in having boys and girls repeat what they have heard or read. It is true that such accumulation of facts may, in some cases, either at the time at which they are learned, or later, be used as the basis for thinking; but a teacher may feel satisfied that she has contributed largely toward the development of the scientific spirit upon the part of children only when this inquiring attitude is commonly found in her classroom. The association of ideas which will result from an honest attempt upon the part of boys and girls to find

the solution of a real problem will furnish the very best possible basis for the recall of the facts or information which may be involved. The attempt to remember pages of history or of geography, or the facts of chemistry or of physics, however well they may be organized in the text-book, is usually successful only until the examination period is passed. Children who have engaged in this type of activity quite commonly show an appalling lack of knowledge of the subjects which they have studied a very short time after they have satisfied the examination requirement. The same amount of energy devoted to the solution of problems in which children may be normally interested may be expected not only to develop some appreciation of scientific method in the fields in which they have worked, but also to result in a control of knowledge or a memory of facts that will last over a longer period of time.

Recitations should be places where children meet for the discussion of problems which are vital to them. The question by the pupil should be as common as the question by the teacher. Laboratory periods should not consist of following directions, but rather in undertaking, in so far as it is possible, real experiments. We may not hope that an investigating or inquiring turn of mind encouraged in school will always be found operating in the solution of problems which occur outside of school, but the school which insists merely upon memory and upon following instructions may scarcely claim to have made any considerable contribution to the equipment of citizens of a democracy who should solve their common problems in terms of the evidence presented. The unthinking acceptance of the words of the book or the statement of the teacher prepares the way for the blind following of the boss, for faith in the demagogue, or even for acceptance of the statements of the quack.

The ideal school situation is one in which the spirit of inquiry and investigation is constantly encouraged and in which children are developing ideals of service by virtue of their *activity*. A high school class in English literature in which children are at work in small groups, asking each other questions and helping each other in the solution of their problems, seems to the writer to afford unusual opportunity for the realization of the social aim of education. A first grade class in beginning reading, in which the stronger children seek to help those who are less able, involves something more significant in education than merely the command of the tool we call reading. A teacher of a class in physics who suggested to his pupils that they find out which was the more economical way to heat their homes,--with hot air, with steam, or with hot water,--evidently hoped to have them use whatever power of investigation they possessed, as well as to have them come to understand and to remember the principles of physics which were involved. In many schools the coöperation of children in the preparation of school plays, or school festivals, in the writing and printing of school papers, in the participation in the school assembly, in the making of shelves, tables, or other school equipment, in the working for community betterment with respect to clean streets and the like, may be considered even more significant from the standpoint of the realization of the social aim of education than are the recitations in which they are commonly engaged.

We have emphasized thus far the meaning of the social aim of education in terms of methods of work upon the part of pupils. It is important to call attention to the fact that the materials or content of education are also determined by the same consideration of purposes. If we really accept the idea of participation upon the part of children in modern social life as the purpose of education, we must include in our courses of study only such subject matter as may be judged to contribute toward the realization of this aim. We must, of course, provide children with the tools of investigation or of inquiry; but their importance should not be overemphasized, and in their acquirement significant experiences with respect to life activities should dominate, rather than the mere acquisition of the tool. Beginning reading, for example, is important not merely from the standpoint of learning to read. The teaching of beginning reading should involve the enlarging and enriching of experience. Thought getting is of primary importance for little children who are to learn to read, and the recognition of symbols is important only in so far as they contribute to this end. The best reading books no longer print meaningless sentences for children to decipher. Mother Goose rhymes, popular stories and fables, language reading lessons, in which children relate their own experience for the teacher to print or write on the board, satisfy the demand for content and aid, by virtue of the interest which is advanced, in the mastering of the symbols.

It is, of course, necessary for one who would understand modern social conditions or problems, to know of the past out of which our modern life has developed. It is also necessary for one who would understand the problems of one community, or of one nation, to know, in so far as it is possible, of the experiences of other peoples. History and geography furnish a background, without which our current problems could not be reasonably attacked. Literature and science, the study of the fine arts, and of our social institutions, all become significant in proportion as they make possible contributions, by the individual who has been educated, to the common good.

Any proper interpretation of the social purpose of education leads inevitably to the conclusion that much that we have taught is of very little significance. Processes in arithmetic which are not used in modern life have little or no worth for the great majority of boys and girls. Partnership settlements involving time, exact interest, the extraction of cube and of square roots, partial payments, and many of the problems in mensuration, might well be omitted from all courses of study in arithmetic. Many of the unimportant dates in history and much of the locational geography should disappear in order that a better appreciation of the larger social movements can be secured, or in order that the laws which control in nature may be taught. In English, any attempt to realize the aim which we have in mind would lay greater stress upon the accomplishment of children in speaking and writing our language, and relatively less upon the rules of grammar.

It may well be asked how our conception of aim can be related to the present tendency to offer a variety of courses of instruction, or to provide different types of schools. The answer is found in an understanding and appreciation of the fact that children vary tremendously in ability, and that the largest contribution by each individual to the welfare of the whole group can be made only when each is trained in the field for which his capacity fits him. The movement for the development of vocational education means, above all else, an attempt to train all members of the group to the highest possible degree of efficiency, instead of offering a common education which, though liberal in its character, is actually neglected or refused by a large part of our population.

Our interest in the physical welfare of children is accounted for by the fact that no individual may make the most significant contribution to the common good who does not enjoy a maximum of physical efficiency. The current emphasis upon moral training can be understood when we accept that conception of morality which measures the individual in terms of his contribution to the welfare of others. However important it may be that individuals be restrained or that they inhibit those impulses which might lead to anti-social activity, of even greater importance must be the part actually played by each member of the social group in the development of the common welfare.

If we think of the problems of teaching in terms of habits to be fixed, we must ask ourselves are these habits desirable or necessary for an individual who is to work as a member of the social group. If we consider the problem of teaching from the standpoint of development in intelligence, we must constantly seek to present problems which are worth while, not simply from the standpoint of the curiosity which they arouse, but also on account of their relation to the life activities with which our modern world is concerned. We must seek to develop the power of appreciating that which is noble and beautiful primarily because the highest efficiency can be secured only by those who use their time in occupations which are truly recreative and not enervating.

As we seek to understand the problem of teaching as determined by the normal mental development of boys and girls, we must have in mind constantly the use to which their capacities and abilities are to be put. Any adequate recognition of the social purpose of education suggests the necessity for eliminating, as far as possible, that type of action which is socially undesirable, while we strive for the development of those capacities which mean at least the possibility of contribution to the common good. We study the principles of teaching in order that we may better adapt ourselves to the children's possibilities of learning, but we must keep in mind constantly that kind of learning and those methods of work which look to the development of socially efficient boys and girls. We must seek to provide situations which are in themselves significant in our modern social life as the subject matter with which children may struggle in accomplishing their individual development. We need constantly to have in mind the ideal of school work which will value most highly opportunities for coöperation and for contribution to the common good upon the part of children, which are in the last analysis entirely like the situations in which older people contribute to social progress. More and more we must seek to develop the type of pupil who knows the meaning of duty and who gladly recognizes his obligations to a social group which is growing larger with each new experience and each new opportunity.

QUESTIONS

1.   Why would you not be satisfied with a statement of the aim of education which was expressed in terms of the harmonious development of an individual's abilities and capacities?

2. Suggest any part of the courses of study now in force in your school system the omission of which would be in accordance with the social aim of education.

3. Name any subjects or parts of subjects which might be added for the sake of realizing the aim of education.

4. How may a teacher who insists upon having children ask permission before they move in the room interfere with the realization of the social aim of education?

5. Can you name any physical habits which may be considered socially undesirable? Desirable?

6. What is the significance of pupil participation in school government?

7. How does the teacher who stands behind his desk at the front of the room interfere with the development of the right social attitude upon the part of pupils?

8. Why is the desire to excel one's own previous record preferable to striving for the highest mark?

9. In one elementary school, products of the school garden were sold and from the funds thus secured apparatus for the playground was bought. In another school, children sold the vegetables and kept the money. Which, in your judgment, was the most worth while from the standpoint of the social development of boys and girls?

10. A teacher of Latin had children collect words of Latin origin, references to Latin characters, and

even advertisements in which Latin words or literary references were to be found. The children in the class were enthusiastic in making these collections, and considerable interest was added to the work in Latin. Are you able to discover in the exercise any other value?

11.   Describe some teaching in which you have recently engaged, or which you have observed, in which the methods of work employed by teacher and pupils seemed to you to contribute to a realization of the social purpose of education.

12.   How can a reading lesson in the sixth grade, or a history lesson in the high school, be conducted to make children feel that they are doing something for the whole group?

13.   In what activities may children engage outside of school which may count toward the betterment of the community in which they live?

II

Original Nature, The Capital With Which Teachers Work

After deciding upon the aims of education, the goals towards which all teaching must strive, the fundamental question to be answered is, "What have we to work with?" "What is the makeup with which children start in life?" Given a certain nature, certain definite results are possible; but if the nature is different, the results must of necessity differ. The possibility of education or of teaching along any line depends upon the presence of an original nature which possesses corresponding abilities. The development of intellect, of character, of interest, or of any other trait depends absolutely upon the presence in human beings of capacity for growth or development. What the child inherits, his original nature, is the capital with which education must work; beyond the limits which are determined by inheritance education cannot go.

All original nature is in terms of a nervous system. What a child inherits is not ideas, or feelings, or habits, as such, but a nervous system whose correlate is human intelligence and emotion. Just what relationship exists between the action of the nervous system and consciousness or intellect or emotion is still an open question and need not be discussed here. One thing seems fairly certain, that the original of any individual is bound up in some way with the kind of nervous system he has inherited. What we have in common, as a human race, of imagination, or reason, or tact, or skill is correlated in some fashion to the inheritance of a human nervous system. What we have as individual abilities, which distinguish us from our fellows, depends primarily upon our family inheritance. Certain traits such as interest in people, and accuracy in perception of details, seem to be dependent upon the sex inheritance. All traits, whether racial, or family, or sex, are inherited in terms of a plastic nervous system.

The racial inheritance, the capital which all normal children bring into the world, is usually discussed under several heads: reflexes, physiological actions, impulsive actions, instincts, capacities, etc., the particular heads chosen varying with the author. They all depend for their existence upon the fact that certain bonds of connection are performed in the nervous system. Just what this connection is which is found between the nerve cells is still open to question. It may be chemical or it may be electrical. We know it is not a growing together of the neurones,[1] but further than that nothing is definitely known.

---

1. The nervous system is composed of units of structure called neurones or nerve cells. "If we could see exactly the structure of the brain itself, we should find it to consist of millions of similar neurones each resembling a bit of string frayed out at both ends and here and there along its course. So also the nerves going out to the muscles are simply bundles of such neurones, each of which by itself is a thread-like connection between the cells of the spinal cord or brain and some muscle. The nervous system is simply the sum total of all these neurones, which form an almost infinitely complex system of connections between the sense organs and the muscles."

    The word synapses, meaning clasping together, is used as a descriptive term for the connections that exist between neurone and neurone.

That there are very definite pathways of discharge developed by the laws of inner growth and independent of individual learning, there can be no doubt. This of course means that in the early days of a child's life, and later in so far as he is governed by these inborn tendencies, his conduct is machine-like and blind--with no purpose and no consciousness controlling or initiating the responses. Only after experience and learning have had an opportunity to influence these responses can the child be held responsible for his conduct, for only then does his conduct become conscious instead of merely physiological.

There are many facts concerning the psychology of these inborn tendencies that are interesting and important from a purely theoretical point of view, but only those which are of primary importance in teaching will be considered here. A fact that is often overlooked by teachers is that these inborn tendencies to connections of various kinds exist in the intellectual and emotional fields just as truly as in the field of action or motor response. The capacity to think in terms of words and of generals; to understand relationships; to remember; to imagine; to be satisfied with thinking,--all these, as well as such special abilities as skill in music, in managing people or affairs, in tact, or in sympathy, are due to just the same factors as produce fear or curiosity. These former types of tendencies differ from the latter in complexity of situation and response, in definiteness of response, in variability amongst individuals of the same family, and in modifiability; but in the essential element they do not differ from the more evident inborn tendencies.

Just what these original tendencies are and just what the situations are to which they come as responses are both unknown except in a very few instances. The psychology of original nature has enumerated the so-called instincts and discussed a few of their characteristics, but has left almost untouched the inborn capacities that are more peculiarly human. Even the treatment of instincts has been misleading. For instance, instincts have been discussed under such heads as the "self-preservative instincts," "the social instincts," just as if the child had an inborn, mystical something that told him how to preserve his life, or become a social king. Original nature does not work in that way; it is only as the experience of the individual modifies the blind instinctive responses through learning that these results can just as easily come about unless the care of parents provides the right sort of surroundings. There is nothing in the child's natural makeup that warns him against eating pins and buttons and poisonous berries, or encourages him to eat milk and eggs and cereal instead of cake and sweets. He will do one sort of thing just as easily as the other. All nature provides him with is a blind tendency to put all objects that attract his attention into his mouth. This response may preserve his life or destroy it, depending on the conditions in which he lives. The same thing is true of the "social instinct"--the child may become the most selfish egotist imaginable or the most self-sacrificing of men, according as his surroundings and training influence the original tendencies towards behavior to other people in one way or the other. Of course it is very evident that no one has ever consistently lived up to the idea indicated by such a treatment of original nature, but certain tendencies in education are traceable to such psychology. What the child has by nature is neither good nor bad, right nor wrong--it may become either according to the habits which grow out of these tendencies. A child's inborn nature cannot determine the goal of his education. His nature has remained practically the same from the days of primitive man, while the goals of education have changed. What nature does provide is an immense number of definite responses to definite situations. These provide the capital which education and training may use as it will.

It is just because education does need to use these tendencies as capital that the lack of knowledge of just what the responses are is such a serious one. And yet the difficulties of determining just what original nature gives are so tremendous that the task seems a hopeless one to many investigators. The fact that in the human being these tendencies are so easily modified means that from the first they are being influenced and changed by the experiences of the child. Because of the quality of our inheritance the response to a situation is not a one-to-one affair, like a key in a lock, but all sorts of minor causes in the individual are operative in determining his response; and, on the other side, situations are so complex in themselves that they contain that which may call out several different instincts. For example, a child's response to an animal will be influenced by his own physical condition, emotional attitude, and recent mental status and by the conditions of size and nearness of the animal, whether it is shaggy or not, moving or still, whether he is alone or with others, on the floor or in his chair, and the like. It will depend on just how these factors combine as to whether the response is one of fear, of curiosity, of manipulation, or of friendliness. When to these facts are added the fact that the age and previous habits of the child also influence his response, the immense complexity of the problem of discovering just what the situations are to which there are original tendencies to respond and just how these tendencies show themselves is evident. And yet this is what psychologists must finally do if the use by teachers of these tendencies is to be both economical and wise. Just as an illustration of the possibilities of analysis, Thorndike in his "Original Nature of Man" lists eleven different situations which call out an instinctive expression of fear and thirty-one different responses which may occur in that expression. Under fighting he says, "There seem, indeed, to be at least six separable sets of connections in the so-called 'fighting instinct,'" in each of which the situation and the response differ from any other one.

Very few of the instincts are present at birth; most of them develop later in the child's life. Pillsbury says, "One may recognize the food-taking instincts, the vocal protests at discomfort, but relatively few others." This delay in the appearance of instincts and capacities is dependent upon the development of the nervous system. No one of them can appear until the connections between nerve centers are ready, making the path of discharge perfect. Just when these various nervous connections mature, and therefore just when the respective tendencies should appear, is largely unknown. In only a few of the most prominent and comparatively simple responses is it even approximately known. Holding the head up is accomplished about the fourth month, walking and talking somewhere near the twelfth, but the more complex the tendency and the more they involve intellectual factors, the greater is the uncertainty as to the time of development. We are told that fear is most prominent at about "three or four" years of age, spontaneous imitation "becomes very prominent the latter part of the first year," the gang instinct is characteristic of the preadolescent period, desire for adventure shows itself in early adolescence, altruism "appears in the early teens," and the sex instinct "after about a dozen years of life." The child of from four to six is largely sensory, from seven to nine he is motor, from then to twelve the retentive powers are prominent. In the adolescent period he is capable of thinking logically and reasoning, while maturity finds him a man of responsibilities and affairs. Although there is some truth in the belief that certain tendencies are more prominent at certain periods in the development of the child than at others, still it must be borne in mind that just when these optimum periods occur is not known. Three of the most important reasons for this lack of knowledge are: first, the fact that all inborn tendencies mature gradually and do not burst into being; second, we do not know how transitory they are; and, third, the fact of the great influence of environment in stimulating or repressing such capacities.

Although the tendency to make collections is most prominent at nine, the beginnings of it may be found before the child is five. Moll finds that the sex instinct begins its development at about six years of age, despite the fact that it is always quoted as the adolescent instinct. Children in the kindergarten can think out their little problems purposively, even though reasoning is supposed to mark the high school pupil. The elements of most tendencies show themselves early in crude, almost unrecognizable, beginnings, and from these they grow gradually to maturity.

In the second place how quickly do these tendencies fade? How transitory are they? It has always been stated in general psychology that instincts are transitory, that therefore it was the business of teachers to strike while the iron was hot, to seize the wave of interest or response at its crest before the ebb had begun. There was supposed to be a "happy moment for fixing in children skill in drawing, for making collections in natural history," for developing the appreciative emotions, for training the social instinct, or the memory or the imagination. Children are supposed to be interested and attracted by novelty, rhythm, and movement,--to be creatures of play and imagination and to become different merely as a matter of the transitoriness of these tendencies due to growth. When the activities of the adult and the child are analyzed to see what tendencies have really passed, are transitory, it is difficult to find any that have disappeared. True, they have changed their form, have been influenced by the third factor mentioned above, but change the surroundings a little and the tendency appears. Free the adult from the restraints of his ordinary life and turn him out for a holiday and the childish tendencies of interest in novelty and the mysterious, in physical prowess and adventure and play, all make their appearance. In how many adults does the collecting instinct still persist, and the instinct of personal rivalry? In how many has the crude desire for material ownership or the impulse to punish an affront by physical attack died out? Experimental evidence is even proving that the general plasticity of the nervous system, which has always been considered to be transitory, is of very, very much longer duration than has been supposed.

In illustration of the third fact, namely, the effect of environment to stimulate or repress, witness the "little mothers" of five and the wage earners of twelve who have assumed all the responsibilities with all that they entail of maturity. On the other side of the picture is the indulged petted child of fortune who never grows up because he has had everything done for him all his life, and therefore the tendencies which normally might be expected to pass and give place to others remain and those others never appear. That inborn tendencies do wax, reach a maximum, and wane is probably true, but the onset is much more gradual and the waning much less frequent than has been taken for granted. Our ignorance concerning all these matters outweighs our knowledge; only careful experimentation which allows for all the other factors involved can give a reliable answer.

One reason why the facts of delayedness and transitoriness in instincts have been so generally accepted without being thoroughly tested has been the belief in the recapitulation or repeating by the individual of racial development. So long as this was accepted as explaining the development of inborn tendencies and their order of appearance, transitoriness and delayedness must necessarily be postulated. This theory is being seriously questioned by psychologists of note, and even its strongest advocate, President Hall, finds many questions concerning it which cannot be answered.

The chief reasons for its acceptance were first, on logical grounds as an outgrowth of the doctrine of evolution, and second, because of an analogy with the growth of the physical body which was pushed to an extreme. On the physiological side, although there is some likeness between the human embryo and that of the lower animals, still the stages passed through by the two are not the same, being alike only in rough outline, and only in the case of a few of the bodily organs is the series of changes similar. In the case of the physical structure which should be recapitulated most closely, if behavior is to follow the same law,--namely, in that of the brain and nervous system,--there is least evidence of recapitulation. The brain of man does not follow in its development at all the same course taken in the development of brains in the lower animals. And, moreover, it is perfectly possible to explain any similarity or parallelism which does exist between the development of man's embryo and that of lower animals by postulating a general order of development followed by nature as the easiest or most economical, traces of which must then be found in all animal life. When it comes to the actual test of the theory, that of finding actual cases of recapitulation in behavior, it fails. No one has been able to point out just when a child passes through any stage of racial development, and any attempt to do so has resulted in confusion. There is no clear-cut marking off into stages, but, instead, overlapping and coexistence of tendencies characterize the development of the child. The infant of a few days old may show the swimming movements, but at the same time he can support his own weight by clinging to a horizontal stick. Which stage is he recapitulating, that of the fishes or the monkeys? The nine-year-old boy loves to swim, climb trees, and hunt like a savage all at the same period, and, what is more, some of these same tendencies characterize the college man. The late maturing of the sex instinct, so old and strong in the race, and the early appearing of the tendencies towards vocalization and grasping, both of late date in the race, are facts that are hard to explain on the basis of the theory of recapitulation.

As has been already suggested, one of the most important characteristics of all these tendencies is their modifiability. The very ease with which they can be modified suggests that this is what has most often to be done with them. On examination of the lists of original tendencies there are none which can be kept and fixed in the form in which they first appear. Even the best of them are crude and impossible from the standpoint of civilized society. Take as an illustration mother-love; what are the original tendencies and behavior? "All women possess originally, from early childhood to death, some interest in human babies, and a responsiveness to the instinctive looks, calls, gestures, and cries of infancy and childhood, being satisfied by childish gurglings, smiles, and affectionate gestures, and moved to instinctive comforting acts of childish signs of pain, grief, and misery." But the mother has to learn not to cuddle the baby and talk to it all the time it is awake and not to run to it and take it up at every cry, to steel her heart against the wheedling of the coaxing gurgles and even to allow the baby to hurt himself, all for his own good. This comes about only as original nature is modified in line with knowledge and ideals. The same need is evidenced by such a valuable tendency as curiosity. So far as original nature goes, the tendency to attend to novel objects, to human behavior, to explore with the eyes and manipulate with the hands, to enjoy having sensations of all kinds merely for their own sakes, make up what is known as the instinct of curiosity. But what a tremendous amount of modification is necessary before these crude responses result in the valuable scientific curiosity. Not blind following where instinct leads, but modification, must be the watchword.

On the other hand, there are equally few tendencies that could be spared, could be absolutely voted out without loss to the individual or the race. Bullying as an original tendency seems to add nothing to the possibilities of development, but every other inborn tendency has its value. Jealousy, anger, fighting, rivalry, possessiveness, fear, each has its quota to contribute to valuable manhood and womanhood. Again, not suppression but a wise control must be the attitude of the educator. Inhibition of certain phases or elements of some of the tendencies is necessary for the most valuable development of the individual, but the entire loss of any save one or two would be disastrous to some form of adult usefulness or enjoyment. The method by which valuable elements or phases of an original tendency are fixed and strengthened is the general method of habit formation and will be taken up under that head in Chapter IV. When the modification involves definite inhibition, there are three possible methods,--punishment, disuse, and substitution. As an example of the use of the three methods take the case of a child who develops a fear of the dark. In using the first method the child would be punished every time he exhibited fear of the dark. By using the second method he would never be allowed to go into a dark room, a light being left burning in his bedroom, etc., until the tendency to fear the dark had passed. In the third method the emotion of fear would be replaced by that of joy or satisfaction by making the bedtime the occasion for telling a favorite story or for being allowed to have the best-loved toy, or for being played with or cuddled. The situation of darkness might be met in still another way. If the child were old enough, the emotion of courage might replace that of fear by having him make believe he was a soldier or a policeman.

The method of punishment is the usual one, the one most teachers and parents use first. It relies for its effectiveness on the general law of the nervous system that pain tends to weaken the connections with whose activity it is associated. The method is weak in that pain is not a strong enough weapon to break the fundamental connections; it is not known how much of it is necessary to break even weaker ones; it is negative in its results--breaking one connection but replacing it by nothing else. The second method of inhibition is that of disuse. It is possible to inhibit by this means, because lack of use of connections in the nervous system results in atrophy. As a method it is valuable because it does not arouse resistance or anger. It is weak in that as neither the delayedness nor the transitoriness of instincts is known, when to begin to keep the situation from the child, and how long to keep it away in order to provide for the dying out of the connections, are not known. The method is negative and very unsure of results. The method of substitution depends for its use upon the presence in the individual of opposing tendencies and of different levels of development in the same tendency. Because of this fact a certain response to a situation may be inhibited by forming the habit of meeting the situation in another way or of replacing a lower phase of a tendency by a higher one. This method is difficult to handle because of the need of knowledge of the original tendencies of children in general which it implies as well as the knowledge of the capacities and development of the individual child with whom the work is being done. The amount of time and individual attention necessary adds another difficulty. However, it is by far the best method of the three, for it is sure, is economical, using the energy that is provided by nature, is educative, and is positive.

To replace what is poor or harmful by something better is one of the greatest problems of human life--and this is the outcome of the method of substitution. All three methods have their place in a system of education, and certain of them are more in place at certain times than at others, but at all times if the method of substitution can be used it should be.

The instinct of physical activity is one of the most noticeable ones in babyhood. The young baby seems to be in constant movement. Even when asleep, the twitchings and squirmings may continue. This continued muscular activity is necessary because the motor nerves offer the only possible path of discharge at first. As higher centers in the brain are developed, the ingoing currents, aroused by all sense stimuli, find other connections, and ideas, images, trains of thoughts, are aroused, and so the energy is consumed; but at first all that these currents can do is to arouse physical activity. The strength of this instinct is but little diminished by the time the child comes to school. His natural inclination is to do things requiring movement of all the growing muscles. Inhibition, "sitting still," "being quiet," takes real effort on his part, and is extremely fatiguing. This instinct is extremely valuable in several ways: it gives the exercise necessary to a growing body, provides the experience of muscle movements necessary for control, and stimulates mental growth through the increase and variety of experiences it gives.

The tendency to enjoy mental activity, to be satisfied with it for its own sake, is peculiarly a human trait. This capacity shows itself in two important ways--in the interest in sensory stimuli, usually discussed under the head of curiosity, and in the delight in "being a cause" or mental control. The interest in tastes, sounds, sights, touches, etc., merely for their own sake, is very evident in a baby. He spends most of his waking time in just that enjoyment. Though more complex, it is still strong when the child enters school, and for years any object of sense which attracts his attention is material which arouses this instinct. The second form in which the instinct for mental ability shows itself is later in development and involves the secondary brain connections. It is the satisfaction aroused by results of which the individual is the cause. For example, the enjoyment of a child in seeing a ball swing or hearing a whistle blown would be a manifestation of curiosity, while the added interest which is always present when the child not only sees the ball swing but swings it, not only hears the whistle but blows it himself, is a result of the second tendency, that of joy in being a cause. As the child grows older the same tendency shows itself on a higher level when the materials dealt with, instead of being sensations or percepts, are images or ideas. The interest in following out a train of ideas to a logical conclusion, of building "castles in the air," of making plans and getting results, all find their taproot in this instinctive tendency towards mental activity.

In close connection with the general tendency towards physical activity is the instinct of manipulation. From this crude root grows constructiveness and destructiveness. As it shows itself at first it has the elements of neither. The child inherits the tendency to respond by "many different arm, hand, and finger movements to many different objects"--poking, pulling, handling, tearing, piling, digging, and dropping objects. Just what habits of using tools, and the like, will grow out of this tendency will depend on the education and training it gets. The habits of constructiveness may be developed in different sorts of media. The order of their availability is roughly as follows: first, in the use of materials such as wood, clay, raffia, etc.; second, in the use of pencil and brush with color, etc.; third, in the use of words. We should therefore expect and provide for considerable development along manual lines before demanding much in the way of literary expression. Indeed, it may be argued that richness of experience in doing is prerequisite to verbal expression.

Acquisitiveness and collecting are two closely allied tendencies of great strength. Every child has a tendency to approach, grasp, and carry off any object not too large which attracts his attention, and to be satisfied by its mere possession. Blind hoarding and collecting of objects sometimes valueless in themselves results. This instinct is very much influenced in its manifestation by others which are present at the same time, such as the food-getting instinct, rivalry, love of approval, etc. The time at which the tendency to collect seems strongest is at about nine years, judged by the number of collections per child.

Rivalry as an instinct shows itself in increased vigor, in instinctive activity when others are engaged in the same activity, and in satisfaction when superiority is attained. There is probably no inborn tendency whereby these responses of increased vigor and satisfaction are aroused in connection with any kind of activity. We do not try to surpass others in the way we talk or in our moral habits or in our intellectual attainments, as a result of nature, but rather as a result of painstaking education. As an instinct, rivalry is aroused only in connection with other instinctive responses. In getting food, in securing attention or approval, in hunting and collecting, the activity would be increased by seeing another doing the same thing, and satisfaction would be aroused at success or annoyance at failure. The use of rivalry in other activities and at other levels comes as a result of experience.

The fighting responses are called out by a variety of situations. These situations are definite and the responses to them differ from each other. In each case the child tries by physical force of some kind, by scratching, kicking, biting, slapping, throwing, and the like, to change the situation into a more agreeable one. This is true whether he be trying to escape from the restraining arms of his mother or to compel another child to recognize his mastery. Original nature endows us with the pugnacious instinct on the physical level and in connection with situations which for various reasons annoy us. If this is to be raised in its manner of response from the physical to the intellectual level, if the occasions calling it out are to be changed from those that merely annoy one to those which involve the rights of others and matters of principle, it must be as a result of education. Nature provides only this crude root.

Imitation has long been discussed as one of the most important and influential of human instincts. It has been regarded as a big general tendency to attempt to do whatever one saw any one else doing. As such a tendency it does not exist. It is only in certain narrow lines that the tendency to imitate shows itself, such as smiling when smiled at, yelling when others yell, looking and listening, running, crouching, attacking, etc., when others do. To this extent and in similar situations the tendency to imitate seems to be truly an instinct. Imitating in other lines, such as writing as another writes, talking, dressing, acting like a friend, trying to use the methods used by others, etc., are a result of experience and education. The "spontaneous," "dramatic," and "voluntary" imitation discussed by some authors are the stages of development of *habits* of imitation.

The desire to be with others of the same species, the satisfaction at company and the discomfort aroused by solitude, is one of the strongest roots of all social tendencies and customs. It manifests itself in young babies, and continues a strong force throughout life. As an instinct it has nothing to do with either being interested in taking one's share in the duties or pleasures of the group or with being interested in people for their own sakes. It is merely that company makes one comfortable and solitude annoys one. Anything further must come as a result of experience.

Motherliness and kindliness have as their characteristic behavior tendencies to respond by instinctive comforting acts to signs of pain, grief, or misery shown by living things, especially, by children, and by the feeling of satisfaction and the sight of happiness in others. Of course very often these instinctive responses are interfered with by the presence of some other instinct, such as fighting, hunting, ownership, or scorn, but that such tendencies to respond in such situations are a part of the original equipment of man seems beyond dispute. They are possessed by both sexes and manifest themselves in very early childhood.

There are original tendencies to respond both in getting and in giving approval and scorn. By original nature, smiles, pats, admiration, and companionship from one to whom submission is given arouses intense satisfaction; and the withdrawal of such responses, and the expression of scorn or disapproval, excites great discomfort. Even the expression of approval or scorn from any one--a stranger or a servant--brings with it the responses of satisfaction or discomfort. Just as strongly marked are original tendencies which cause responses of approval and cause as a result of "relief from hunger, rescue from fear, gorgeous display, instinctive acts of strength, daring and victory," and responses of scorn "to the observation of empty-handedness, deformity, physical meanness, pusillanimity, and defect." The desire for approval is never outgrown--it is one of the governing forces in society. If it is to be shown or desired on any but this crude level of instinctive response, it can only come by education.

Children come to school with both an original nature determined by their human inheritance and by their more immediate family relationship, and with an education more significant, perhaps, than any which the school can provide. From earliest infancy up to the time of entering a kindergarten or a first grade, the original equipment in terms of instincts, capacities, and abilities has been utilized by the child and directed by his parents and associates in learning to walk and to talk, to conform to certain social standards or requirements, to accept certain rules or precepts, or to act in accordance with certain beliefs or superstitions. The problem which the teacher faces is that of directing and guiding an individual, who is at the same time both educated and in possession of tendencies and capacities which make possible further development.

Not infrequently the education which children have when they come to school may in some measure handicap the teacher. It is unfortunate, but true, that in some homes instinctive tendencies which should have been overcome have been magnified. The control of children is sometimes secured through the utilization of the instinct of fear. The fighting instinct may often have been overdeveloped in a home in which disagreement and nagging, even to the extent of physical violence, have taken the place of reason. Pride and jealousy may have taken deep root on account of the encouragement and approval which have been given by thoughtless adults.

The teacher does not attack the problem of education with a clean slate, but rather it is his to discover what results have already been achieved in the education of the child, whether they be good or bad, for it is in the light of original nature or original tendencies to behave, and in the light of the education already secured, that the teacher must work.

When one realizes the great variety or differences in ability or capacity, as determined by heredity, and when there is added to this difference in original nature the fact of variety in training which children have experienced prior to their school life, he cannot fail to emphasize the necessity for individualizing children. While it is true that we may assume that all children will take delight in achievement, it may be necessary with one child to stir as much as possible the spirit of rivalry, to give as far as one can the delight which comes from success, while for another child in the same class one may need to minimize success on account of a spirit of arrogance which has been developed before school life began. It is possible to conceive of a situation in which some children need to be encouraged to fight, even to the extent of engaging in physical combat, in order to develop a kind of courage which will accept physical discomfort rather than give up a principle or ideal. In the same group there may be children for whom the teacher must work primarily in terms of developing, in so far as he can, the willingness to reason or discuss the issue which may have aroused the fighting instinct.

For all children in elementary and in high schools the possibility of utilizing their original nature for the sake of that development which will result in action which is socially desirable is still present. The problem which the teacher faces will be more or less difficult in proportion as the child's endowment by original nature is large or small, and as previous education has been successful or unsuccessful. The skillful teacher is the one who will constantly seek to utilize to the full those instincts or capacities which seem most potent. This utilization, as has already been pointed out, does not mean a blind following of the instinctive tendencies, but often the substitution of a higher form of action for a lower, which may seem to be related to the instinct in question. It is probably wise to encourage collections of stamps, of pictures, of different kinds of wood, and the like, upon the part of children in the elementary school, provided always that the teacher has in mind the possibility of leading these children, through their interest in objects, to desire to collect ideas. Indeed, a teacher might measure her success in utilizing the collecting instinct in proportion as children become relatively less interested in things collected, and more interested in the ideas suggested by them, or in the mastery of fields of knowledge or investigation in which objects have very little signif-icance. The desire for physical activity upon the part of children is originally satisfied by very crude performanc-es. Development is measured not simply in an increase in manual dexterity, but also in terms of the higher sat-isfaction which may come from producing articles which have artistic merit, or engaging in games of skill which make for the highest physical efficiency.

During the whole period of childhood and adoles-cence we may never assume that the results of previous education, whether they be favorable or unsatisfactory, are permanent. Whether we succeed or not in achieving the ends which we desire, the fact of modifiability, of do-cility, and of plasticity remains. The teacher who seeks to understand the individuals with whom he works, both in terms of their original nature and in terms of their previous education, and who at the same time seeks to substitute for a lower phase of an instinctive tendency a higher one, or who tries to have his pupils respond to a situation by inhibiting a particular tendency by forming the habit of meeting the situation in another way, need not despair of results which are socially desirable.

QUESTIONS

1.   May a teacher ever expect the children in his class to be equal in achievement? Why?

2.   Why is it not possible to educate children satisfac-torily by following where instincts lead?

3.   Which of the instincts seem most strong in the children in your class?

4. Can you give any example of an instinctive tendency which you think should have been outgrown but which seems to persist among your pupils?

5. Give examples of the inhibition of undesirable actions based upon instinctive tendencies by means of (1) punishment, (2) disuse, (3) substitution.

6. How can you use the tendency to enjoy mental activity?

7. Why does building a boat make a stronger appeal to a boy than engaging in manual training exercises which might involve the same amount of activity?

8. Cite examples of collections made by boys and girls in which the ideas associated with the objects collected may be more important than the objects themselves.

9. In what degree are we justified in speaking of the social instinct? The instinct to imitate?

10. How can you use the fighting instinct in your work with children?

11. What can teachers do to influence the education which children have received or are getting outside of school?

12. What differences in action among the children in your class do you attribute to differences in original nature? What to differences in education?

III

Attention and Interest in Teaching

Attention is a function of consciousness. Wherever consciousness is, attention must perforce be present. One cannot exist without the other. According to most psychologists, the term attention is used to describe the form consciousness takes, to refer to the fact that consciousness is selective. It simply means that consciousness is always focal and marginal--that some ideas, facts, or feelings stand out in greater prominence than do others, and that the presence of this "perspective" in consciousness is a matter of mechanical adjustment. James describes consciousness by likening it to a series of waves, each having a crest and sides which correspond to the focus and margin of attention. The form of the wave changes from a high sharp crest with almost straight sides in pointed, concentrated attention, to a series of mere undulations, when crests are difficult to distinguish, in so-called states of dispersed attention. The latter states are rare in normal individuals, although they may be rather frequent in certain types of low-grade mental defectives. This of course means that states of "inattention" do not exist in normal people. So long as consciousness is present one must be attending to something. The "day dream" is often accompanied by concentrated attention. Only when we are truly thinking of nothing, and that can only be as unconsciousness approaches, is attention absent. What is true of attention is also true of interest, for interest is coming more and more to be considered the "feeling side" of attention, or the affective accompaniment of attention. The kind of interest may vary, but some kind is always present. The place the interest occupies may also vary: sometimes the affective state itself is so strong that it forces itself into the focal point and becomes the object of attention. The chief fact of importance, however, is that attention and interest are inseparable and both are coexistent with consciousness.

This selective action of consciousness is mechanical, due to the inborn tendencies toward attention possessed by human beings. The situations which by their very nature occupy the focal point in consciousness are color and brightness, novelty, sudden changes and sharp contrasts, rhythm and cadence, movement, and all other situations to which there are other instinctive responses, such as hunting, collecting, curiosity, manipulation, etc. In other words, children are born with tendencies to attend to an enormous number of situations because of the number of instinctive responses they possess. So great is this number that psychologists used to talk about the omnivorousness of children's attention, believing that they attended to everything. Such a general attention seems not to be true. However, it is because so many situations have the power to force consciousness to a crest that human beings have developed the intellectual power that puts them so far above other animals. That these situations do attract attention is shown by the fact that individuals respond by movements which enable them to be more deeply impressed or impressed for a longer time by the situations in question. For example, a baby will focus his eyes upon a bright object and then move eyes and head to follow it if it moves from his field of vision. Just what the situations are, then, which will arouse responses of attention in any given individual will depend in the first place upon his age, sex, and maturity, and in the second place upon his experience. The process of learning very quickly modifies the inborn tendencies to attention by adding new situations which demand it. It is the things we learn to attend to that make us human rather than merely animal.

The fact of attention or selection must of necessity involve also inhibition or neglect. The very fact of the selection of certain objects and qualities means the neglect of others. This fact of neglect is at first just as mechanical as that of attention, but experiences teach us to neglect some situations which by original nature attracted attention. From the standpoint of education what we neglect is quite as important as what is selected for attention.

The breadth of a person's attention, *i.e.,* the number of lines along which attention is possible, must vary with age and experience. The younger or the more immature an individual is, the greater the number of different lines to which attention is given. It is the little child whose attention seems omnivorous, and it is the old person for whom situations worthy of attention have narrowed down to a few lines. This must of necessity be so, due to the interrelation of attention and neglect. The very fact of continuing to give attention along one line means less and less ability and desire to attend along other lines.

The question as to how many things, whether objects or ideas, can be attended to at the same time, has aroused considerable discussion. Most people think that they are attending to several things, if not to many, at the same second of consciousness. Experiments show that if four or five unrelated objects, words, or letters be shown to adults for less than one quarter of a second, they can be apprehended, but the probability is that they are photographed, so to speak, on the eye and counted afterwards. It is the general belief of psychologists at present that the mind attends to only one thing at a time, that only one idea or object can occupy the focal point in consciousness.

The apparent contradiction between ordinary experience and psychological experience along this line is due to three facts which are often overlooked. In the first place, the complexity of the idea or thing that can be attended to as a unit varies tremendously. Differences in people account for part of this variation, but training and experience account for still more. Our ideas become more and more complex as experience and familiarity build them up. Qualities which to a little child demand separate acts of attention are with the adult merged into his perception of the object. Just as simple words, although composed of separate letters, are perceived as units, so with training, more complex units may be found which can be attended to as wholes. So (to the ignorant or the uninstructed) what is apparently attending to more than one thing at a time may be explained by the complexity of the unit which is receiving the attention.

In the second place *doing* more than one thing at a time does not imply attending to more than one thing at a time. An activity which is habitual or mechanical does not need attention, but can be carried on by the control exercised by the fringe of consciousness. Attention may be needed to start the activity or if a difficulty of any kind should arise, but that is all. For the rest of the time it can be devoted to anything else. The great speed with which attention can flash from one thing to another and back again must be taken into consideration in all this discussion. So far as attention goes, one can *do* as many things at a time as he can make mechanical plus one unfamiliar one. Thus a woman can rock the baby's cradle, croon a lullaby, knit, and at the same time be thinking of illustrations for her paper at the Woman's Club, because only one of these activities needs attention. When no one of the activities is automatic and the individual must depend on the rapid change of attention from one to the other to keep them going, the results obtained are likely to be poor and the fatigue is great. The attempt to take notes while listening to a lecture is of this order, and hence the unsatisfactoriness of the results.

The third fact which helps to explain the apparent contradiction under discussion is closely related to this one. It is possible when engaged with one object to have several questions or topics close by in the fringe of consciousness so that one or the other may flash to the focal point as the development of the train of thought demands. The individual is apparently considering many questions at the same time, when in reality it is the readiness of these associations plus the oscillations of attention that account for the activity. The ability to do this sort of thing depends partly on the individual,--some people will always be "people of one idea,"--but training and experience increase the power. The child who in the primary can be given only one thing to look for when he goes on his excursion may grow into the youth who can carry half a dozen different questions in his mind to which he is looking for answers.

By concentration of attention is meant the depth of the attention, and this is measured by the ease with which a person's attention can be called off the topic with which he is concerned. The concentration may be so great that the individual is oblivious to all that goes on about him. He may forget engagements and meals because of his absorption. Sometimes even physical pain is not strong enough to distract attention. On the other hand, the concentration may be so slight that every passing sense impression, every irrelevant association called up by the topic, takes the attention away from the subject. The depth of concentration depends upon four factors. Certain mental and physical conditions have a great deal to do with the concentration of attention, and these will be discussed later. Individual differences also account for the presence or absence of power of concentration--some people concentrate naturally, others never get very deeply into any topic. Maturity is another factor that is influential. A little child cannot have great concentration, simply because he has not had experience enough to give him many associations with which to work. His attention is easily distracted. Although apparently absorbed in play, he hears what goes on about him and notices many things which adults suppose he does not see. This same lack of power shows itself in any one's attention when a new subject is taken up if he has few associations with it. Of course this means that other things being equal the older one is, up to maturity at least, the greater one's power of concentration. Little children have very little power, adolescents a great deal, but it is the adult who excels in concentration. Although this is true, the fourth factor, that of training in concentration, does much toward increasing the power before full maturity is reached. One can learn to concentrate just as he can learn to do anything else. Habits of concentration, of ignoring distinctions and interruptions, of putting all one's power into the work in hand, are just as possible as habits of neatness. The laws of habit formation apply in the field of attention just as truly as in every other field of mental life. Laboratory experiments prove the large influence which training has on concentration and the great improvement that can be made. It is true that few people do show much concentration of attention when they wish. This is true of adults as well as of children. They have formed habits of working at half speed, with little concentration and no real absorption in the topic. This method of work is both wasteful of time and energy and injurious to the mental stability and development of the individual. Half-speed work due to lack of concentration often means that a student will stay with a topic and fuss over it for hours instead of working hard and then dropping it. Teachers often do this sort of thing with their school work. Not only are the results less satisfactory, because the individual never gets deeply enough into the topic to really get what is there, but the effect on him is bad. It is like "constant dripping wears away the stone." Children must be taught to "work when they work and play when they play," if they are to have habits of concentration as adults.

The length of time which it is possible to attend to the same object or idea may be reckoned in seconds. It is impossible to hold the attention on an object for any appreciable length of time. In order to hold the attention the object must change. The simple experiment of trying to pay attention to a blot of ink or the idea of bravery proves that change is necessary if the attention is not to wander. What happens is that either the attention goes to something else, or that you begin thinking about the thing in question. Of course, the minute you begin thinking, new associations, images, memories, come flocking in, and the attention occupies itself with each in turn. All may concern the idea with which you started out, but the very fact that these have been added to the mental content of the instant makes the percept of ink blot or the concept of bravery different from the bare thing with which the attention began. If this change and fluctuation of the mental state does not take place, the attention flits to something else. The length of time that the attention may be engaged with a topic will depend, then, upon the number of associations connected with it. The more one knows about a topic, the longer he can attend to it. If it is a new topic, the more suggestive it is in calling up past experience or in offering incentive for experiment or application, the longer can attention stay with it. Such a topic is usually called "interesting," but upon analysis it seems that this means that for one of the above reasons it develops or changes and therefore holds the attention. This duration of attention will vary in length from a few seconds to hours. The child who is given a problem which means almost nothing, which presents a blank wall when he tries to attend to it, which offers no suggestions for solution, is an illustration of the first. Attention to such a problem is impossible; his attention must wander. The genius who, working with his favorite subject, finds a multitude of trains of thought called up by each idea, and who therefore spends hours on one topic with no vacillation of attention, is an illustration of the second.

Attention has been classified according to the kind of feeling which accompanies the activity. Sometimes attention comes spontaneously, freely, and the emotional tone is that accompanying successful activity. On the other hand, sometimes it has to be forced and is accompanied by feelings of strain and annoyance. The first type is called Free[2] attention; the second is Forced attention.

Free attention is given when the object of attention satisfies a need; when the situation attended to provides the necessary material for some self-activity. The activity of the individual at that second needs something that the situation in question gives, and hence free, spontaneous attention results. Forced attention is given when there is a lack of just such feeling of need in connection with the object of attention. It does not satisfy the individual--it is distinct from his desires at the time. He attends only because of fear of the results if he does not, and hence the condition is one of strain. All play takes free attention. Work which holds the worker because it is satisfying also takes free attention. Work which has in it the element of drudgery needs forced attention. The girl making clothes for her doll, the boy building his shack in the woods, the inventor working over his machine, the student absorbed in his history lesson,--all these are freely attending to the thing in hand. The girl running her seam and hating it, the, boy building the chicken coop while wishing to be at the ball game, the inventor working over his machine when his thoughts and desires are with his sick wife, the student trying to study his history when the debate in the civics club is filling his mind,--these are cases when forced attention would probably be necessary.

---

2. This is synonymous with James's Involuntary Attention, Angell's Non-Voluntary Attention, and Titchener's Secondary-Passive Attention.

It is very evident that there is no one situation which will necessarily take either free or forced attention because the determining factor is not in the situation *per se*, but in the relation it bears to the mind engaged with it. Sometimes the same object will call forth forced attention from one person and free from another. Further, the same object may at one time demand free attention and at another time forced attention from the same person, depending on the operation of other factors. It is also true that attention which was at first forced may change into free as the activity is persevered in.

Although these two types of attention are discussed as if they were entirely separated from each other, as if one occurred in this situation and the other in that, still as a matter of fact the actual conditions involve an interplay between the two. It is seldom true that free attention is given for any great length of time without flashes of forced attention being scattered through it. Often the forced attention may be needed for certain parts of the work, although as a whole it may take free attention. The same thing is true of occasions when forced attention is used. There are periods in the activity when free attention will carry the worker on. Every activity, then, is likely to be complex so far as the kind of attention used, but it is also characterized by the predominance of one or the other type.

The question as to the conditions which call out each type of attention is an important one. As has already been said, free attention is given when the situation attended to satisfies a need. Physiologically stated, free attention is given when a neurone series which is ready to act is called into activity. The situations which do this, other things being equal, will be those which appeal to some instinctive tendency or capacity, or to the self-activity or the personal experience of the individual and which therefore are in accord with his stage of development and his experience. Forced attention is necessary when the neurone tracts used by the attention are for some reason unready to act. Situations to which attention is given through fear of punishment, or when the activity involves a choice of ideal ends as opposed to personal desires, or when some instinctive tendency must be inhibited or its free activity is blocked or interfered with, or when the laws of growth and experience are violated, take forced attention. Of course fatigue, disease, and monotony are frequent breeders of forced attention.

From the above discussion it must be evident that one of the chief characteristics of free attention is its unity. The mental activity of the person is all directed along one line, that which leads to the satisfying of the need. It is unified by the appeal the situation makes. As a result of such a state the attention is likely to be concentrated, and can be sustained over a long period. Of course this means that the work accomplished under such conditions will be greater in amount, more thorough, and more accurate than could be true were there less unity in the process. The opposite in all respects is true of forced attention. It is present when there is divided interest. The topic does not appeal to the need of the individual. He attends to it because he must. Part of his full power of attention is given to keeping himself to the work, leaving only a part to be given to the work itself. If there is any other object in the field of attention which is particularly attractive, as there usually is, that claims its share, and the attention is still further divided. Divided attention cannot be concentrated; it cannot last long. The very strain and effort involved makes it extremely fatiguing. The results of work done under such conditions must be poor. There can be but little thoroughness, for the worker will do just as much as he must to pass muster, and no more. Inaccuracy and superficiality will characterize such work. Just as training in giving concentrated attention results in power along that line, so frequent necessity for forced attention develops habits of divided attention which in time will hinder the development of any concentration.

From a psychological viewpoint there can be no question but what free attention is the end to be sought by workers of all kinds. It is an absolutely false notion that things are easy when free attention is present. It is only when free attention is present that results worth mentioning are accomplished. It is only under such conditions that the worker is willing to try and try again, and put up with disappointment and failure, to use his ingenuity and skill to the utmost, to go out of his way for material or suggestions; in other words, to put himself into his work in such a way that it is truly educational. On the other hand, forced attention has its own value and could not be dispensed with in the development of a human being. Its value is that of means to end--not that of an end in itself. It is only as it leads into free attention that forced attention is truly valuable. In that place the part it plays is tremendous because things are as they are. There will always be materials which will not appeal to a need in some individual because of lack of capacity or experience; there will always be parts of various activities and processes which seem unnecessary and a waste of time to some worker; there will always be choices to be made between instinctive desires and ideal needs, and in each case forced attention is the only means, perhaps, by which the necessary conditions can be acquired that make possible free attention. It is evident, therefore, that forced attention should be called into play only when needed. When needed, it should be demanded rigorously, but the sooner the individual in question can pass from it to the other type, the better. This is true in all fields whether intellectual or moral.

A second classification of attention has been suggested according to the answer to the question as to why attention is given. Sometimes attention is given simply because the material itself demands it; sometimes for some ulterior reason. The former type is called immediate or intrinsic attention; the latter is called derived, mediate, or extrinsic attention. The former is given to the situation for its own sake; the latter because of something attached to it. Forced attention is always derived; free attention may be either immediate or derived. It is immediate and derived free attention that needs further discussion.

It should be borne in mind that there is no sharp line of division between immediate and derived attention. Sometimes it is perfectly evident that the attention is given for the sake of the material--at other times there can be no doubt but that it is the something beyond the material that holds the attention. But in big, complex situations it is not so evident. For instance, the musician composing just for the love of it is an example of immediate attention, while the small boy working his arithmetic examples with great care in order to beat his seatmate is surely giving derived attention. But under some conditions the motives are mixed and the attention may fluctuate from the value of the material itself to the values to be derived from it. However this may be, at the two extremes there is a clear-cut difference between these two types of attention. The value of rewards and incentives depends on the psychology of derived free attention, while that of punishment and deterrents is wrapped up with derived forced attention.

Immediate free attention is the more valuable of the two types because it is the most highly unified and most strongly dynamic of all the attention types. The big accomplishments of human lives have been brought to pass through this kind of attention. It is the kind the little child gives to his play--the activity itself is worth while. So with the artist, the inventor, the poet, the teacher, the physician, the architect, the banker--to be engaged in that particular activity satisfies. But this is not true of all artists, bankers, etc., nor with the others all the time. Even for the child at play, sometimes conditions arise when the particular part of the activity does not seem worth while in itself; then if it is to be continued, another kind of attention must be brought in--derived attention. This illustration shows the place of derived attention as a means to an end--the same part played by forced attention in its relation to free. Derived attention must needs be characteristic of much of the activity of human beings. People have few well-developed capacities, and there are many kinds of things they are required to do. If these are to be done with free attention, heartily, it will only be because of some value that is worth while that is attached to the necessary activity. As activities grow complex and as the results of activities grow remote, the need for something to carry over the attention to the parts of the activity that are seen to be worth while in the first place, or to the results in the second, grows imperative. This need is filled by derived attention, and here it shows its value as means to an end, but it is only when the need for this carrier disappears, and the activity as a whole for itself seems worth while, that the best results are obtained.

There is a very great difference between the kinds of motives or values chosen for derived attention, and their value varies in accordance with the following principles. Incentives should be closely connected naturally with the subject to which they are attached. They should be suited to the development of the child and be natural rather than artificial. Their appeal should be permanent, *i.e.*, should persist in the same situation outside of school. They should really stimulate those to whom they are offered. They should not be too attractive in themselves. Applying these principles it would seem that derived interests that have their source in instincts, in special capacities, or in correlation of subjects are of the best type, while such extremely artificial incentives as prizes, half holidays, etc., are among the poorest.

The value of derived attention is that it gets the work done or the habit formed. Of course the hope is always there that it will pass over into the immediate type, but if it does not, at least results are obtained. It has already been shown that results may also be obtained by the use of forced attention, which is also derived. Both derived free attention and forced attention are means to an end. The question as to the comparative value of the two must be answered in favor of the derived free attention. The chief reasons for this conclusion are as follows. First, derived free attention is likely to be more unified than forced attention. Second, it arouses greater self-activity on the part of the worker. Third, the emotional tone is that of being satisfied instead of strain. Fourth, it is more likely to lead to the immediate attention which is its end. Despite these advantages of derived free attention over forced attention, it still has some of the same disadvantages that forced attention has. The chief of these is that it also may result in division of energy. If the means for gaining the attention is nothing but sugar coating, if it results in the mere entertainment of the worker, there is every likelihood that the attention will be divided between the two. The other disadvantage is that because of the attractiveness of the means used to gain attention it may be given just so long as the incentive remains, and no longer. These difficulties may be largely overcome, however, by the application of the principles governing good incentives. This must mean that the choice of types of attention and therefore the provision of situations calling them out should be in this order: immediate free attention, derived free attention, forced attention. All three are necessary in the education of any child, but each should be used in its proper place.

The conditions which insure the best attention of whatever type have to do with both physical and mental adjustments. On the physical side there is need for the adaptation of the sense organ and the body to the situation. For this adaptation to be effective the environmental conditions must be controlled by the laws of hygiene. A certain amount of bodily freedom yields better results than rigidity because the latter draws energy from the task in hand for purposes of inhibition. On the mental side there is need for preparation in terms of readiness of the nerve tracts to be used. James calls this "ideational" preparation. This simply means that one can attend better if he knows something of what he is to attend to. Experimental evidence proves without doubt that if the subject knows that he is to see a color, instead of a word, his perception of it is much more rapid and accurate than if he does not have this preparation. This same result is obtained in much more complex sensory situations, and it also holds when the situation is intellectual. Contrary to expectation, great quietness is not the best condition for the maximum of attention; a certain amount of distraction is beneficial.

The problem of interest and of attention, from the point of view of teaching, is not simply to secure attention, but rather to have the attention fixed upon those activities which are most desirable from the standpoint of realizing the aim or purpose of education. As has already been suggested, children are constantly attending to something. They instinctively respond to the very great variety of stimuli with which they come in contact. Our schools seek to provide experiences which are valuable. In school work when we are successful children attend to those stimuli which promise most for the formation of habits, or the growth in understanding and appreciation which will fit them for participation in our social life. We seek constantly in our work as teachers to secure either free or forced attention to the particular part of our courses of study or to the particular experiences which are allotted to the grade or class which we teach. One of the very greatest difficulties in securing attention upon the part of a class is found in the variety of experiences which they have already enjoyed, and the differences in the strength of the appeal which the particular situation may make upon the several members of the group. In class teaching we have constantly to vary our appeal and to differentiate our work to suit the individual differences represented in the class, if we would succeed in holding the attention of even the majority of the children.

Boys and girls do their best work only when they concentrate their attention upon the work to be done. One of the greatest fallacies that has ever crept into our educational thought is that which suggests that there is great value in having people work in fields in which they are not interested, and in which they do not freely give their attention. Any one who is familiar with children, or with grown-ups, must know that it is only when interest is at a maximum that the effort put forth approaches the limit of capacity set by the individual's ability. Boys concentrate their attention upon baseball or upon fishing to a degree which demands of them a maximum of effort. A boy may spend hours at a time seeking to perfect himself in pitching, batting, or fielding. He may be uncomfortable a large part of the time, he may suffer considerable pain, and yet continue in his practice by virtue of his great enthusiasm for perfecting himself in the game. Interest of a not dissimilar sort leads a man who desires position, or power, or wealth, to concentrate his attention upon the particular field of his endeavor to the exclusion of almost everything else. Indeed, men almost literally kill themselves in the effort which they make to achieve these social distinctions or rewards. We may not hope always to secure so high a degree of concentration of attention or of effort, but it is only as we approach a situation in which children are interested, and in which they freely give their attention to the subject in hand, that we can claim to be most successful in our teaching.

The teacher who is able in beginning reading to discover to children the tool which will enable them to get the familiar story or rhyme from the book may hope to get a quality of attention which could never be brought about by forcing them to attend to formal phonetic drill. The teacher of biology who has been able to awaken enthusiasm for the investigation of plant and animal life, and who has allowed children to conduct their own investigations and to carry out their own experiments, may hope for a type of attention which is never present in the carrying out of the directions of the laboratory manual or in naming or classifying plants or animals merely as a matter of memory. Children who are at work producing a school play will accomplish more in the study of the history in which they seek to discover a dramatic situation, by virtue of the concentration of attention given, than they would in reciting many lessons in which they seek to remember the paragraphs or pages which they have read. The boy who gives his attention to the production of a story for his school paper will work harder than one who is asked to write a composition covering two pages. Children who are allowed to prepare for the entertainment of the members of their class a story with which they alone are familiar will give a quality of attention to the work in hand which is never secured when all of the members of the class are asked to reproduce a story which the teacher has read.

It is necessary at times to have children give forced attention. There are some things to be accomplished that must be done, regardless of our success in securing free attention. It is entirely conceivable that some boy or girl may not want to learn his multiplication tables, or his words in spelling, or his conjugation or declension in French, and that all that the teacher has done may fail to arouse any great amount of interest or enthusiasm for the work in question. In these cases, and in many others which might be cited, the necessity for the particular habit may be so great as to demand that every pupil do the work or form the habit in question. In these cases we may not infrequently hope that after having given forced attention to the work of the school, children may in time come to understand the importance of the experiences which they are having, or even become interested in the work for its own sake. It is not infrequently true that after a period of forced attention there follows a time during which, on account of the value which children are able to understand as attached to or belonging to the particular exercise, they give free derived attention. Many boys and girls have worked through their courses in science or in modern languages because they believed that these subjects.

The importance of making children conscious of their power of concentrating their attention needs to be kept constantly in mind. Exercises in which children are asked to do as much as they can in a period of five or ten minutes may be used to teach children what concentration of attention is and of the economy involved in work done under these conditions. The trouble with a great many adults, as well as with children, is that they have never learned what it is to work up to the maximum of their capacity. All too frequently in our attempts to teach children in classes we neglect to provide even a sufficient amount of work to demand of the more able members of the group any considerable amount of continued, concentrated attention.

We seek in our work as teachers not only to secure a maximum of attention to the fields of work in which children are engaged, but also to arouse interests and enthusiasms which will last after school days are over. We think of interest often, and properly too, as the means employed to secure a maximum of attention, and, in consequence, a maximum of accomplishment. It is worth while to think often in our work in terms of interest as the end to be secured. Children should become sufficiently interested in some of the subjects that we teach to care to be students in these fields, or to find enjoyment in further work or activity along these lines, either as a matter of recreation or, not infrequently, as a means of discovering their true vocation in life. That teacher who has aroused sufficient interest in music to enable the student of musical ability to venture all of the hard work which may be necessary in order to become a skillful musician, has made possibly his greatest contribution by arousing interest or creating enthusiasm. The teacher whose enthusiasm in science has led a boy to desire to continue in this field, even to the extent of influencing him to undertake work in an engineering school, may be satisfied, not so much in the accomplishment of his pupil in the field of science, as in the enthusiasm which has carried him forward to more significant work. Even for children who go no farther than the elementary school, interest in history, or geography, in nature study, or in literature, may mean throughout the life of the individuals taught a better use of leisure time and an enjoyment of the nobler pleasures.

Successful teaching in any part of our school system demands an adjustment in the amount of work to be done, to the abilities, and even to the interest of individual children. Much may be accomplished by the organization of special classes or groups in large school systems, but even under the most favorable conditions children cannot be expected to work up to the maximum of their capacity except as teachers recognize these differences in interest and in ability, and make assignments and conduct exercises which take account of these differences.

QUESTIONS

1. Why do all children attend when the teacher raps on the desk, when she writes on the board, when some one opens the door and comes into the room?

2. Some teachers are constantly rapping with their pencils and raising their voices in order to attract attention. What possible weakness is indicated by this procedure?

3. Why do adults attend to fewer things than do children?

4. In what sense is it possible to attend to two things at the same time?

5. Why are children less able to concentrate their attention than are most adults?

6. Will a boy or girl in your class be more or less easily distracted as he gives free attention or forced attention to the work in hand?

7. What educational value is attached to an exercise which requires that a boy sit at his desk and work, even upon something in which he is not very much interested, for twenty minutes?

8. In what sense is it true that we form the habit of concentrating our attention?

9. Why is it wrong to extend a lesson beyond the period during which children are able to concentrate

their attention upon the work in hand, or beyond the period during which they do concentrate their attention?

10.   How is it possible to extend the period devoted to a lesson in reading, or in geography, or in Latin, beyond the time required to read a story or draw a map, or translate a paragraph?

11.   Why is it possible to have longer recitation periods in the upper grades and in the high school than in the primary school?

12.   Give examples from your class work of free attention; of forced attention; of free derived attention.

13.   In what sense is it true that we work hardest when we give free attention?

14.   In what sense is it true that we work hardest when we give forced attention?

15.   Can you give any example of superficiality or inaccuracy which has resulted from divided attention, upon the part of any member of one of your classes?

16.   Does free attention imply lack of effort?

17.   Name incidents which you think might properly be offered boys and girls in order to secure free derived attention.

18.   Can you cite any example in your teaching in which children have progressed from forced to free attention?

19.   What interests have been developed in your classes which you think may make possible the giving of free attention in the field in question, even after school days are over?

20.   How can you teach children what it is to concen-
      trate their attention and the value of concentrated
      attention?

IV

The Formation of Habits

Habit in its simplest form is the tendency to do, think, or act as one has done, thought, or acted in the past. It is the tendency to repeat activities of all kinds. It is the tendency which makes one inclined to do the familiar action rather than a new one. In a broader sense, habit formation means learning. It is a statement of the fact that conduct *is* modifiable and that such modifications may become permanent.

The fact of learning depends physiologically on the plasticity of the nervous system. The neurones, particularly those concerned with intellectual life, are not only sensitive to nerve currents but are modified by them. The point where the greatest change seems to take place is at the synapses, but what this modification is, no one knows. There are several theories offered as explanations of what happens, but no one of them has been generally accepted, although the theory of chemical change seems to be receiving the strongest support at present. There can be no disagreement, however, as to the effects of this change, whatever it may be. Currents originally passing with difficulty over a certain conduction unit later pass with greater and greater ease. The resistance which seems at first to be present gradually disappears, and to that extent is the conduct modified. This same element of plasticity accounts for the breaking of habits. In this case the action is double, for it implies the disuse of certain connections which have been made and the forming of others; for the breaking of a bad habit means the beginning of a good one.

The plasticity of neurone groups seems to vary in two respects--as to modifiability and as to power to hold modifications. The neurone groups controlling the reflex and physiological operations are least easily modified, while those controlling the higher mental processes are most easily modified. The neurone groups controlling the instincts hold a middle place. So far as permanence goes, connections between sensorimotor neurone groups seem to hold modifications longer than do connections between either associative-motor or associative-association.

It is probably because of this fact that habit in the minds of so many people refers to some physical activity. Of course this is a misconception. Wherever the nervous system is employed, habits are formed. There are intellectual, moral, emotional, temperamental habits, just as truly as physical habits. In the intellectual field every operation that involves association or memory also involves habits. Good temper, or the reverse, truthfulness, patriotism, thoughtfulness for others, open-mindedness, are as much matters of learning and of habit as talking or skating or sewing. Habit is found in all three lines of mental development: intellect, character, and skill.

Not only does the law of habit operate in all fields of mental activity, but the characteristics which mark its operation are the same. Two of these are important. In the first place, habit formation results in a lessening of attention to the process. Any process that is habitual can be taken care of by a minimum of attention. In other words, it need no longer be in the focal point, but can be relegated to the fringe. At the beginning of the modification of the neurone tract focal attention is often necessary, but as it progresses less and less attention is needed until the activity becomes automatic, apparently running by itself. Not all habits reach this stage of perfection, but this is the general tendency. This lessening of the need for attention means that less energy is used by the activity, and the individual doing the work is less likely to be fatigued. In the second place, habit tends to make the process more and more sure in its results. As the resistance is removed from the synapses, and the one particular series of units come to act more and more as a unit, the current shoots along the path with no side-tracking, and the act is performed or the thought reached unwaveringly with very little chance of error. If the habit being formed is that of writing, the appropriate movements are made with no hesitation, and the chances that certain ones will be made the first time increase in probability. This means a saving of time and an increase in confidence as to the results.

A consideration of these characteristics of habits makes clear its dangers as well as its values. The fact that habit is based on actual changes which take place in the nervous system, that its foundation is physical, emphasizes its binding power. Most people in talking and thinking of habit regard it as something primarily mental in nature and therefore believe all that is necessary to break any habit is the sufficient exercise of will power. But will power, however strong, cannot break actual physical connections, and it is such connections that bind us to a certain line of activity instead of any other, when once the habit is formed. It is just as logical to expect a car which is started on its own track to suddenly go off on to another track where there is no switch, as to expect a nerve current traveling along its habitual conduction unit to run off on some other line of nervous discharge. Habit once formed binds that particular line of thought to action, either good or bad. Of course habits may be broken, but it is a work of time and must result from definite physical changes. Every habit formed lessens the likelihood of any other response coming in that particular situation. Every interest formed, every act of skill perfected, every method of work adopted, every principle or ideal accepted, limits the recognition of any other possible line of action in that situation. Habit binds to one particular response and at the same time blinds the individual to any other alternative. The danger of this is obvious. If the habits formed are bad or wasteful ones, the individual is handicapped in his growth until new ones can be formed. On the other hand, habit makes for limitation.

Despite these dangers, habit is of inestimable value in the development of both the individual and the human race. It is through it that all learning is possible. It makes possible the preservation of our social inheritance. As James says, "Habit is the enormous fly-wheel of society, its most precious conservative agent." Because of its power of limitation it is sometimes considered the foe of independence and originality, but in reality it is the only road to progress. Other things being equal, the more good habits a person has, the greater the probability of his doing original work. The genius in science or in art or in statesmanship is the man who has made habitual many of the activities demanded by his particular field and who therefore has time and energy left for the kind of work that demands thinking. Habit won't make a genius, but all men of exceptional ability excel others in the number and quality of their habits in the field in which they show power. As the little child differs from the adult in the number and quality of his habits, so the ordinary layman differs from the expert. It is scarcity, not abundance, of habits that forces a man into a rut and keeps him mediocre. Just as the three year old, having taken four or five times as long as the adult to dress himself, is tired out at the end of the task, so the amateur in literature or music or morals as compared with the expert. The more habits any one has in any line, the better for him, both from the standpoint of efficiency and productivity, provided that the habits are good and that among them is found the habit of breaking habits.

The two great laws of habit formation are the laws of exercise and effect. These laws apply in all cases of habit formation, whether they be the purposeless habits of children or the purposive habits of maturity. The law of exercise says that the oftener and the more emphatically a certain response is connected with a certain situation, the more likely is it to be made to that situation. The two factors of repetition and intensity are involved. It is a common observance that the oftener one does a thing, other things being equal, the better he does it, whether it be good or bad. Drill is the usual method adopted by all classes of people for habit formation. It is because of the recognition of the value of repetition that the old maxim of "Practice makes Perfect" has been so blindly adhered to. Practice may make perfect, but it also may make imperfect. All that practice can do is to make more sure and automatic the activity, whatever it is. It cannot alone make for improvement. A child becomes more and more proficient in bad writing or posture, in incorrect work in arithmetic and spelling, with practice just as truly as under other conditions he improves in the same activities. Evidence from school experiments, which shows that as many as 40 per cent of the children examined did poorer work along such lines in a second test than in the first which had been given several months earlier, bears witness to the inability of mere repetition to get "perfect" results. To get such results the repetition must be only of the improvements. There must be a constant variation towards the ideal, and a selection of just those variations for practice, if perfect as well as invariable results are to be obtained.

The amount of repetition necessary in the formation of any given habit is not known. It will, of course, vary with the habit and with the individual, but experimental psychology will some day have something to offer along this line. We could make a great saving if we knew, even approximately, the amount of practice necessary under the best conditions to form some of the more simple and elementary habits, such as learning the facts of multiplication.

One other fact in connection with repetition should be noted, namely, that the exercise given any connection by the learner, freely, of his own initiative counts more than that given under purposive learning. This method of learning is valuable in that it is incidental and often saves energy and possible imitation on the part of the child, but it has certain drawbacks. Habits formed this way are ingrained to such an extent that they are very difficult to modify. They were not consciously attended to when they were formed, and hence it is difficult later to raise them to the focal point. Hence it is best whenever habits are partial and will need to be modified later, or when the habits must later be rationalized, or when bad habits must be broken, to have the process focalized in attention. The methods of gaining attention have already been discussed.

In the second place, if the habit being formed is connected with an instinct, the element of intensity is added. This, of course, means that a connection already made and one which is strongly ready to act is made to give its support to the new connection being formed. Of course the instinct chosen for this purpose must be in accord with the particular habit and with the nature of the learner. They may vary from the purely personal and physical up to those which have to do with groups and intellectual reactions. The added impetus of the instinct hastens the speed of the direction or supervision. The psychology of the value of self-activity is operative. It should be borne in mind, however, that the two kinds of exercise must be of the same degree of accuracy if this better result in self-initiated practice is to be obtained.

Not only is it true that repetition makes for automaticity, but intensity is also an aid. Connections which are made emphatically as well as often tend to become permanent. This is particularly true of mental habits. There are two factors of importance which make for intensity in habit formation. First, the focalization of attention on the connections being made adds intensity. Bagley in his discussion of this topic makes "focalization in attention" a necessity in all habits. Although habits may be formed without such concentration, still it is true that if attention is given to the process, time is saved; for the added intensity secured increases the speed of learning. In certain types of habits, however, when incidental learning plays a large part, much skill may be acquired without focalization of attention in the process. Much of the learning of little children is of this type. Their habits of language, ways of doing things, mannerisms, and emotional attitudes often come as a result of suggestion and imitation rather than as a result of definite formation of the new habit.

The second great law of habit formation is the law of effect. This law says that any connection whose activity is accompanied by or followed by satisfaction tends thereby to be strengthened. If the accompanying emotional tone is annoyance, the connection is weakened. This law that satisfaction stamps connections in, and annoyance inhibits connections, is one of the greatest if not the greatest law of human life. Whatever gives satisfaction, that mankind continues to do. He learns only that which results in some kind of satisfaction. Because of the working of this law animals learn to do their tricks, the baby learns to talk, the child learns to tell the truth, the adult learns to work with the fourth dimension. Repetition by itself is a wasteful method of habit formation. The law of effect must work as well as the law of exercise, if the results are to be satisfactory. As has already been pointed out, it is not the practice alone that makes perfect, but the *stressing* of improvements, and that fixing is made possible only by satisfaction. Pleasure, in the broad sense, must be the accompaniment or the result of any connection that is to become habitual. This satisfaction may be of many different sorts, physical, emotional, or intellectual. It may be occasioned by a reward or recognition from without or by appreciation arising from self-criticism. In some form or other it must be present.

Two further suggestions in habit formation which grow out of the above laws should be borne in mind.

The first is the effect of primacy. In everyday language, "first impressions last longest." The character of the first responses made in any given situation have great influence on all succeeding responses. They make the strongest impression, they are the hardest to eradicate. From a physiological point of view the explanation is evident. A connection untraversed or used but a few times is much more plastic than later when it has been used often. Hence the first time the connection is used gives a greater set or bent than any equal subsequent activity. This is true both of the nervous system as a whole and of any particular conduction unit. Thus impressions made in childhood count more than those of the same strength made later. The first few attempts in pronouncing foreign words fixes the pronunciation. The first few weeks in a subject or in dealing with any person influences all subsequent responses to a marked degree.

The second suggestion has to do with the effect of exceptions. James says, "Never allow an exception to occur" in the course of forming a habit. Not only will the occurrence of one exception make more likely its recurrence, but if the exception does not recur, at least the response is less sure and less accurate than it otherwise would be. It tends to destroy self-confidence or confidence in the one who allowed the exception. Sometimes even one exception leads to disastrous consequences and undoes the work of weeks and months. This is especially true in breaking a bad habit or in forming a new one which has some instinctive response working against it.

There has been a great deal of work done in experimental laboratories and elsewhere in the study of the formation of particular habits. The process of habit formation has been shown by learning curves. When these learning curves are compared, it becomes clear that they have certain characteristics in common. This is true whether the learning be directed to such habits as the acquisition of vocabularies in a foreign language or to skill in the use of a typewriter. Several of the most important characteristics follow.

In the first place it is true of all learning that there is rapid improvement at first. During the beginning of the formation of a habit more rapid advance is made than at any other time. There are two principal reasons for this fact. The adjustments required at the beginning are comparatively simple and easily made and the particular learning is new and therefore is undertaken with zest and interest. After a time the work becomes more difficult, the novelty wears off, therefore the progress becomes less marked and the curve shows fluctuations.

Another characteristic of the learning curve is the presence of the so-called "plateaus." Plateaus show in the curve as flat, level stretches during which there has apparently been no progress. The meaning of these level stretches, and whether or not they can be entirely done away with in any curve, is a matter of dispute. These pauses may be necessary for some of the habits to reach a certain degree of perfection before further progress can be made. However this may be, there are several minor causes which tend to increase the number of plateaus and to lengthen the time spent in any one. In the first place an insecure or an inaccurate foundation must result in an increase of plateaus. If at the beginning, during the initial spurt, for instance, the learner is allowed to go so fast that what he learns is not thoroughly learned, or if he is pushed at a pace that for him makes thoroughness impossible, plateaus must soon occur in his learning curve. In the second place a fruitful cause of plateaus is loss of interest,--monotony. If the learner is not interested, he will not put forth the energy necessary for continued improvement, and a time of no progress is the result. The attitude of the learner toward the work is extremely important, not only in the matter of interest, but in the further attitude of self-confidence. Discouragement usually results in hindering progress, whereas confidence tends to increase it. The psychological explanation of this is very evident. Both lack of interest in the learning and the presence of discouragement are likely to result in divided attention and that, as has already been shown, results in unsatisfactory work. A third cause for plateaus is physiological. Not only must the learner be in the right attitude towards the work, but he must feel physically "fit." There seem to be certain physiological rhythms that may disturb the learning process whose cause cannot be directly determined, but generally the feeling of unfitness can be traced to a simple cause,--such as physical illness, loss of sleep, exercise, or food, or undue emotional strain.

The older psychology has left an impression that improvement in any function is limited both as to amount and as to the period during which it must be attained. The physiological limit of improvement has been thought of as one which was rather easily reached. The loss of plasticity of the nervous system has been supposed to be rather rapid, so that marked improvement in a habit after one has passed well into the twenties was considered improbable. Recent experiments, however, seem to show that no such condition of affairs exists. There is very great probability that any function whatsoever is improvable with practice, and in most cases to a very marked degree. To find a function which has reached the physiological limit has been very rare, even in experimental research, and even with extended practice series it has been unusual to reach a stage of zero improvement even with adults. Thorndike says, "Let the reader consider that if he should now spend seven hours, well distributed, in mental multiplication with three place numbers, he would thereby much more than double his speed and also reduce his errors; or that, by forty hours of practice, he could come to typewrite (supposing him to now have had zero practice) approximately as fast as he can write by hand; or that, starting from zero knowledge, he could learn to copy English into German script at a rate of fifty letters per minute, in three hours or a little more."[3] It is probably true that the majority of adults are much below their limit of efficiency in most of the habits required by their profession, and that in school habits the same thing is true of children. Spurious levels of accomplishment have been held up as worthy goals, and efficiency accepted as ultimate which was only two thirds, and often less than that, of what was possible. Of course it may not be worth the time and energy necessary to obtain improvement in certain lines,--that must be determined by the particular case,--but the point is, that improvement; is possible with both children and adults in almost every habit they possess with comparatively little practice. Neither the physiological limit of a function nor the age limit of the individual is reached as easily or as soon as has been believed.

There are certain aids to improvement which must be used in order that the best results may be obtained.

---

3.   Educational Psychology, Briefer Course.

Some of them have already been discussed and others will be discussed at a later time, so they need only be listed here, the right physiological conditions, the proper distribution of the practice periods, interest in the work, interest in improvement, problem attitude, attention, and absence of both excitement and worry.

Habits have been treated in psychology as wholes, just as if each habit was a unit. This has been true, whether the habits being discussed were moral habits, such as sharing toys with a younger brother; intellectual habits, such as reading and understanding the meaning of the word "and"; or motor habits, such as sitting straight. The slightest consideration of these habits makes obvious that they differ tremendously in complexity. The moral habit quoted involves both intellectual and motor habits--and not one, but several. From a physiological point of view, this difference in the complexity of habits is made clear by an examination of the number of neural bonds used in getting the habit response to a given situation. In some cases they are comparatively few--in others the number necessary is astonishing. In no case of habit will the bonds used involve but a single connection.

Just what bonds are needed in order that a child may learn to add, or to spell, to appreciate music, or to be industrious, is a question that only experiment and investigation can answer. At present but little is known as to just what happens, just what connections are formed, when from the original tendency towards vocalization the child just learns to say the word "milk," later reads it, and still later writes it. One thing is certain, the process is not a unitary one, nor is it a simple one. Just so long as habit is discussed in general terms, without any recognition of the complexity of the process or to the specific bonds involved, just so long will the process of habit formation be wasteful and inefficient.

As a sample of the kind of work being done in connection with special habits, investigation seems to give evidence that in the habit of simple column addition eight or nine distinct functions are involved, each of which involves the use of several bonds. Besides these positive connections, a child in learning must inhibit other connections which are incorrect, and these must often outnumber the correct ones. And yet column addition has always been treated as a simple habit--with perhaps one element of complexity, when carrying was involved. It is evident that, if the habit concerned does involve eight or nine different functions, a child might go astray in any one. His difficulty in forming the habit might be in connection with one or several of the processes involved. Knowledge on the part of the teacher of these different steps in the habit, and appreciation by him of the possibilities of making errors, are the prerequisites of efficient teaching of habits.

In each one of the subjects there is much need of definite experimental work, in order that the specific bonds necessary in forming the habits peculiar to the subject be determined. The psychology of arithmetic, or of physics, or of spelling should involve such information. Meanwhile every teacher can do much if she will carefully stop and think just what she is requiring in the given response. An analysis of the particular situation and response will make clear at least some of the largest elements involved, some of the most important connections to be made. It is the specific nature of the connections to be made and the number of those connections that need emphasis in the teaching of habits. Not only must the specific nature of the bonds involved in individual habits be stressed, but also the specific nature of the entire complex which is called the habit. There is no such thing as a general curve of learning that will apply equally well, no matter what the habit. The kind of curve, the rate of improvement, the possibilities of plateaus, the permanence of the improvement, all these facts and others vary with the particular habit.

In habit formation, as is the case in other types of activity, we get the most satisfactory results only when we secure a maximum of interest in the work to be done. The teacher who thinks that she can get satisfactory results merely by compelling children to repeat over and over again the particular form to be mastered is doomed to disappointment. Indeed, it is not infrequently true that the dislike which children get for the dreary exercises which have little or no meaning for them interferes to such a degree with the formation of the habit we hope to secure as to develop a maximum of inaccuracies rather than any considerable improvement. The teacher who makes a game out of her word drill in beginning reading may confidently expect to have children recognize more words the next day than one who has used the same amount of time, without introducing the motive which has made children enjoy their work. Children who compare their handwriting with a scale, which enables them to tell what degree of improvement they have made over a given period, are much more apt to improve than are children who are merely asked to fill up sheets of paper with practice writing. A vocabulary in a modern language will be built up more certainly if students seek to make a record in the mastery of some hundreds or thousands of words during a given period, rather than merely to do the work which is assigned from day to day. A group of boys in a continuation school have little difficulty in mastering the habits which are required in order to handle the formal processes in arithmetic, or to apply the formula of algebra or trigonometry, if the application of these habitual responses to their everyday work has been made clear. Wherever we seek to secure an habitual response we should attempt to have children understand the use to which the given response is to be put, or, if this is not possible, to introduce some extraneous motive which will give satisfaction.

We cannot be too careful in the habits which we seek to have children form to see to it that the first response is correct. It is well on many occasions, if we have any doubt as to the knowledge of children, to anticipate the response which they should give, and to make them acquainted with it, rather than to allow them to engage in random guessing. The boy who in writing his composition wishes to use a word which he does not know how to spell, should feel entirely free to ask the teacher for the correct spelling, unless there is a dictionary at hand which he knows how to use. It is very much better for a boy to ask for a particular form in a foreign language, or to refer to his grammar, than it is for him to use in his oral or written composition a form concerning which he is not certain. A mistake made in a formula in algebra, or in physics, may persist, even after many repetitions might seem to have rendered the correct form entirely automatic.

In matters of habit it does not pay to take it for granted that all have mastered the particular forms which have supposedly been taught, and it never pays to attempt to present too much at any one time. More satisfactory work in habit formation would commonly be done were we to *teach* fewer words in any one spelling lesson, or attempt to fix fewer combinations in any particular drill lesson in arithmetic, or assign a part of a declension or conjugation in a foreign language, or to be absolutely certain that one or two formulas were fixed in algebra or in chemistry, rather than in attempting to master several on the same day. Teachers ought constantly to ask themselves whether every member of the class is absolutely sure and absolutely accurate in his response before attempting new work. It is of the utmost importance that particular difficulties be analyzed, and that attention be fixed upon that which is new, or that which presents some unusual difficulty.

As has already been implied, it is important not simply to start with as strong a motive as possible, but it is also necessary to keep attention concentrated during the exercises which are supposed to result in habit formation. However strong the motive for the particular work may have been at the beginning, it is likely after a few minutes to lack power, if the particular exercise is continued in exactly the same form. Much is to be gained by varying the procedure. Oral work alternated with written work, concert work alternated with individual testing, the setting of one group over against another, the attempt to see how much can be done in a given period of minutes,--indeed, any device which will keep attention fixed is to be most eagerly sought for. In all practice it is important that the pupil strive to do his very best. If the ideal of accuracy or of perfection in form is once lost sight of, the responses given may result in an actual loss rather than in gain in fixing the habit. When a teacher is no longer able to secure attention to the work in hand, it is better to stop rather than to continue in order to provide for a given number of repetitions. Drill periods of from five to fifteen minutes two or three times a day may almost always be found to produce better results than the same amount of time used consecutively. Systematic reviews are most essential in the process of habit formation. The complaint of a fifth-grade teacher that the work in long division was not properly taught in the fourth grade may be due in considerable measure to the fact that she has neglected at the beginning of the fifth grade's work to spend a week or two in careful or systematic review of the work covered in the previous year. The complaint of high school teachers that children are not properly taught in the elementary school would often be obviated if in each of the fields in question some systematic review were given from time to time, especially at the beginning of the work undertaken, in any particular subject which involves work previously done in the elementary school. During any year's work that teacher will be most successful who reviews each day the work of the day before, who reviews each third or fourth day the particularly difficult parts of the work done during the previous periods, who reviews each week and each month, and even each two or three months, the work which has been covered up to that time. When teachers understand that the intervals between repetitions which seem to have fixed a habit may only be gradually lengthened, then will the formation of habits upon the part of boys and girls become more certain, and the difficulties arising from lapses and inaccuracies become less frequent.

As has been suggested in previous discussions, it will be necessary in habit formation to vary the requirements among the individuals who compose a group. The motive which we seek to utilize may make a greater appeal to one child than to another. Physiological differences may account for the fact that a small number of repetitions will serve to fix the response for one individual as over against a very much larger number of repetitions required for another. It is of the utmost importance that all children work up to the maximum of their capacity. It is very much better, for example, to excuse a boy entirely from a given drill exercise than to have him dawdle or loaf during the period. In some fields a degree of efficiency may be reached which will permit the most efficient children to be relieved entirely from certain exercises in order that they may spend their time on other work. On the other hand, those who are less capable may need to have special drill exercises arranged which will help them to make up their deficiency. The teacher who is acquainted with the psychology of habit formation should secure from the pupils in her class a degree of efficiency which is not commonly found in our schools.

QUESTIONS

1. In what sense is it true that we have habits of thought?

2. What habits which may interfere with or aid in your school work are formed before children enter school?

3. Why is it hard to break a habit of speech?

4. Distinguish among actions to which we attribute a moral significance those which are based upon habit and those which are reasoned.

5. Professor James said, "Habits are the stuff of which behavior consists." Indicate the extent to which this is true for the children in your classes.

6. In how far is it advantageous to become a creature of habit?

7. Which of our actions should be the result of reason?

8. Should school children reason their responses in case of a fire alarm, in passing pencils, in formal work in arithmetic? Name responses which should be the result of reason; others which should be habitual.

9. Why do we sometimes become less efficient when we fix our attention upon an action that is ordinarily habitual?

10. Why do children sometimes write more poorly, or make more mistakes in addition, or in their conjugations or declensions, at the end of the period than they do at the beginning?

11. How would you hope to correct habits of speech learned at home? What particular difficulty is involved?

12. When, are repetitions most helpful in habit formation?

13. When may repetitions actually break down or eliminate habitual responses?

14. How may the keeping of a record of one's improvement add in the formation of a habit?

15.   What motives have you found most usable in keeping attention concentrated during the exercises in habit formation which you conduct?

16.   The approval or disapproval of a group of boys and girls often brings about a very rapid change in physical, moral, or mental habits on the part of individual children. Why?

17.   Why should drill work be discontinued when children grow tired and cease to concentrate their attention?

18.   Why should reviews be undertaken at the beginning of a year's work? How can reviews be organized to best advantage during the year?

19.   What provision do you make in your work to guard against lapses?

V

How to Memorize

There is no sharp distinction between habit and memory. Both are governed by the general laws of association. They shade off into each other, and what one might call habit another with equal reason might call memory. Their likenesses are greater than their differences. However, there is some reason for treating the topic of association under these two heads. The term memory has been used by different writers to mean at least four different types of association. It has been used to refer to the presence of mental images; to refer to the consciousness of a feeling or event as belonging to one's own past experience; to refer to the presence of connections between situation and motor response; and to refer to the ability to recall the appropriate response to a particular situation. The last meaning of the term is the one which will be used here. The mere flow of imagery is not memory, and it matters little whether the appropriate response be accompanied by the time element and the personal element or not. In fact, most of the remembering which is done in daily life lacks these two elements.

Memory then is the recall of the appropriate response in a given situation. It differs from habit in that the responses referred to are more often mental rather than motor; in that it is less automatic, more purposeful.

The fact that the elements involved are so largely mental makes it true that the given fact is usually found to have several connections and the given situation to be connected with many facts. Which particular one will be "appropriate" will depend on all sorts of subtle factors, hence the need of the control of the connection aeries by a purpose and the diminishing of the element of automaticity. As was said before, there is no hard and fast line of division between habit and memory. The recall of the "sqrt" or of how to spell "home" or of the French for "table" might be called either or both. All that was said in the discussion of habit applies to memory.

This ability to recall appropriate facts in given situations is dependent primarily on three factors: power of retention, number of associations, organization of associations. The first factor, power of retention, is the most fundamental and to some extent limits the usefulness of the other two. It is determined by the character of the neurones and varies with different brains. Neurones which are easily impressed and retain their impression simply because they are so made are the gift of nature and the corner stone of a good memory. This retention power is but little, if at all, affected by practice. It is a primary quality of the nervous system, present or absent to the degree determined by each individual's original nature. Hence memory as a whole cannot be unproved, although the absence of certain conditions may mean that it is not being used up to its maximum capacity. Change in these conditions, then, will enable a person to make use of all the native retentiveness his nervous system has. One of the most important of these conditions is good health. To the extent that good blood, sleep, exercise, etc., put the nervous system in better tone, to that extent the retentive power present is put in better working order. Every one knows how lack of sleep and illness is often accompanied by loss in memory. Repetition, attention, interest, vividness of impression, all appeal primarily to this so-called "brute memory," or retentive power. Pleasurable results seem not to be quite so important, and repetition to be more so when the connections are between mental states instead of between mental states and motor responses. An emphasis on, or an improvement in, the use of any one of these factors may call into play to a greater extent than before the native retentive power of a given child.

The power to recall a fact or an event depends not only upon this quality of retentiveness, but also upon the number of other facts or events connected with it. Each one of these connections serves as an avenue of approach, a clew by means of which the recall may operate. Any single blockade therefore may not hinder the recall, provided there are many associates. This is true, no matter how strong the retentive power may be. It is doubly important if the retentive power is weak. Suppose a given fact to be held rather weakly because of comparatively poor retentive power, then the operation of one chain of associates may not be energetic enough to recall it. But if this same fact may be approached from several different angles by means of several chains of associations, the combined power of the activity in the several neurone chains will likely be enough to lift it above the threshold of recall. Other things being equal, the likelihood that a needed fact will be recalled is in proportion to the number of its associations.

The third factor upon which goodness in memory depends is the organization of associates. Number of connections is an aid to memory--but systematization among these connections is an added help. Logical arrangement of facts in memory, classification according to various principles, orderly grouping of things that belong together, make the operation of memory more efficient and economical. The difference between mere number of associations and orderly arrangement of those associations may be illustrated by the difference in efficiency between the housekeeper who starts more or less blindly to look all over the house for a lost article, and the one who at least knows that it must be in a certain room and probably in a certain bureau drawer. Although memory as a whole cannot be improved because of the limiting power of native retentiveness, memory for any fact or in any definite field may be improved by emphasizing these two factors: number of associations and organization among associations.

Although all three factors are operative in securing the best type of memory, still the efficiency of a given memory may be due more to the unusual power of one of them than to the combined effect of the three. It is this difference in the functioning of these three factors which is primarily responsible for certain types of memory which will be discussed later. It must also be borne in mind that the power of these factors to operate in determining recall varies somewhat with age. Little children and old people are more dependent upon mere retentiveness than upon either of the others, the former because of lack of experience and lack of habits of thought, the latter because of the loss of both of these factors. The adult depends more on the organization of his material, while in the years between the number of the clews is probably the controlling factor. Here again there is no sharp line of division; all three are needed. So in the primary grades we begin to require children to organize, and as adults we do all we can to make the power of retention operate at its maximum.

Many methods of memorizing have been used by both children and adults. Recently experimental psychology has been testing some of them. So far as the learner is concerned, he may use repetition, or concentration, or recall as a primary method. Repetition means simply the going over and over again the material to be learned--the element depended upon being the number of times the connection is made. Concentration means going over the material with attention. Not the number of connections is important, but the intensity of those connections. In recall the emphasis is laid upon reinstating the desired connections from within. In using this method, for instance, the learner goes over the material as many times as he sees necessary, then closes the book and recalls from memory what he can of it.

The last of the three methods is by far the best, whether the memory desired be rote or logical, for several reasons. In the first place it involves both the other methods or goes beyond them. Second, it is economical, for the learner knows when he knows the lesson. Third, it is sure, for it establishes connections as they will be used--in other words, the learning provides for recall, which is the thing desired, whereas the other two methods establish only connections of impression. Fourth, it tends to establish habits that are of themselves worth while, such as assuming responsibility for getting results, testing one's own power and others. Fifth, it encourages the use of the two factors upon which memory depends, which are most capable of development, *i.e.*, number and organization of associations.

In connection with the use of the material two methods have been employed--the part method and the whole method. The learner may break the material up into sections, and study just one, then the next, and so on, or he may take all the material and go through with it from the beginning to the end and then back again. Experimental results show the whole method to be the better of the two. However, in actual practice, especially with school children, probably a combination of the two is still better, because of certain difficulties arising from the exclusive use of the whole method. The advantages of the whole method are that it forms the right connections and emphasizes the complete thought and therefore saves time and gives the right perspective. Its difficulties are that the material is not all of equal difficulty and therefore it is wasteful to put the same amount of time on all parts; it is discouraging to the learner, as no part may be raised above the threshold of recall at the first study period (particularly true if it is rote memory); it is difficult to use recall, if the whole method is rigidly adhered to. A combination of the two is therefore wise. The learner should be encouraged to go over the material from beginning to end, until the difficult parts become apparent, then to concentrate on these parts for a time and again go over from the beginning--using recall whenever possible.

A consideration of the time element involved in memorizing has given use to two other methods, the so-called concentrated and distributive. Given a certain amount of time to spend on a certain subject, the learner may distribute it in almost an infinite number of ways, varying not only the length of the period of practice, but also the length of time elapsing between periods. The experimental work done in connection with these methods has not resulted in agreement. No doubt there is an optimum length of period for practice and an optimum interval, but too many factors enter in to make any one statement. "The experimental results justify in a rough way the avoidance of very long practice periods and of very short intervals. They seem to show, on the other hand, that much longer practice periods than are customary in the common schools are probably entirely allowable, and that much shorter intervals are allowable than those customary between the just learning and successive 'reviews' in schools."[4] This statement leaves the terms very long and very short to be defined, but at present the experimental results are too contradictory to permit of anything more specific. However, a few suggestions do grow from these results. The practice period should be short in proportion as these factors are present: first, young or immature minds; second, mechanical mental processes as opposed to thought material; third, a learner who "warms up" quickly; the presence of fatigue; a function near its limit. Thus the length of the optimum period must vary with the age of the learner, the subject matter, the stage of proficiency in the subject, and the particular learner. The same facts must be taken into consideration in deciding on the optimum interval. One fact seems pretty well established in connection with the interval, and that is that a comparatively short period of practice with a review after a night's rest counts more than a much longer period added to the time spent the evening before.

---

4.   Thorndike, *Psychology of Learning*.

There are certain suggestions which if carried out help the learner in his memorizing. In the first place, as the number of associates is one factor determining recall, the fact to be remembered should be presented in many ways, *i.e.*, appealing to as many senses as possible. In carrying this out, it has been the practice of many teachers to require the material to be remembered to be acted out or written. This is all right in so far as the muscular reactions required are mechanical and take little attention. If, on the other hand, the child has to give much attention to how he is to dramatize it, or if writing in itself is as yet a partially learned process, the attention must be divided between the fact to be memorized and its expression, and hence the desired result is not accomplished. Colvin claims that "writing is not an aid to learning until the sixth or seventh grade in the schools." This same fact that an association only partly known is a hindrance rather than a help in fixing another is often violated both in teaching spelling and language. If the spelling of "two" is unknown or only partly known, it is a hindrance instead of a help to teach it at the same time "too" is being taught. Second, the learner should be allowed to find his own speed, as it varies tremendously with the individual. Third, rhythm is always an aid when it can be used, such as learning the number of days in each month in rhyme. Fourth, after a period of hard mental work a few minutes (Pillsbury thinks three to six) should elapse before definitely taking up a new line of work. This allows for the so-called "setting" of associations, due to the action of the general law of inertia, and tends to diminish the possibility of interference from the bonds called into play by the new work. Fifth, mnemonic devices of simple type are sometimes an aid. Most of these devices are of questionable value, as they themselves require more memory work than the facts they are supposed to be fixing. However, if devised by the learner, or if suggested by some one else after failure on the part of the learner to fix the material, they are permissible.

Memory has been classified in various ways, according to the time element, as immediate and permanent. Immediate memory is the one which holds for a short time, whereas permanent memory holds for a long time. People differ markedly in this respect. Some can if tested after the study period reproduce the material with a high degree of accuracy, but lose most of it in a comparatively short time. Others, if tested in the same way, reproduce less immediately, but hold what they have over a long period. Children as a whole differ from adults in having poorer immediate memories, but in holding what is fixed through years. Of course permanent memory is the more valuable of the two types for most of life, but on the other hand immediate memory has its own special value. Lawyers, physicians, politicians, ministers, lecturers, all need great power of immediate memory in their particular professions. They need to be able to hold a large amount of material for a short time, but then they may forget a great deal of it.

Memory is also classified according to the arrangement of the material as desultory, rote, and logical memory. In desultory memory the facts just "stick" because of the great retentive power of the brain, there are few connections, the material is disconnected and disjointed. Rote memory depends on a special memory for words, aided by serial connections and often rhythm. Logical is primarily a memory for meanings and depends upon arrangement and system for its power. Little children as a class have good desultory memories and poor logical memories. Rote memory is probably at its best in the pre-adolescent and early adolescent years. Logical memory is characteristic of mature, adult minds. However, some people excel in one rather than another type, and each renders its own peculiar service. A genius in any line finds a good desultory memory of immense help, despite the fact that logical memory is the one he finds most valuable. Teachers, politicians, linguists, clerks, waiters, and others need a well-developed desultory memory. Rote memory is, of course, necessary if an individual is to make a success as an actor, a singer, or a musician.

According to the rate of acquisition memory has been classified into quick and slow. One learner gets his material so much more quickly than another. Up to rather recent years the quick learner has been commiserated, for we believed, "quickly come, quickly go." Experimental results have proved this not to be true, but in fact the reverse is more true, *i.e.*, "quickly come, slowly go." The one who learns quickly, provided he really learns it, retains it just as long and on the average longer than the one who learns much more slowly. The danger, from a practical point of view, is that the quick learner, because of his ability, gets careless and learns the material only well enough to reproduce at the time, whereas the slow learner, because of his lack of ability, raises his efficiency to a higher level and therefore retains. If the quick learner had spent five minutes more on the material, he would have raised his work to the same level as that of the slow one and yet have finished in perhaps half the time.

All through the discussion of kinds of memory the term "memory" should have been used in the plural, for after all we possess "memories" and not a single faculty memory which may be quick, or desultory, or permanent. The actual condition of affairs is much more complex, for although it has been the individual who has been designated as quick or logical, it would be much more accurate to designate the particular memory. The same person may have a splendid desultory memory for gossip and yet in science be of the logical type. In learning French vocabularies he may have only a good immediate memory, whereas his memory for faces may be most lasting. His ability to learn facts in history may class him as a quick learner, whereas his slowness in learning music may be proverbial. The degree to which quickness of learning or permanence of memory in one line is correlated with that same ability in others has not yet been ascertained. That there is some correlation is probable, but at present the safest way is to think in terms of special memories and special acquisitions. Some experimental work has been done to discover the order in which special memories develop in children. The results, however, are not in agreement and the experiments themselves are unsatisfactory. That there is some more or less definite order of development, paralleling to a certain extent the growth of instincts, is probable, but nothing more definite is known than observation teaches. For instance, every observer of children knows that memory for objects develops before memory for words; that memory for gestures preceded memory for words; that memory for oral language preceded memory for written language; that memory for concrete objects preceded memory for abstractions. Further knowledge of the development of special memories should be accompanied by knowledge as to how far this development is dependent on training and to what extent lack of memory involves lack of understanding before it can be of much practical value to the teacher.

Just as repetition or exercise tends to fix a fact in memory, so disuse of a connection results in the fact fading from memory. "Forgetting" is a matter of everyday experience for every one. The rate of forgetting has been the subject of experimental work. Ebbinghaus's investigation is the historical one. The results from this particular series of experiments are as follows: During the first hour after study over half of what was learned had been forgotten; at the end of the first day two thirds, and at the end of a month about four fifths. These results have been accepted as capable of rather general application until within the last few years. Recent experiments in learning poetry, translation of French into English, practice in addition and multiplication, learning to toss balls and to typewrite, and others, make clear that there is no general curve of forgetting. The rate of forgetting is more rapid soon after the practice period than later, but the total amount forgotten and the rate of deterioration depend upon the particular function tested. No one function can serve as a sample for others. No one curve of forgetting exists for different functions at the same stage of advancement or for the same function at different stages of advancement in the same individual, much less for different functions, at different stages of advancement, in different individuals. Much more experimental work is needed before definite general results can be stated.

This experimental work, however, is suggestive along several lines,

(1) It seems possible that habits of skill, involving direct sensori-motor bonds, are more permanent than memories involving connections between association bonds. In other words, that physical habits are more lasting than memories of intellectual facts.

(2) Overlearning seems a necessary correlate of permanence of connection. That is, what seems to be overlearning at beginning stages is really only raising the material to the necessary level above the threshold for retention. How far overlearning is necessary and when it becomes wasteful are yet to be determined.

(3) Deterioration is hastened by competing connections. If during the time a particular function is lying idle other bonds of connection are being formed into some parts or elements of it, the rate of forgetting of the function in question is hastened and the possibility of recall made more problematic. The less the interference, the greater will be the permanence of the particular bonds.

A belief maintained by some psychologists is in direct opposition to this general law that disuse causes deterioration. It is usually stated something like this, that periods of incubation are necessary in acquiring skill, or that letting a function lie fallow results in greater skill at the end of that period, or briefly one learns to skate in summer and swim in winter. To some extent this is true, but as stated it is misleading. The general law of the effect of disuse on a memory is true, but under some circumstances its effect is mitigated by the presence of other factors whose presence has been unnoted. Sometimes this improvement without practice is explained by the fact that at the last practice period the actual improvement was masked by fatigue or boredom, so that disuse involving rest and the disappearance of fatigue and boredom produces apparent gain, when in reality it but allows the real improvement to become evident. Sometimes a particular practice period was accompanied by certain undesirable elements such as worry, excitement, misunderstandings, and so on, and therefore the improvement hindered or masked, whereas at the next period under different conditions there would be less interference and therefore added gain. All experimental evidence is against the opinion that mere disuse in and of itself produces gain. In fact, all results point to the fact that disuse brings deterioration.

In the case of memory, as has already been described in habit formation, reviews which are organized with the period between repetitions only gradually lengthened may do much to insure permanence. It is entirely feasible to have children at the end of any school year able to repeat the poems or prose selections which they have memorized, provided that they have been recalled with sufficient frequency during the course of the year. In a subject like geography or history, or in the study of mathematics or science, in which logical memory is demanded, systematic reviews, rather than cramming for examinations, will result in permanence of command of the facts or principles involved, especially when these reviews have involved the right type of organization and as many associations as is possible.

It is important in those subjects which involve a logical organization of ideas to have ideas associated around some particular problem or situation in which the individual is vitally interested. Children may readily forget a large number of facts which they have learned about cats in the first grade, while the same children might remember, very many of them, had these facts been organized round the problem of taking care of cats, and of how cats take care of themselves. A group of children in an upper grade may forget with great rapidity the facts of climate, soil, surface drainage, industries, and the like, while they may remember with little difficulty facts which belong under each of these categories on account of the interest which they have taken in the problem, "Why is the western part of the United States much more sparsely populated than the Mississippi Valley?" Boys and girls who study physics in the high school may find it difficult to remember the principles involved in their study of heat if they are given only in their logical order and are applied only in laboratory exercises which have little or no meaning for them, while the same group of high school pupils may remember without difficulty these same laws or principles if associated round the issue of the most economical way of heating their houses, or of the best way to build an icehouse.

There has been in our school system during the past few years more or less of a reaction against verbatim memorization, which is certainly justified when we are considering those subjects which involve primarily an organization of ideas in terms of problems to be solved, rather than memory for the particular form of expression of the ideas in question. It is worth while, however, at every stage of education to use whatever power children may possess for verbatim memorization, especially in the field of literature, and to some extent in other fields as well. It seems to the writers to be worth while to indicate as clearly as possible in the illustration which follows the method to be employed in verbatim memorization. As will be easily recognized, the number and organization of associations are an important consideration. It is especially important to call attention to the fact that any attempt at verbatim memorization should follow a very careful thinking through of the whole selection to be memorized. An organization of the ideas in terms of that which is most important, and that which can be subordinated to these larger thoughts, a combination of method of learning by wholes and by parts, is involved.

It is not easy to indicate fully the method by which one would attempt to teach to a group of sixth-grade boys or girls Wordsworth's "Daffodils." The main outline of the method may, however, be indicated as follows: The first thing to be done is to arouse, in so far as is possible, some interest and enthusiasm for the poem in question. One might suggest to the class something of the beauty of the high, rugged hills, and of the lakes nestling among them in the region which is called the "Lake Region" in England. The Wordsworth cottage near one of the lakes, and at the foot of one of the high hills, together with the walk which is to this day called Wordsworth's Walk, can be brought to the mind, especially by a teacher who has taken the trouble to know something of Wordsworth's home life. The enthusiasm of the poet for the beauties of nature and his enjoyment in walking over the hills and around the lakes, is suggested by the poem itself. One might suggest to the pupils that this is the story of a walk which he took one morning early in the spring.

The attempt will be made from this point on to give the illustration as the writer might have hoped to have it recorded as presented to a particular class. The poet tells us first of his loneliness and of the surprise which was his when he caught sight for the first time of the daffodils which had blossomed since the last time that he had taken this particular walk:

> "I wandered lonely as a cloud
>
> That floats on high o'er vales and hills,
>
> When all at once I saw a crowd,
>
> A host, of golden daffodils;
>
> Beside the lake, beneath the trees,
>
> Fluttering and dancing in the breeze."

You see, he was not expecting to meet any one or to have any unusual experience. He "wandered lonely as a cloud that floats on high o'er vales and hills," and his surprise was complete when he saw suddenly,--"all at once I saw a crowd, a *host* of *golden* daffodils, beside the lake, beneath the trees." You might have said that they were waving in the wind, but he saw them "fluttering and dancing in the breeze."

The daffodils as they waved and danced in the breeze suggested to him the experience which he had had on other walks which he had taken when the stars were shining, and he compares the golden daffodils to the shining, twinkling stars:

> "Continuous as the stars that shine
>
> And twinkle on the Milky Way,
>
> They stretched in never-ending line
>
> Along the margin of a bay;

> Ten thousand saw I at a glance,
>
> Tossing their heads in sprightly dance."

The daffodils were as "continuous as the stars that shine and twinkle on the Milky Way." There was no beginning and no end to the line,--"They stretched in never-ending line along the margin of a bay." He saw as many daffodils as one might see stars,--"Ten thousand saw I at a glance, tossing their heads in sprightly dance."

The poet has enjoyed the beauty of the little rippling waves in the lake, and he tells us that

> "The waves beside them danced; but they
>
> Outdid the sparkling waves in glee:
>
> A poet could not but be gay,
>
> In such a jocund company:
>
> I gazed--and gazed,--but little thought
>
> What wealth the show to me had brought:"

The daffodils have really left the poet with a great joy,--the waves beside the daffodils are dancing, "but they outdid the *sparkling* waves in glee," and of course "a poet could not but be gay in such a jocund company." Had you ever thought of flowers as a jocund company? You remember they fluttered and danced in the breeze, they lifted their heads in sprightly dance. Do you wonder that the poet says of his experience, "I gazed--and gazed,--but little thought what wealth the show to me had brought"? I wonder if any of you have ever had a similar experience. I remember the days when I used to go fishing, and there is a great joy even now in recalling the twitter of the birds and the hum of the bees as I lay on the bank and waited for the fish to bite.

And what is the great joy which is his, and which may belong to us, if we really see the beautiful things in nature? He tells us when he says

"For oft, when on my couch I lie

In vacant or in pensive mood,

They flash upon that inward eye

Which is the bliss of solitude;

And then my heart with pleasure fills,

And dances with the daffodils."

There are days when we cannot get out of doors,--"For oft, when on my couch I lie in vacant or in pensive mood,"--these are the days when we recall the experiences which we have enjoyed in the days which are gone,--"they flash upon that inward eye which is the bliss of solitude." And then for the poet, as well as for us, "And then my heart with pleasure fills, and dances with the daffodils."

Now let us get the main ideas in the story which the poet tells us of his adventure. "I wandered lonely as a cloud that floats on high o'er vales and hills," "I saw a crowd, a host, of golden daffodils," they were "beside the lake, beneath the trees, fluttering and dancing in the breeze." They reminded me as I saw the beautiful arched line of "the stars that shine and twinkle on the Milky Way," because "they stretched in never-ending line along the margin of a bay"; and as I watched "ten thousand" I saw, "tossing their heads in sprightly dance." And then they reminded me of the waves which sparkled near by, "but they outdid the sparkling waves in glee," and in the happiness which was mine, "I gazed--and gazed,--but little thought what wealth the show to me had brought." And that happiness I can depend upon when upon my couch I lie in vacant or in pensive mood, for "they flash upon that inward eye which is the bliss of solitude," and my heart will fill with pleasure and dance with the daffodils.

These, then, are the big ideas which the poet has,-- he wanders lonely as a cloud, he enjoys the great surprise of the daffodils, the great crowd, the host, of golden daf- fodils, fluttering and dancing in the breeze; he thinks of the stars that twinkle in the Milky Way, because the line of daffodils seems to have no beginning and no end,--he sees ten thousand of them at a glance, tossing their heads in sprightly dance. And as he looks at them he thinks of the beauty of the sparkling waves, and thinks of them as they dance with glee, and he gazes and gazes without thinking of the wealth of the experience. But later when he writes the poem, he tells us of the wealth of the expe- rience which can last through all of the days when he lies on his couch in vacant or in pensive mood, for it is then that this experience flashes upon that inward eye which is the bliss of solitude, and his heart fills with pleasure and dances with the daffodils.

Now let us say it all over again, and see how nearly we are able to recall the story of his experience in just the words that he used. I will read it for you first, and then you may all try to repeat it after me.

The teacher then reads the whole poem through, possibly more than once, and then asks all of the chil- dren to recite it with him, repeating possibly the first stanza twice or three times until they get it, and then the second stanza two or three times, then the third as often as may be necessary, and finally the fourth. It may be well then to go back and again analyze the thought, and indicate, using as far as possible the author's own words, the development of ideas through the poem. Then the poem should be recited as a whole by the teacher and children. The children may then be left to study it so that they may individually on the next day recite it verbatim. The writer has found it possible to have a number of children in a sixth grade able to repeat the poem verbatim after the kind of treatment indicated above, and at the end of a period of fifteen minutes.

QUESTIONS

1. Distinguish in so far as you can between habit and memory.

2. Name the factors which determine one's ability to recall.

3. How can you hope to improve children's memories? Which of the factors involved are subject to improvement?

4. In what way can you improve the organization of associations upon the part of children in any one of the subjects which you teach? How increase the number of associations?

5. What advantage has the method of concentration over the method of repetition in memorization?

6. Give the reasons why the method of recall is the best method of memorization.

7.   If you were teaching a poem of four stanzas, would you use the method of memorization by wholes or by parts? Indicate clearly the degree to which the one or the other method should be used or the nature of the combination of methods for the particular selection which you use for the purposes of illustration.

8.   How long do children in your classes seem to be able to work hard at verbatim memorization?

9.   Under what conditions may the writing of the material being memorized actually interfere with the process? When may it help?

10.   Why may it not be wise to attempt to teach "their" and "there" at the same time?

11.   What is the type of memory employed by children who have considerable ability in cramming for examinations? Is this type of memory ever useful in later life?

12.   What precaution do we need to take to insure permanence in memory upon the part of those who learn quickly?

13.   What is meant by saying that we possess memories rather than a power or capacity called memory?

14.   Do we forget with equal rapidity in all fields in which we have learned? What factors determine the rate of forgetting?

15.   Why should a boy think through a poem to be memorized rather than beginning his work by trying to repeat the first two lines?

VI

The Teacher's Use of the Imagination

Imagination is governed by the same general laws of association which control habit and memory. In these two former topics the emphasis was upon getting a desired result without any attention to the form of that result. Imagination, on the other hand, has to do with the way past experience is used and the form taken by the result. It merges into memory in one direction and into thinking in another. No one definition has been found acceptable--in fact, in no field of psychology is there more difference of opinion, in no topic are terms used more loosely, than in this one of imagination. Stated in very general terms, imagination is the process of reproducing, or reconstructing any form of experience. The result of such a process is a mental image. When the fact that it is reproduction or reconstruction is lost sight of, and the image reacted to as if it were present, an illusion or hallucination results.

Images may be classified according to the sense through which the original experience came, into visual, auditory, gustatory, tactile, kinæsthetic, and so on. In many discussions of imagery the term "picture" has been used to describe it, and hence in the thought of many it is limited rather definitely to the visual field. Of course this is entirely wrong. The recall of a melody, or of the touch of velvet, or of the fragrance of a rose, is just as much mental imagery as the recall of the sight of a friend.

Three points of dispute in connection with image types are worth while noting. First, the question is raised by some psychologists as to whether kinæsthetic or motor images really exist. An example of such an image would be to imagine yourself as dancing, or walking downstairs, or writing your name, or saying the word "bubble." Those who object to such an image type claim that when one tries to get such an image, the attempt initiates slight muscle movements and the result is a sense experience instead of an imaged one. They believe this always happens and that therefore a motor image is an impossibility. Others agree that this reinstatement of actual movements often happens, but contend that in such cases the image precedes the movement and that the resulting movement does not always take place. The question is still in dispute.

The second question in dispute is as to the possibility of classifying people according to the predominant type of their imagery. People used to be classed as "visualizers," "audiles." etc., the supposition being that their mental imagery was predominantly in terms of vision or hearing. This is being seriously questioned, and experimental work seems to show that such a classification, at least with the majority of people, is impossible. The results which are believed to warrant such a conclusion are as follows: First, no one has ever been tested who always used one type of image. Second, the type of image used changed with the following factors: the material, the purpose of the subject, the familiarity of the subject with the experience imagined. For example, the same person would, perhaps, visualize if he were imaging landscape, but get an auditory image of a friend's voice instead of a visual image of him. He might, when under experimental conditions with the controlling purpose,--that of examining his images,--get visual images, but, when under ordinary conditions, get a larger number of auditory and kinæsthetic images. He might when thought was flowing smoothly be using auditory and motor images, but upon the appearance of some obstacle or difficulty in the process find himself flooded with visual images. Third, subjects who ranked high in one type of imagery ranked high in others, and subjects who ranked low in one type ranked low also in others. The ability seems to be that of getting clear image types, or the lack of it, rather than the ability to get one type. Fourth, most of the subjects reported that the first image was usually followed by others of different types. The conclusions then, that individuals, children as well as adults, are rarely of one fixed type, the mixed type being the usual one, is being generally accepted. In fact, it seems much more probable that materials and outside conditions can more easily be classified as usually arousing a certain type of image, than people can be classified into types.

The third point of controversy grows out of the second. Some psychologists are asking what is the value of such a classification? Suppose people could be put under types in imagery, what would be the practical advantage? Such an attempt at classification is futile and not worth while, for two reasons. First, the result of the mental processes--the goal arrived at is the important thing, and the particular type of image used is of little importance. Does it make any difference to the business man whether his clerk thinks in terms of the visual images of words or in terms of motor images so long as he sells the goods? To the teacher of geography, does it make any difference whether John in his thinking of the value of trees is seeing them in his mind's eye, or hearing the wind rustle through the leaves, or smelling the moist earth, leaf-mold, or having none of these images, if he gets the meaning, and reaches a right conclusion? Second, the sense which gives the clearest, most dependable impressions is not the one necessarily in terms of which the experience is recalled. One of the chief values urged for a classification according to image type of people, especially children, has been that the appeal could then be made through the corresponding sense organs. For instance, Group A, being visualizers, will be asked to read the material silently; Group B, audiles, will have the material read to them; Group C, motiles, will be asked to read the material orally, or asked to dramatize it. For each group the major appeal should be made in terms of the sense corresponding to their image type. But such a correspondence as this does not exist. An individual may learn best by use of his eyes and yet very seldom use visual images in recall. This is true of most people in reading. Most people grasp the meaning of a passage better when they read it than when they hear it read, and yet the predominant type of word image is auditory-motor. Hence if any classification of children is attempted it should be according to the sense by means of which they learn best, and not according to some supposed image type. Many methods of appeal for all children is the safest practical suggestion.

Images may also be classified according to the use made of past experience. Past experience may be recalled in approximately the same form in which it occurred, or it may be reconstructed. In the former case the image is called reproductive image or memory image; in the latter form it is called productive or creative image, or image of the imagination. The reproductive image never duplicates experience, but in its major features it closely corresponds to it, whereas the productive image breaks up old experiences and from them makes new wholes which correspond to no definite occurrence. The elements found in both kinds of imagery must come from experience. One cannot imagine anything the elements of which he has not experienced. Creative imagination transcends experience only in the sense that it remodels and remakes, but the result of that activity produces new wholes as far removed from the actual occurrences as "Alice in Wonderland" is from the humdrum life of a tenement dweller. Just the same, the fact that the elements used in creative work must be drawn from experience is extremely suggestive from a practical point of view. It demonstrates the need of a rich sensory life for every child. It also explains the reason for the lack of appreciation on the part of immature children of certain types of literature and certain moral questions.

No more need be said here of the reproductive image, as it is synonymous with the memory image and was therefore treated fully under the topic of memory. One fact should be borne in mind, however, and that is, that the creative image is to some extent dependent on the reproductive image as it involves recall. However, as productive imagery involves the recall of elements or parts rather than wholes, an individual may have talent in creative imagery without being above the average in exact reproduction.

Productive imagery may be classified as fanciful, realistic, and idealistic according to the character of the material used. Fanciful productive imagery is characterized by its spontaneity, its disregard of the probable and possible, its vividness of detail. It is its own reward, and does not look to any result beyond itself. Little children's imaginations are of this type--it is their play world of make-believe. The incongruity and absurdity of their images have been compared to the dreams of adults. Lacking in experience, without knowledge of natural laws, their imagination runs riot with the materials it has at its command. Some adults still retain it to a high degree--witness the myths and fairy stories, "Alice in Wonderland," and the like. All adults in their "castle-building" indulge in this type of imagery to some extent. Realistic productive imagery, as its name implies, adheres more strictly to actual conditions, it deals with the probable. It usually is constructed for a purpose, being put to some end beyond itself. It lacks much of the emotional element possessed by the other two types. This is the kind most valuable in reasoning and thinking. It deals with new situations--constructs them, creates means of dealing with them, and forecasts the results. It is the type of productive imagery called into play by inventors, by craftsmen, by physicians, by teachers--in fact, by any one who tries to bring about a change in conditions by the functioning of a definite thought process. This is the kind of imagery which most interests grammar school pupils. They demand facts, not fancies. They are most active in making changes in a world of things.

Idealistic productive imagery does not fly in the face of reality as does the fanciful, nor does it adhere so strictly to facts as does the realistic. It deals with the possible--with what may be, but with what is not yet. It always looks to the future, for if realized it is no longer idealistic. It is enjoyed for its own sake but does not exist for that alone, but looks towards some result. It is concerned primarily with human lives and has a strong emotional tone. It is the heart of ideals. The adolescent revels in this type of productive imagery. His dreams concerning his own future, his service to his fellow men, his success, and the like involve much idealistic imagery. Hero worship involves it. It is one of the differences between the man with "vision" and the man without.

The importance of productive imagery cannot be overemphasized. This power to create the new out of the old is one of the greatest possessions of mankind. All progress in every field, whether individual or racial, depends upon it. From the fertility and richness of man's productive imagination must come all the suggestions which will make this world other than what it is. Therefore one of the greatest tasks of education at present is to cherish and cultivate this power. One cannot fail to recognize, however, that with the emphasis at present so largely upon memory, the cultivation of the imagination is being pushed into the background despite all our theories to the contrary. Not only is productive imagery as a whole worth while, but each type is valuable. An adult lacking power of fanciful imagination lacks power to enjoy certain elements in life and lacks a very definite means of recreation. Lacking in realistic imagination he is unable to deal successfully with new situations, but must forever remain in bondage to the past. Without idealistic imagination he lacks the motive which makes men strive to be better, more efficient--other than what they are. At certain times in child development one type may need special encouragement, and at another time some other. All should, however, be borne in mind and developed along right and wholesome lines; otherwise, left to itself, any one of these, and especially the last, may be a source of danger to the character.

Images may be classified according to the material dealt with into object images or concrete images and into word or abstract images. No one of these terms is very good as a name of the image referred to. The first group--object or concrete image--refers to an image in which the sensory qualities, such as color, size, rhythm, sweetness, harmony, etc., are present. The images of a friend, of a text-book, of the national anthem, of an orange, of the schoolroom, and so on, would all be object images. A word or abstract image is one which is a symbol. It stands for and represents certain sensory experiences, the quality of which does not appear in the image. Any word, number, mathematical or chemical symbol--in fact, any abstract symbol will come under this type of image. If in the first list of illustrations, instead of having images of the real objects, an individual had images of words in each case, the images would be abstract or verbal images. Abstract images shade into concrete by gradual degrees--there is no sharp line of division between the two; however, they do form two different kinds of images, two forms which may have the same meaning.

The question as to the respective use and value of these two kinds of images is given different answers. There is no question but that the verbal image is more economical than the object image. It saves energy and time. It brings with it less of irrelevant detail and is more stable than the object image, and therefore results in more accurate thinking. It is abstract in nature and therefore has more general application. On the other hand, it has been claimed for the object image that it necessarily precedes the verbal image--is fundamental to it; that it is essential in creative work dealing with materials and sounds and in the appreciation of certain types of descriptive literature, and that in any part of the thinking process when, because of difficulty of some kind, a percept would help, an object image would be of the same assistance. It is concerning these supposed advantages of the object image that there has been most dispute. There is no proof that the line of growth is necessarily from percept, through object image, to verbal image. In certain fields, notably smell, the object image is almost absent and yet the verbal images in that field carry meaning. It is also true that people whose power of getting clear-cut, vivid object images is almost nil seem to be in nowise hampered by that fact in their use of the symbols. Knowing the unreliability of the object image, it would seem very unsafe to use it as the link between percept and symbol. Much better to connect the symbol directly with the experience and let it gain its meaning from that. As to its value in constructive work in arts, literature, drama, and invention, the testimony of some experts in each field bears witness that it is not a necessary accompaniment of success. The musician need not hear, mentally, all the harmonies, changes, intervals; he may think them in terms of notes, rests, etc., as he composes. The poet need not see the scene he is describing; verbal images may bear his meanings. Of course this does not mean that object images may not be present too, but the point is that the worker is not dependent on them. The aid offered by object images in time of difficulty is still more open to doubt. As an illustration of what is meant by this: Suppose a child to be given a carpeting example in arithmetic which he finds himself unable to solve. The claim is made that if he will then call up a concrete image of the room, he will see that the carpet is laid in strips and that suggestion may set him right. But it has been proved experimentally over and over again that if he doesn't know that carpets are laid that way, he will never get it from the image, and if he does know it, he doesn't need an object image. It seems to be a fact that object images do not function, in the sense that one cannot get a correct answer as to color, or form, or number from them. One can read off from a concrete image what he knows to be true of it--or else it is just guessing. "Knowing" in each case involves observation and judgment, and that means verbal images. Students whose power of concrete imagery is low do, on the average, in situations where a concrete image would supposedly help, just as well as students whose power in this field is high. It does seem to be true that object images give a vividness and color to mental life which may result in a keener appreciation of certain types of literature. This warmth and vividness which object images add to the mental processes of those who have them is a boon.

On the whole, then, word images are the more valuable of the two types. Upon them depends, primarily, the ability to handle new situations, and even in the constructive fields they are all sufficient. These two facts, added to the fact that they are more accurate, speedy, and general in application, makes them a necessary part of the mental equipment of an efficient worker, and means that much more attention must be given to the development of productive symbol images.

Two warnings should be borne in mind: First, although the object images are not necessary in general, as discussed above, to any given individual, because of his particular habits of thought, they may be necessary accompaniments to his mental processes. Second, although object images may not help in giving understanding or appreciation under new conditions, still the method of asking students to try to image certain conditions is worth while because it makes them stop and think, which is always a help. Whether they get object or word images in the process makes no difference.

The discussion concerning the possibility of "imageless" thought, while an interesting one, cannot be entered into here. Whether "meanings" can exist in the human mind apart from any carrier in the form of some sensory or imaginal state is unsettled, but the discussion has drawn attention to at least the very fragmentary nature of those carriers. A few fragments of words, a mental shrug of the shoulder, a feeling of the direction in which a certain course is leading, a consciousness of one's attitude towards a plan or person--and the conclusion is reached. The thinking, or it may even have been reasoning, involved few clear-cut images of any kind. The fragmentary, schematic nature of the carriers and the large part played by feelings of direction and attitude are the rather astonishing results of the introspective analysis resulting from this discussion. This sort of thinking is valuable for the same reasons that thinking in terms of words is valuable--it only goes a step further, but it needs direction and training.

Images of all kinds have been discussed as if they stood out clearly differentiated from all other types of mental states. This is necessary in order that their peculiar characteristics and functions may be clear. However, they are not so clearly defined in actual mental life, but shade into each other and into other mental states, giving rise to confusion and error. The two greatest sources of error are: first, the confusion of image with percept, and second, the confusion of memory image with image of the imagination. The chief difference between these mental states as they exist is a difference in kind and amount of associations. These different associates usually give to the percept a vividness and material reality which the other two lack. They give to the memory image a feeling of pastness and trueness which the image of imagination lacks. Therefore lack of certain associations, due to lack of experience or knowledge, or presence of associations due to these same causes and to the undue vividness of other connections, could easily result in one of these states being mistaken for another. There is no inherent difference between them. The first type of confusion, between percept and image, has been recently made the subject of investigation. Perky found that even with trained adults, if the perceptual stimulus was slight, it was mistaken for an image. All illusions would come under this head. Children's imaginary companions, when really believed in, are explained by this confusion. However, the confusion is much more general than these illustrations would seem to imply. The fact that "Love is blind," that "We see what we look for" are but statements of this same confusion, and these two facts enter into multitudes of situations all through life. The need to "see life clearly and see it whole" is an imperative one.

The second type of confusion, between reproductive and productive memory, is even more common. The "white lies" of children, the embroidering of a story by the adult, the adding to and adding to the original experience until all sense of what really happened is lost, are but ordinary facts of everyday experiences. The unreliability of witness and testimony is due, in part, to this confusion.

QUESTIONS

1. How is the process of imagination like memory?

2. What is the relation of imagination to thinking?

3. What kind of images do you seek to have children use in their work in the subjects which you teach?

4. Can you classify the members of your class as visualizers, audiles, and the like?

5. If one learns most readily by reading rather than hearing, does it follow that his images will be largely visual? Why?

6. Give examples from your own experience of memory images; of creative images.

7. To what degree does creative imagination depend upon past experiences?

8. What type of imagery is most important for the work of the inventor? The farmer? The social reformer?

9. Of what significance in the life of an adult is fanciful imagery?

10. What, if any, is the danger involved in reveling in idealistic productive imagery?

11. What advantages do verbal images possess as over against object images?

12. Why would you ask children to try to image in teaching literature, geography, history, or any other subject for which you are responsible?

13. How would you handle a boy who is hi the habit of confusing memory images with images of imagination?

14. In what sense is it true that all progress, is dependent upon productive imagination?

VII

How Thinking May be Stimulated

The term "thinking" has been used almost as loosely as the term "imagination," and used to mean almost as many different things. Even now there is no consensus of opinion as to just what thinking is. Dewey says, "Active, persistent, and careful consideration of any belief or supposed form of knowledge in the light of the grounds that support it, and the further conclusions to which it tends, constitutes reflective thought."[5] Miller says, "Thinking is not so much a distinct conscious process as it is an organisation of all the conscious processes which are relevant in a problematic situation for the performance of the function of consciously adjusting means to end."[6] Thinking always presupposes some lack in adjustment, some doubt or uncertainty, some hesitation in response. So long as the situation, because of its simplicity or familiarity, receives immediately a response which satisfies, there is no need for thinking. Only when the response is inadequate or when no satisfactory response is forthcoming is thinking aroused. By far the majority of the daily adjustments made by people, both mental and physical, require no thinking because instinct, habit, and memory suffice. It is only when these do not serve to pro-

---

5. How We Think.
6. The Psychology of Thinking.

duce a satisfactory response that thinking is needed--only when there is something problematic in the situation. Even in new situations thinking is not always used to bring about a satisfactory adjustment. Following an instinctive prompting when confronted by a new situation; blindly following another's lead; using the trial and error method of response; reacting to the situation as to the old situation most like it; or response by analogy: all are methods of dealing with new situations which often result in correct adjustments, and yet none of which need involve thinking. This does not mean that these methods, save the first mentioned, may not be accompanied by thinking; but that each of them may be used without the conscious adjustment of means to end demanded by thinking. That these methods, and not thinking, are the ones most often used, even by adults, in dealing with problems, cannot be denied. They offer an easy means of escape from the more troublesome method of thinking. It is so much easier to accept what some one else says, so much easier to agree with a book's answer to a question than to think it out for oneself. Following the first suggestion offered, just going at things in a hit-or-miss fashion, uncritical response by analogy, saves much time and energy apparently, and therefore these methods are adopted and followed by the majority of people in most of the circumstances of life. It is human nature to think only when no other method of mental activity brings the desired response. We think only when we must.

Not only is it true that problems are often solved correctly by other methods than that of thinking, but on the other hand much thinking may take place and yet the result be an incorrect conclusion, or perhaps no solution at all be reached. Think of the years of work men have devoted to a single problem, and yet perhaps at the end of that time, because of a wrong premise or some incorrect data, have arrived at a result that later years have proved to have been utterly false. Think of the investigations being carried on now in medicine, in science, in invention, which because of the lack of knowledge are still incomplete, and yet in each case thinking of the most technical and rigorous type has been used. Thinking cannot be considered in terms of the result. Correct results may be obtained, even in problematic situations, with no thinking, and on the other hand much thinking may be done and yet the results reached be entirely unsatisfactory. Thinking is a process involving a certain definite procedure. It is the organisation of all mental states toward a certain definite end, but is not any one mental state. In certain types of situations this procedure is the one most certain of reaching correct conclusions, in some situations it is the only possible one, but the conclusion is not the thinking and its correctness does not differentiate the process from others.

From the foregoing discussions it must not be deduced that because of the specific nature and the difficulty of thinking that the power is given only to adults. On the contrary, the power is rooted in the original equipment of the human race and develops gradually, just as all other original capacities do. Children under three years of age manifest it. True, the situations calling it out are very simple, and to the adult seem often trivial, as they most often occur in connection with the child's play, but they none the less call for the adjustment of means to end, which is thinking. A lost toy, the absence of a playmate, the breaking of a cup, a thunderstorm, these and hundreds of other events of daily life are occasions which may arouse thinking on the part of a little child. It is not the type of situation, nor its dignity, that is the important thing in thinking, but the way in which it is dealt with. The incorrectness of a child's data, their incompleteness and lack of organization, often result in incorrect conclusions, and still his thinking may be absolutely sound. The difference between the child and the adult in this power is a difference in degree--both possess the power. As Dewey says, "Only by making the most of the thought-factor, already active in the experience of childhood, is there any promise or warrant for the emergence of superior reflective power at adolescence, or at any later period."[7]

Thinking, then, is involved in any response which comes as a result of the conscious adaptation of means to end in a problematic situation. Many of the processes of mental activity which have been given other names may involve this process. Habit formation--when the learner analyzes his progress or failure, when he tries to find a short cut, or when he seeks for an incentive to insure greater improvement--may serve as a situation calling for thinking. The process of apperceiving or of assimilation may involve it. Studying and trying to remember may involve it. Constructive imagination often calls for it. Reasoning, always requires it. In the older psychology reasoning and thinking were often used as synonyms, but more recently it has been accepted by most psychologists that reasoning is simply one type of thinking, the most advanced type, and the most demanding type, but not the only one. Thinking may go on (as in the other processes just mentioned) without reasoning, but all reasoning must involve thinking. It is this lack of differen-

---

7. How We Think.

tiation between reasoning and thinking, the attempt to make of all thinking, reasoning, that has limited teachers in their attempts to develop thinking upon the part of their pupils.

The essentials of the thinking process are three:

(1)   a state of doubt or uncertainty, resulting in suspended judgment;

(2)   an organization and control of mental states in view of an end to be attained;

(3)   a critical attitude involving selection and rejection of suggestions offered.

The recognition of some lack of adjustment, the feeling of need for something one hasn't, is the only stimulus toward thinking. This problematic situation, resulting in suspended judgment, caused by the inadequacy of present power or knowledge, may arise in connection with any situation. It is unfortunate that the terms "problematic situation" and "feeling of inadequacy" have been discussed almost entirely in connection with situations when the result has some pragmatic value. There is no question but what the situation arousing thinking must be a live one and a real one, but it need not be one the answer to which will be useful. It is true that with the majority of people, both children and adults, a problem of this type will be more often effective in arousing the thinking process than a problem of a more abstract nature, but it is not always so, nor necessarily so. Most children sometimes, and some children most of the time, enjoy thinking simply for the sake of the activity. They do not need the concrete, pragmatic situation--anything, no matter how abstract, that arouses their curiosity or appeals to their love of mastery offers enough of a problem. Sometimes children are vitally interested in working geometrical problems, translating difficult passages in Latin, striving to invent the perpetual motion machine, even though there is no evident and useful result. It is not the particular type of situation that is the thing to be considered, but the attitude that it arouses in the individual concerned. Educators in discussion of the situations that make for thinking must allow for individual differences and must plan for the intellectually minded as well as for others.

The thinker confronted by a situation for which his present knowledge is not adequate, recognizes the difficulty and suspends judgment; in other words, does not jump at a conclusion but undertakes to think it out. To do this control is continually necessary. He must keep his problem continually before him and work directly for its solution, avoiding delays, avoiding being side-tracked. This means, of course, the critical attitude towards all suggestions offered. Each one as it comes must be inspected in the light of the end to be reached--if it does not seem to help towards that goal, it must be rejected. Criticism, selection, and rejection of suggestions offered must continue as long as the thinking process goes on. "To maintain the state of doubt and to carry on systematic and protracted inquiry--these are the essentials of thinking."

In order to maintain this critical attitude to select and reject suggestions with reference to a goal, the suggestions as they come cannot be accepted as units and followed. Such a procedure is possible only when the mental process is not controlled by an end. Control by a goal necessitates analysis of the suggestions and abstraction of what in them is essential for the particular problem in hand. It is because no complete association at hand offers a satisfactory response to the situation that the need for thinking arises. Each association as it comes must be broken up, certain parts or elements emerge, certain relationships, implications, or functions are made conscious. Each of these is examined in turn; as they seem to be valueless for the purpose of the thinker, they are rejected. If one element or relationship seems significant for the problem, it is seized upon, abstracted from its fellows, and becomes the center of the next series of suggestions. A part, element, quality, or what not, of the situation is accepted as significant of it for the time being. The part stands for the whole--this is characteristic of all thinking. As a very simple illustration, consider the following one reported by Dewey:

"Projecting nearly horizontally from the upper deck of the ferryboat on which I daily cross the river, is a long white pole, bearing a gilded ball at its tip. It suggested a flag pole when I first saw it; its color, shape, and gilded ball agreed with this idea, and these reasons seemed to justify me in this belief. But soon difficulties presented themselves. The pole was nearly horizontal, an unusual position for a flag pole; in the next place, there was no pulley, ring, or cord by which to attach a flag; finally, there were elsewhere two vertical staffs from which flags were occasionally flown. It seemed probable that the pole was not there for flag-flying.

"I then tried to imagine all possible purposes of such a pole, and to consider for which of these it was best suited:

(*a*)   Possibly it was an ornament. But as all the ferryboats and even the tugboats carried like poles, this hypothesis was rejected.

(*b*)   Possibly it was the terminal of a wireless telegraph. But the same considerations made this improbable. Besides, the more natural place for such a terminal would be the highest part of the boat, on top of the pilot house,

(*c*)   Its purpose might be to point out the direction in which the boat is moving.

"In support of this conclusion, I discovered that the pole was lower than the pilot house, so that the steersman could easily see it. Moreover, the tip was enough higher than the base, so that, from the pilot's position, it must appear to project far out in front of the boat. Moreover, the pilot being near the front of the boat, he would need some such guide as to its direction. Tugboats would also need poles for such a purpose. This hypothesis was so much more probable than the others that I accepted it. I formed the conclusion that the pole was set up for the purpose of showing the pilot the direction in which the boat pointed, to enable him to steer correctly."[8]

The problem was to find out the use of the flag pole. No adequate explanation came as the problem presented itself; it therefore caused a state of uncertainty, of suspended judgment, and a process of thinking in order to get an answer. Each suggestion that came was analyzed, its requirements and possibilities checked up by the actual facts and the goal. The suggestions that the pole was simply to carry a flag, was an ornament, was the terminal

---

8.   How We Think.

of a wireless telegraph, were examined and rejected. The final one, that the pole was to point out the direction in which the boat was moving, upon analysis seemed most probable and was accepted. The one characteristic of the pole, that it points direction, and its position, need to be accepted as the essential facts in the situation, for the particular problem. Without control of the process, without the two steps of analysis and abstraction, no conclusion could have been reached.

Analysis and abstraction may be facilitated in three ways. First, by attentive piecemeal examination. The total situation is examined, element by element, attentively, until the element needed is reached or approximated. This method of procedure helps to emphasize minor bonds of association which the element possesses in the learner's experience but which he needs to have brought to his attention. It can only be used when the element is known to some degree. It is the method to use when elements are known in a hazy, incomplete, or indefinite way and need clearing up. Second, by varying the concomitant. An element associated with many situations, which vary in other respects, comes to be felt and recognized as independent. This is the method to use when a new element in a complex is to be taught. Third, by contrast. A new element is brought into consciousness more quickly if it is set side by side with its opposite. Of course, this is only true provided the opposite has already been learned. To present opposites, both of which are new or only partially learned, confuses the analysis instead of facilitating it.

Reasoning, as the highest type of thinking, includes all that thinking in general does, and adds some particular requirement which differentiates it from the simpler forms. Further discussion of it, then, should make clearer the essential in thinking as a process, as well as make clear its most difficult form. Reasoning is defined by Miller as "controlled thinking,--thinking organized and systematized according to laws and principles and carried on by use of superior technique."[9] Reasoning, then, is the kind of thinking that deals directly with laws and principles. Much thinking may be carried on without any overt, definite use of laws and principles, as in constructive imagination or in apperception, but, if this is so, it seems better to call the thinking by one of the other names. Of course this classification is somewhat arbitrary, but there can be no question that types of thinking do differ. As has already been noted, some psychologists have used the terms thinking and reasoning as synonyms, but such usage has resulted in confusion and has not been of practical value. It is only as the mental process desired becomes clearly conceived of, its connotations and denotation clearly defined, that it becomes a real goal towards Which a teacher or learner may strive. This, then, is the primary criterion of reasoning--that the thinker be dealing consciously with laws and principles. An acceptance of this first essential makes clear that the particular process of reasoning cannot be carried on in subjects which lack laws and principles. Spelling, elementary reading, vocabulary study, most of the early work in music and art, the acquisition of facts wherever found--these situations may offer opportunity for thinking, but little if any for reasoning. Because a teacher is using the development method does not mean necessarily that her students are reasoning. The two terms are not in any way synonymous.

---

9.   Psychology of Thinking.

The second essential in reasoning is the presence of a definite technique. This technique consists of two factors: first, certain definite mental states, and second, the use of the process of thinking by either the inductive or the deductive method.

First as to the mental states involved. The fact that the thinking deals with laws and principles necessitates the presence, in the thinking process, of constructive verbal or symbolic imagery, logical relationships, logical concepts, and explicit judgments. This does not at all exclude other types of these mental states and entirely different mental states. The kind of analysis involved simply necessitates the presence of these types, whatever others may be present. Constructive symbolic imagery has already been discussed. Logical relationships are those that are independent of accidental conditions, are not dependent on mere contiguity in time and space, but are inherent in the association involved. Such relationships are those of likeness and difference, cause and effect, subject and object, equality, concession, and the like. Logical concepts are those which are the result of thinking, whose definite meaning has been brought clearly into consciousness so that a definition could be framed. A child has some notion of the meaning of tree, or man, or chemist, and therefore possesses a concept of some kind, but the exact meaning, the particular qualities necessary, are usually lacking, and so it could not be called a logical concept. Explicit judgments are those which contain within themselves the reasons for the inference. They, too, are the result of thinking. One may say that "cheating is wrong," or that "water will not rise above its source level," or that "cleanliness is necessary to health," or that "this is a Rembrandt"--as a matter of experience, habit, but without any reflection and with no reasons for such judgment. If, on the other hand, the problems to which these judgments are answers had been a matter of thinking, the reasons or the ground for such judgment would have become conscious and the judgment then become explicit. It must be evident that in any problems dealing with laws and principles the mental states involved must be definite, clear cut, logically sound, and their implications thoroughly appreciated and understood.

The second element in the technique necessary in reasoning is the use of either the inductive or the deductive method in the process. Induction requires--a problem, search for facts with which to solve it, comparison and analysis of those facts, abstraction of the essential likenesses, and conclusion. Deduction requires--a problem, the analysis of the situation and abstraction of its essential elements, search for generals under which to classify it, comparison of it with each general found, and conclusion. It is unfortunate that in the discussions of induction and deduction the differences have been so emphasized that they have been regarded as different processes, whereas the likenesses far outweigh the differences. An examination of the requirements of each as stated above shows that the process in the two is the same. Not only do both involve reasoning and therefore require the major steps of analysis and abstraction present in all thinking, but both also involve search and comparison. Both, of course, involve the same kind of mental states. At times it is very difficult to distinguish between them. Although for practical purposes it is necessary, sometimes, to stress the differences, the inherent similarity should not be lost sight of.

The differences between these two methods of reasoning are, first, in the locus of the problem; second, in the order of the steps of the process; third, in the relative proportion of particulars and generals used; fourth, in the devices used,

(1)   In induction the problem is concerned with a general. In some situation a concept, law, or principle has proven inadequate as a response. The question is then raised as to what is wrong with it and the inductive process is instigated. The problem is solved when the principle or concept is perfected or enlarged--in other words, is made adequate. In deduction the problem is concerned with the individual situation. Some problem is raised by a particular fact or experience and is answered when it is placed under the law or concept to which it belongs. Deduction is, practically the classification of particulars.

(2)   The order of steps is different. In induction, because present knowledge falls short, the major step of analysis necessary to abstraction of the essential is impossible, and therefore the search for new facts must come first, whereas in deduction, the analysis of the particular situation results in a search for generals and a classification of the situation in question.

(3)   In induction many particular facts may be necessary before one concept or principle is made adequate, while in deduction many concepts or principles may be examined before one particular is classified.

> (4)   In induction the hypothesis is used as a device to make clear the possible goal; in deduction the syllogism is used as a device to make clear the conclusion which has been reached, to throw into relief the classification and the result coming from it.

In this discussion, induction and deduction have been treated, for the sake of clearness, as if they acted independently of each other, as if a thinker might at one time use deduction and at another time induction. They have been outlined in such a way that one might think that the movement of the mind in one process was such that it precluded the possibility of the other process. This is not so--the two are inextricably mingled in the actual process of reasoning, and further, induction as used in practical life always involves deduction at two points, as an initial starting point and as an end point. The knowledge that a certain principle is inadequate comes to consciousness through the attempt to classify some particular experience under it. Failure results and the inductive process may then be initiated, but this initial attempt is deductive and if it had been successful there would have been no need of induction. After the inductive process is complete and the general principle has been classified or perfected, the final step is testing it to see if it is adequate, first by applying it to the particular problem which caused the whole process, and then to new situations. If it tests, it is accepted,--if not, further induction is necessary. This again is deduction. Not only is induction not complete without deduction, but each deduction influences the principle which is applied, making it more sure and more flexible. Even in the process of induction, there are attempts to classify these facts which are being gathered under suggested old principles, or half-formed new ones, before the process is completed. This is a deductive movement, even though it prove unsatisfactory or impossible. Dewey describes this interaction by saying, "There is thus a double movement in all reflection: a movement from the given partial and confused data to a suggested comprehension (or inclusive) entire situation; and back from this suggested whole--which as suggested is a meaning, an idea--to the particular facts, so as to connect these with one another and with additional facts to which the suggestion has directed attention."[10] However true this intermingling of induction and deduction may be, the fact still remains true that in any given case the major movement is in one direction or the other, and that therefore in order to insure effective thinking measures must be taken accordingly. As a child formulates his conception of a verb, or words the characteristic essentials of the lily-family, or frames the rule for addition of fractions or the action of a base on a metal, he is concerned primarily with the form of the reasoning process known as induction. When he classes a certain word as a conjunction, a certain city as a trade center, a certain problem as one in percentage, he is using deduction. Complexes and gradual shadings of one state into another, not clearly defined and sharply differentiated processes and states, are characteristic of all mental life.

Another unfortunate statement with regard to induction and deduction is that the former "proceeds from particulars to generals" and the latter from "generals to particulars." Both of these statements omit the starting point and leave the thinker with no ground for either the particulars or the generals with which he works. The

---

10. How We Think.

thinker is supposed, let us say, to collect specimens of flowers in order to arrive at a notion of the characteristics of a certain class--but why collect these rather than any others? True, in the artificial situation of a schoolroom or college, the learner often collects in a certain field rather than another, simply because he is told to. But in daily life he would not be told to---the incentive must come from some particular situation which presents a problem and therefore limits the field of search. The starting point must be a particular experience or situation. The same thing is true in deduction, although the syllogistic form has often been misleading. "Metals are hard; iron is a metal, therefore iron is hard." But why talk about metals at all--and if so why hardness rather than color or effect on bases or some other characteristic? Of course, here again it is some particular problem that defines the search for the general and directs attention to some class characteristics rather than to others. Not only is the starting point of all reasoning some definite situation for which there is no adequate response, but the end point must naturally be the same. A particular problem demanding solution is the cause for reasoning, and, of course, the end of the process must be the solution of that problem.

From the foregoing it must not be concluded that the processes of induction and deduction are manifested only in connection with reasoning. In fact, their use as a conscious tool of technique in reasoning comes only after considerable experience of their use when there was no conscious purpose and no control. A little child's notion of dog, or tree, or city--in fact, all his psychological concepts necessitate the inductive movement, but it has taken place in his spontaneous thinking and the meanings have evolved after considerable experience without any definite control on his part. So with deduction. As he recognizes this as a chestnut tree, that as a rocking chair, as he decides that this is wrong or that it is going to clear, he is classifying things, or conduct, or conditions, and so is following the deductive movement. But the judgments may come as a result of past experience, may be spontaneous and involve no protracted controlled activity which has been defined as thinking. Man's mind works spontaneously both inductively and deductively, and hence the possibility of control of these operations later. Thinking is an outgrowth of spontaneous activity; reasoning is but an application of the natural laws of mental activity to certain situations.

The laws of readiness, exercise, and effect govern thinking just as they do all other mental processes. Thinking is not independent of habit; it is not a mysterious force other than association which deals with novel data. Thinking is merely an exhibition of the laws of habit under certain definite situations. At first sight this seems to be impossible, because, as has been emphasized throughout this chapter, thinking takes place when no satisfactory response is at hand and when nothing is offered by past experience which is adequate. As a result of the thinking, responses are reached which never before have occurred as a result of that situation. Just the same they are reached only because of the operation of the laws of habit. It must be borne in mind that the laws of association do not work in such a way that only gross total situations are bound to total responses. In man particularly, situations are being continually broken up into elements, and those elements connected with responses. Responses are being continually disintegrated, and elements, instead of the whole response, being bound to situations. Analysis is continually taking place merely as a result of the working of these laws. If the nervous mechanism of man were not of this hair-trigger variety, if elements did not emerge from a total complex as a result of bonds formed, of readiness of certain tracts, no willing, no attention on the part of the thinker, would ever bring about analysis. This is made very vivid when one is met by a problem he cannot solve. If the situation does not break up, if the right element does not emerge, if the right cue is not given, he is helpless. All he can do is to hold fast to his problem and wait. As the associations are offered, he can select and reject, but that is all. The marvelous power of the genius, the inventor, the reasoner in all fields, is merely an exhibition of the laws of association working with extremely subtle elements. It seems to transcend all experience because these elements and the bonds which experience has formed cannot be observed. A child fails in his thinking often because he uses his past experience and responds by analogy--we note that fact and criticize him for it. But he succeeds for just the same reason and by the use of just the same laws. James long ago showed conclusively that association by similarity, which is one of the prominent types used in reasoning, was only the law of habit working with elements of novel data.

The fact that thinking is determined by its aim rather than by its antecedents has also been given a mysterious place as apart from association. The thinker who chose the right associate, the one that led him towards his goal rather than some other, was called sagacious. But, after all, this being governed by an aim is nothing more than the operation of the law of readiness among intellectual bonds. One associate is chosen and another rejected because one is more satisfying than another. Certain bonds are made more ready than others because of the general set or attitude of the thinker, and therefore any associate using those bonds brings satisfaction and is retained. "The power that moves the man of science to solve problems correctly is the same that moves him to eat, sleep, rest, and play. The efficient thinker is not only more fertile in ideas and more often productive of the 'right' ideas than the incompetent is; he is also more satisfied by them when he gets them, and more rebellious against the futile and misleading ones. We trust to the laws of cerebral nature to present us spontaneously with the appropriate idea, and also *to prefer that idea to others.*"[11]

The reasons for failure of teachers and educators of all kinds to train people to think are numerous.

(1) Scarcity of brains which work primarily in terms of connections between subtle elements, relationships, etc.

(2) Lack of knowledge or incorrect knowledge, due to narrow experience or poor memory.

(3) Lack of the necessary habits of attention and criticism.

(4) Lack of power of the more abstract and intellectual operations to bring satisfaction, due partly to original equipment and partly to training.

(5) Lack of power to do independent work, due to poor training. Schools cannot in any way make

---

11. Thorndike, *Educational Psychology, Briefer Course.*

good the deficiency which is due to a lack of mental capacity.

They can, and should, do something to provide knowledge which is well organized around experiences which have proved vital to pupils. Something can undoubtedly be done in the way of cultivating the habit of concentration of attention, and of making more or less habitual the critical attitude. Within the range of the ability which the individuals to be educated possess, the school may do much to give training which will make independent work or thinking more common in the experience of school pupils, and therefore much more apt to be resorted to in the case of any problematic situation.

Possibly the greatest weakness in our schools, as they are at present constituted, is in the dependence of both teachers and children upon text-books, laboratory manuals, lectures, and the like. In almost every field of knowledge which is presented in our elementary and high schools, more opportunity should be given for contact with life activities. Such contacts should, in so far as it is possible, involve the organization of the observations which are made with relation to problems and principles which the subject seeks to develop. In nature study or in geography in the elementary school many of the principles involved are never really mastered by children, by virtue of the fact that they merely memorize the words which are involved, rather than solve any of the problems which may occur, either by virtue of their intellectual interests, or on account of their meaning in everyday life. The following of the instructions given in the laboratory manual does not necessarily result in developing the spirit of inquiry or investigation, nor even acquaint pupils with the method of the science which is supposed to be studied.

Possibly the greatest contribution which a teacher can make to the development of thinking upon the part of children is in discovering to them problems which challenge their attention, the solution of which for them is worth while. As has already been indicated, an essential element in thinking is constantly to select from among the many associations which may be available that one which will contribute to the particular problem which we have in mind. The mere grouping of ideas round some topic does not satisfy this requirement, for such a reciting of paragraphs or chapters may amount simply to memorization and nothing more. If a teacher can in geography or in history send children to their books to find such facts as are available for the solution of a particular problem, she is stimulating thought upon their part, and may at the same time be giving them some command of the technique of inquiry or of investigation. The class that starts to work, either in the discussion during the recitation period, or when they work at their seats, or at home, with a clear statement of the aim or problem may be expected to do much more in the way of thinking than will occur in the experience of those who are merely told to read certain parts of a book. In a well-conducted recitation which involves thinking, the aim needs to be restated a number of times in order that the selection of those associations which are important, and the rejection of those which are not pertinent, may continue over a considerable period.

In so far as it is possible, children should be made to feel responsibility for the progress which is made in the solution of their problems. They should be critical of the contributions made by each other. They should be sincere in their expression of doubt, and in questioning whenever they do not understand. Above all, if they are really thinking, they need to have an opportunity for free discussion. In classrooms in which children are seated in rows looking at the backs of each other's heads and reciting to the teacher, the tendency is simply to satisfy what the pupils conceive to be the demands of the teacher, rather than to think and to attempt to resolve one's doubts. In classes in which teachers provide not only for a statement of the problem which is to be solved during the study period, but also for a variety in assignments, children may be expected to bring to class differences in points of view and in the data which they have collected. In such a situation discussion is a perfectly normal process, and thinking is stimulated.

As children pass through the several grades of the school system, they ought to become increasingly conscious of the process of reasoning. They should be asked to tell how they have arrived at their conclusions. They should give the reason for their judgments. A great deal of loose thinking would be avoided if we could in some measure establish the habit upon the part of boys and girls of asking, "Will it work in all cases?"; "What was assumed as a basis for arriving at the conclusion which I have accepted?"; "Are the data which have been brought together adequate?"; "To what degree have the fallacies which are more or less common in reasoning entered into my thinking?" It is not that one would hope to give a course in logic to elementary or to high school children, but rather that they should learn, out of the situations which demand thought, constantly to check up their conclusions and to verify them in every possible way. We may not expect by this method to create any unusual power of thought, but we may in some degree provide for the development of a critical attitude which will enable these same boys and girls, both now and as they grow older, to discriminate between those who merely dogmatize, and those who present a sound basis for their reasoning, either in terms of a principle which can be accepted, or in terms of observations or experiments which establish the conclusions which they are asked to accept.

In all of the work which involves thinking, it is of the utmost importance that we preserve upon the part of pupils, in so far as it is possible, an open-minded attitude. It is well to have children in the habit of saying with respect to their conclusions that in so far as they have the evidence, this or that conclusion seems to be justified. It may even be well to have them reach the conclusion in some parts of their work that there are not sufficient data available upon which to base a generalization, or that certain principles which are accepted as valid by some thinkers are questioned by others, and that the conclusions which are based upon principles which are not commonly accepted must always be stated by saying: it follows, if you accept a particular principle, that this particular conclusion will hold.

We need more and more to encourage the habit of independent work. We must hope as children pass through our school system that they will grow more and more independent in their statement of conclusions and of beliefs. We can never expect that boys and girls, or men and women, will reach conclusions on all of the questions which are of importance to them, but it ought to be possible, especially for those of more than usual capacity, to distinguish between the conclusions of a scientific investigation and the statements of a demagogue. The use of whatever capacity for independent thought which children possess should result in the development of a group of open-minded, inquiring, investigating boys and girls, eager and willing in confronting their common community problems to do their own thinking, or to be guided by those who present conclusions which are recognized as valid. They should learn to act in accordance with well-established conclusions, even though they may have to break with the traditions or superstitions which have operated to interfere with the development of the social welfare of the group with which they are associated.

QUESTIONS

1.   How do children (and adults) most frequently solve their problems?

2.   Under what conditions do children think and yet reach wrong conclusions? Give examples.

3.   Can first-grade children think? Give examples which prove your contention.

4.   What are the important elements to be found in all thinking?

5.   Show how these elements may be involved in a first-grade lesson in nature study. In an eighth-grade lesson in geography. In the teaching of any high school subject.

6.   When may habit formation involve thinking? Memorization?

7.   Give five examples of problems which you believe will challenge the brightest pupils in your class. Which would seem real and worth solving to the duller members of the group?

8.   How may the analysis of such ideas as come to mind, and the abstraction of the part which is valuable for the solution of a particular problem, be facilitated?

9.   How do you distinguish between thinking and reasoning?

10.   What are the essential elements in reasoning? Give an example of reasoning as carried on by one solving a problem in arithmetic or geometry, in geography, physics, or chemistry.

11.   In what respects are the processes of induction and deduction alike? In what do they differ?

12.   At what stage of the inductive process is deduction involved?

13.   Give examples of reasoning demanded in school work in which the process is predominantly inductive. Deductive.

14.   Why are the statements "Induction proceeds from particulars to generals" and "Deduction from generals to particulars" inadequate to describe either process?

15.   In what sense is thinking dependent upon the operation of the laws of habit?

16.   To what degree is it possible to teach your pupils to think? Under what limitations do you work?

VIII

Appreciation, An Important Element in Education

Appreciation belongs to the general field of feeling rather than that of knowing. The element which distinguishes appreciation from memory or imagination or perception is an affective one. Any one of these mental states may be present without the state being an appreciative one. But appreciation does not occur by itself as an elementary state, it is rather a complex--a feeling tone accompanying a mental state or process and coloring it. In other words, appreciation involves the presence of some intellectual states, but its addition makes the total complex of an emotional rather than a cognitive nature. The difficulty found in discussing emotions in general, that of defining or describing them in language, which is a tool of the intellect, is felt here. The only way to know what appreciation means is to appreciate. No phase of feeling can be adequately described--its essence is then lost--it must be felt. Nevertheless something may be done to differentiate this type of feeling from others.

Appreciation is an attitude of mind which is passive, contemplative. It may grow out of an active attitude or emotion, or it may lead to one, but in either case the state changes from one of appreciation to something else.

In appreciation the individual is quiescent. Appreciation, therefore, has no end outside of itself. It is a sufficient cause for being. The individual is satisfied with it. This puts appreciation into the category of recreation. Appreciation then always involves the pleasure tone, otherwise it could not be enjoyed. It is always impersonal. It takes the individual outside and beyond his own affairs; it is an other-regarding feeling. Possession, achievement, and the like do not arouse appreciation, but rather an egoistical emotion.

One of the salient characteristics of emotions is their unifying power. It has aptly been said that in extreme emotional states one *is* the emotion. The individual and his emotional state become one--a very different state of affairs from what is true in cognition. This element of unification is present to some extent in appreciation, although, because of its complex nature, to a lesser extent than in a simpler, more primitive feeling state. Still, in true appreciation one does become absorbed in the object of appreciation; he, for the time being, to some extent becomes identified with what he is appreciating. In, order to appreciate this submerging of one's self, this identification is necessary.

Appreciation is bound up with four different types of situations which are of most importance to the teacher--

    (1)   appreciation of the beautiful,

    (2)   appreciation of human nature,

    (3)   appreciation of the humorous,

    (4)   appreciation of intellectual powers.

The appreciation found in these four types of situations must vary somewhat because of the concomitants, but the characteristics which mark appreciation as such seem to be present in all four. True, in certain of the situations occurring under these types the emotional element may be stronger than in others--in some the intellectual element may seem to almost outweigh the affective, but still the predominant characteristics will be found to be those of an attitude which has the earmarks of appreciation.

Appreciation of beauty has usually been discussed under the head of aesthetic emotions. As to what rightfully belongs under the head of aesthetics is in dispute--writers on the subject varying tremendously in their opinions. Most of the recent writers, however, agree that the stimulus for aesthetic appreciation must be a sense percept or an image of some sense object. Ideas, meanings, in and of themselves, are not then objects of aesthetic enjoyment. The two senses which furnish the stimuli for this sort of appreciation are the eye and the ear--the former combining sensations under space form and the latter under time form to produce aesthetic feelings. Our senses may cause feelings of pleasure, but the enjoyment is sensuous rather than aesthetic. Nature, in all its myriad forms, art, architecture, music, literature, and the dance are the chief sources of aesthetic appreciation. That there is a definite connection between physiological processes and the feeling of appreciation is without doubt true, but just what physiological conditions in connection with visual and auditory perception are fulfilled when some experience gives rise to aesthetic appreciation, and just what is violated when there is lack of such appreciation, is not known. It is known that both harmony and rhythm must be considered in music, and that the structure and muscular control of the eye plus the ease of mental apprehension play important parts in rousing aesthetic feelings in connection with vision, but further than that little is known.

The chief danger met in developing the aesthetic appreciation is the tendency to overestimate its dependence on, in the first place, skill in creative work and the active emotions involved in achievement, and in the second place, the intellectual understanding of the situation. It has been largely taken for granted that the constructive work in the arts or in music increased one's power of appreciation. That, if a child used color and painted a little picture, or composed a melody, or modeled in clay, he would therefore be able to appreciate better in these fields. And further that the very development of this power to do necessarily developed the power to appreciate. These two beliefs are true to some extent, but only to a limited extent, and not nearly so far as practice has taken for granted. It is true that some power to do increases power to appreciate, but they parallel each other only for a short time and then diverge, and either may be developed at the expense of the other. In most people the power to appreciate, the passive, contemplative enjoyment, far surpasses the ability to create. On the other hand, men of creative genius often lack power of aesthetic appreciation. This result is natural if one thinks of the mental processes involved in the two. Power to do is associated with muscular skill, with technique, and with the personal emotions of active achievement. Æsthetic appreciation, on the other hand, is associated with neither, but with a mental attitude and feelings which are quite different. Cultivating one set of processes will not develop the other to any great extent and may, on the other hand, be antagonistic to their development. If the aesthetic emotions, if appreciations of the beautiful, are desired, they must be trained and developed directly.

The second danger to be avoided in developing aesthetic appreciation is that of magnifying its dependence on the intellectual factors. To understand, to be able to analyze, to pick out the flaws in a musical selection, or a painting, is not necessary to its appreciation. True, some understanding is necessary, but, as in the case of skill, it is much less than has been taken for granted. Appreciation can go far ahead of understanding. The intellectual factor and the feeling response are not absolutely interdependent in degree. Not only so, but the prominence of the intellectual factor precludes that of the feeling. When one is emphasized the other cannot be, as they are different sorts of mental stuff. Continuous and emphatic development of the intellectual may result in the atrophy of the power of appreciation in any given field either temporarily or permanently. Many a boy's power to enjoy the rhythm and melody of poetry has been destroyed by the overemphasis of the critical facility during his high school course. The fact that a person can analyze the painting, point out the plans in its composition, and so on, does not at all mean that he can aesthetically appreciate. Contemplative enjoyment may be impossible for him--it bores him. Botanists are not noted for their power of aesthetic appreciation. It is an acknowledged fact that some art and music critics have lost their power of appreciation of the things they are continually criticizing. This discussion is not intended to minimize the value of creative skill, or of power of intellectual criticism. Both are talents that are well worth while cultivating.

But it is necessary for one to decide which of the three, aesthetic appreciation, creative skill, or intellectual criticism, in the fields of art, nature, and music, is most worth while for the majority of people and then make plans accordingly. No one of the three can be best developed and brought to its highest perfection by emphasizing any one of the others.

The second type of appreciation is appreciation of human nature: appreciation of the value of human life, appreciation of its virtues and trials, appreciation of great characters, and so on. Some writers would probably class this type of appreciation under moral feelings--but moral feelings usually are thought of as active, as accompaniments of conduct, whereas these appreciations are feelings aroused in the onlooker--they are passive and for the time being are an end in themselves. These feelings are stimulated by such studies as literature and history particularly. Geography and civics offer some opportunity for their development, and, of course, contact with people is the greatest stimulus. In this latter type of situation the feelings of appreciation easily pass over into active emotions, but so long as one remains an onlooker, they need not do so. This appreciation, sympathy with and enjoyment and approval of human nature, finds its source in the social instincts, but it needs development and training if it is to be perfected. Very much of the time this appreciation is inhibited by the emphasis put on understanding. The intellectual faculties of memory, judgment, and criticism are the ones called into play in the study of history and often of literature. These studies leave the learner cold. He knows, but it does not make any difference to him. He can analyze the period or the character, but he lacks any feeling response, any appreciation of the qualities of endurance and loyalty portrayed, lacks any *sympathetic* understanding of the difficulties met and conquered. As was true of the aesthetic appreciation, a certain amount of understanding is necessary for true appreciation of any kind, but overemphasis of the intellectual element destroys the feeling element.

The third type of appreciation to be discussed is the appreciation of humor. Perhaps this does not belong with the other type, but it certainly has many of the same characteristics. Calkins defines a sense of humor as "enjoyment of an unessential incongruity.... This incongruity must be, as has been said, an unessential one, else the mood of the observer changes from happiness to unhappiness, and the comic becomes the pathetic. A fall on the ice which seemed to offer only a ludicrous contrast between the dignity and grace of the man erect and the ungainly attitude of the falling figure ceases utterly to be funny when it is seen to entail some physical injury; and wit which burns and sears is not amusing to its victim."[12] The ability to appreciate the humorous in life is a great gift and should be cultivated to a much greater extent than it is at present.

A fourth type of appreciation has been called appreciation of intellectual powers--a poor name perhaps, but the feeling is a real one. Enjoyment of style, of logical sequence, of the harmony of the whole, of the clear-cut, concise, telling sentences, are illustrations of what is meant. Enjoyment of a piece of literature, of a debate, of an argument, of a piece of scientific research, is not limited to the appreciation of the meanings expressed--in fact, in many cases the only factor that can arouse

---

12. Introduction to Psychology

the feeling element, the appreciation, is this element of form. One may*understand* an argument or a debate as he hears it, but appreciation, enjoyment of it, comes only as a result of the consciousness of these elements of form.

That one possesses these feelings of appreciation, at least to some degree, is a matter of human equipment, but *what* one appreciates in art, literature, human nature, etc., depends primarily on training. There is almost no situation in life that with all people at all times will arouse appreciative feelings. Although there are a few fundamental conditions established by the physical make-up of the sense organs and by the original capacities of the human race, still they are few, and at present largely unknown, and experience does much to modify even these. What is crude, vulgar, inharmonious, in art and music to some people, arouses extreme aesthetic appreciation in others. Literature that causes one person to throw the book down in disgust will give greatest enjoyment to another. What is malice to one person is humorous to another. What people enjoy and appreciate depends primarily on their experience for the development of these feelings, depends upon the laws of association, readiness, exercise, and effect. To raise power of appreciation from low levels to high, from almost nothing to a controlling force, needs but the application of these laws. But no one of them can be neglected with impunity. It must be a gradual growth, beginning with tracks that are ready, because of the presence of certain instincts, and working on to others through the law of association. To expect a child of seven to appreciate a steel engraving, or a piece of classic music, or moral qualities in another person is to violate the law of readiness. To expect any one in adult life to enjoy music, or art, or nature, who has not had experience with each and enjoyed each continually as a child, is to violate the laws of exercise and effect.

Two or three suggestions as to aids in the application of these laws may be in place. First, a wealth of images is an aid to appreciation. Second, the absence for the time of the critical attitude. Third, an encouragement of the passive contemplative attitude. Fourth, the example of others. Suggestion and association with other people who do appreciate and enjoy are among the best means of securing it.

The value of feelings of appreciation are threefold: First, they serve as recreation. It is in enjoyment of this kind that most of the leisure of civilized races is spent. It serves on the mental level much the same purpose that play does, in fact, much of it is mental play of a kind. Second, they are impersonal. They are valuable in that they take us out of ourselves, away from self-interests, and therefore make for mental health and sanity as well as for a sympathetic character. They are also a means of broadening one's experience. Third, they have a close relationship with ideals and therefore have an active bearing on conduct. It is not necessarily true that one will tend in himself or in his surroundings to be like what he enjoys and appreciates, but the tendency will be strongly in that direction. If an individual truly appreciates, enjoys, beautiful pictures, good music and books, he will be likely, so far as he can, to surround himself with them. If he appreciates loyalty, openmindedness, tolerance, as he meets them in literature and history, he may become more so himself. At least, the developing of appreciations is the first step towards conduct in those lines. In order to insure the conduct, other means must be taken, but without the appreciation the conduct will be less sure.

One who would count most in developing power of appreciation upon the part of children may well inquire concerning his own power of appreciation. There is not very much possibility of the development of joy in poetry, in music, or any other artistic form of expression through association with the teacher who finds little satisfaction in these artistic forms, who has little power of aesthetic appreciation. It is only as teachers themselves are sincere in their appreciation of the nobility of character possessed by the men and women whose lives are portrayed in history, in literature, or in contemporary social life that one may expect that their influence will be important in developing such appreciation upon the part of children. Those pupils are fortunate who are taught by teachers who have a sense of humor, who are able to grow enthusiastic over the intellectual achievement of the leaders in the field of study or investigation in which the children are at work. Children are, indeed, quick to discover sentimentalism or pseudo-appreciation upon the part of teachers, but even though they may not give any certain expression to their enjoyment, they are usually largely influenced by the attitude and genuine power of appreciation possessed by the teacher.

In our attempt to have children grow in the field of appreciation we have often made the mistake of attempting to impose upon them adult standards. A great librarian in one of our eastern cities has said that he would rather have children read dime novels than to have them read nothing. From his point of view it was more important to have children appreciating and enjoying something which they read than to have their lives barren in this respect. In literature, in music, and in fine art the development in power of appreciation is undoubtedly from the simple, cruder forms to those which we as adults consider the higher or nobler forms of expression. Mother Goose, the rhymes of Stevenson, of Field, or of Riley, may be the beginning of the enjoyment of literature which finds its final expression in the reading and in the possession of the greatest literature of the English language. The simple rote songs which the children learn in the first grade, or which they hear on the phonograph, may lead through various stages of development to the enjoyment of grand opera. Pictures in which bright color predominates may be the beginning of power of appreciation which finds its fruition in a home which is decorated with reproductions of the world's masterpieces.

It is not only in the artistic field that this growth in power of appreciation from the simpler to the more complex is to be found. Children instinctively admire the man who is brave rather than the man who endures. Achievement is for most boys and girls of greater significance than self-sacrifice. It is only as we adapt our material to their present attainment, or to an attempt to have them reach the next higher stage of development, that we may expect genuine growth. All too often instead of growth we secure the development of a hypocritical attitude, which accepts the judgment of others, and which never really indicates genuine enjoyment.

While it is best not to insist upon an analysis of the feelings that one has in enjoying a picture or a poem or a great character, it is worth while to encourage choice. Of many stories which have been told, children may very properly choose one which they would like to tell to others. Of many poems which have been read in class, a group of boys may admire one and commit it to memory, while the girls may care for another and be allowed to memorize it. Wherever such coöperation is possible, the picture which you enjoy most is the one that will mean most in power of appreciation if placed in your room at home. Spontaneous approval, rather than an agreement with an adult teacher who is considered an authority, is to be sought for. There is more in the spontaneous laughter which results as children read together their "Alice in Wonderland" than could possibly result from an analysis of the quality of humor which is involved.

We are coming to understand as a matter of education that we may hope to develop relatively few men and women of great creative genius. The producers of work of great artistic worth are, for the most part, to be determined by native capacity rather than by school exercises. We must think of the great majority of school children as possible consumers rather than as producers. Schools which furnish a maximum of opportunity to enjoy music and pictures may hope to develop in their community a power of discrimination in these fields which will result in satisfaction with nothing less than the best. The player-piano and the phonograph may mean more in the development of musical taste in a community than all of the lessons which are given in the reading of music. The art gallery in the high school, the folk dances which have been produced as a part of the school festivals, the reading of the best stories, may prepare the way for the utilization of leisure time in the pursuit of the nobler pleasures. The teacher with a saving sense of humor, large in his power of appreciation of the great men and women of his time, and all of the time keen in his own enjoyment and in his ability to interpret for others those things which are most worth while in literature and in art, may count more largely in the life of the community than the one who is a master in some field of investigation.

QUESTIONS

1. What are the characteristics of the mental states which are involved in appreciation?

2. Name the different types of situations in which appreciation may be developed. Give examples.

3. Does the power to criticize poetry or music necessarily involve appreciation?

4. To what degree may skill in creative work result in power of appreciation?

5. What are the elements involved in appreciating human nature?

6. Give an example of appreciation of intellectual powers.

7. What is the essential element in the appreciation of humor?

8. Explain how the power of appreciation is dependent upon training.

9. What values in the education of an individual are realized through growth in power of appreciation?

10. Why is it important for a teacher to seek to cultivate his own power of appreciation?

11. What poems, or pictures, or music would you expect first-grade children to enjoy? Why?

12. Would you expect fifth-grade children to grow in appreciation of poetry by having them commit to

memory selections from Milton's Paradise Lost? Why?

13.   Why is it important to allow children to choose the poems that they commit to memory, or the pictures which they hang on their walls?

14.   Why would you accept spontaneous expression of approval of the characters in literature or in history, rather than seek to control the judgments of children in this respect?

15.   How may teachers prove most effective in developing the power of appreciation upon the part of children?

IX

The Meaning of Play in Education

All human activity might be classified under three heads,--play, work, and drudgery,--but just what activities belong under each head and just what each of the terms means are questions of dispute. That the boundaries between the three are hazy and undefined, and that they shade gradually into each other, are without doubt true, but after all play is different from work, and work from drudgery. Much of the disagreement as to the value of play is due to this lack of definition. Even to-day when the worth of play is so universally recognized, we still hear the criticism's of "soft pedagogy" and "sugar coating" used in connection with the application of the principle of play in education.

Although what we call play has its roots in original equipment, still there is no such thing as the play instinct, in the sense that there is a hunting instinct or a fighting instinct. Instead of being a definite instinct, which means a definite response to a definite situation, it is rather a tendency characteristic of all instincts and capacities. It is an outgrowth of the general characteristic of all original nature towards activity of some kind. This tendency is so broad and so complex, the machinery governing it is so delicate, that it produces responses that vary tremendously with subtle changes in the individual, and with slight modifications of the situation. What we call play, then, is nothing more than the manifestations of the various instincts and capacities as they appear at times when they are not immediately useful. The connections in the nervous system are ripe and all other factors have operated to put them in a state of readiness: a situation occurs which stimulates these connections and the child plays. These connections called into activity may result in responses which are primarily physical, intellectual, or emotional--all are manifestations of this tendency towards activity. All habits of all kinds grow out of this same activity: habits which we call work and those which we call play. Man has not two original natures, one defined in terms of the play instinct, and the other in terms of work. Most of the original tendencies involved in play are not peculiar to it, but also are the source of work. Manifestation results in making "mud pies and apple pies"; physical activity results in the kicking, squirming, and wriggling of the infant and the monotonous wielding of the hammer of the road mender. The conditions under which an activity occurs, its concomitants, and the attitude of the individual performing it determine whether it is play or work--not its source or root.

Much, then, of what we call play is simply the manifestation of instincts and capacities not immediately useful to the child. If they were immediately useful, they would probably be put under the head of work, not play. Many of the activities which seem playful to us and not of immediate service do so because of the conditions of civilized life. Were the infants living under primitive conditions, "in such a community as a human settlement seems likely to have been twenty-five thousand years ago, their restless examination of small objects would perhaps seem as utilitarian as their fathers' hunting."[13] Certainly the tendency of little children to chase a small object going away from them, and to run from a large object approaching slowly, their tendency to collect and hoard, their tendency to outdo another engaged in any instinctive pursuit, would under primitive conditions have a distinct utilitarian value, and yet all such tendencies are ranked as play when manifested by the civilized child.

Other tendencies become playful rather than useful because of the complexity of the environment and of the nervous system responding to it. In actual life we don't find activity following a neatly arranged situation--response system. On the contrary, a situation seldom stimulates one response, and a response seldom occurs in the typical form required by theory. It is this mingling of responses brought about by varying elements in the situation that gives the playful effect. In a less complex environment this complexity would be lessened. Also experience, habit, tends to pin one type of response to a given situation and the minor connections gradually become eliminated. For example, if a boy of nine, alone in the woods, was approached by another with threatening gestures and scowls, the fighting response would be called out, and we would not call it play, because it served as protection. If the same boy in his own garden, with a group of companions, was approached by another with scowls, a perfectly good-natured tussle might take place and we would call it play. The difference between the two would be in minor elements of the situation. Some of these differences are absence or presence of companions, the strangeness or familiarity of the surroundings, the suddenness of the appearance of the other boy, and so on.

13. Thorndike, Origin of Man.

Most of the older theories of play did not take into account these three facts, *i.e.*, the identity in original nature of the roots of play and work; the fact that man's original nature fits him for primitive not civilized society; the complexity of the situation--response connection and its necessary variation with minor elements in the external situation and in the individual. Earlier writers, therefore, felt the need of special theories of play. The best known of these theories are, first, the Schiller-Spencer surplus energy theory; second, the Groos preparation for life theory; third, the G. Stanley Hall atavistic theory; fourth, the Appleton biological theory. Each of the theories has some element of truth in it, for play is complex enough to include them all, but each, save perhaps the last, falls short of an adequate explanation.

Two facts growing out of the theory of play accepted by the last few paragraphs need further discussion. First, the order of development in play. The play activities must follow along the line of the developing instincts and capacities. As the nerve tracts governing certain responses become ready to act, these responses become the controlling ones in play. So it is that for a time play is controlled largely by the instinct of manipulation, at another time physical activity combined with competition is most prominent, at another period imagination controls, still later the puzzle-solving tendency comes to the point followed by all the games involving an intellectual factor. This being true, it is not surprising to find certain types of play characterizing certain ages and to find that though the particular games may vary, there is a strong resemblance between plays of children of the same age all over the world. It must not be forgotten, however, that the readiness of nerve tracts to function, and therefore the play responses, depends on other factors as well as maturity. The readiness of other tracts to function; past experience and habits; the stimulus provided by the present situation; absence of competing stimuli; sex, health, fatigue, tradition--all these and many more factors modify the order of development of the play tendencies. Still, having these facts in mind, it is possible to indicate roughly the type of play most prominent at different ages.

Children from four to seven play primarily in terms of sensory responses, imagination, imitation, and curiosity of the cruder sort. Love of rhythm also is strong at this period. From seven to ten individual competition or rivalry becomes very strong and influences physical games, the collecting tendency, and manipulation, all of which tendencies are prominent at this time. Ten to twelve or thirteen is characterized by the "gang" spirit which shows itself in connection with all outdoor games and adventures; memory is a large factor in some of the plays of this period, and independent thinking in connection with situations engendered by manipulation and the gang spirit becomes stronger. At this period the differences between girls and boys become more marked. The girls choose quieter indoor games, chumming becomes prominent, and interest in books, especially of the semi-religious and romantic type, comes to the front. In the early adolescent period the emotional factor is strong and characterizes many of the playful activities; the intellectual element takes precedence over the physical; the group interest widens, although the interest in leadership and independent action still remains strong; teasing and bullying are also present. This summary is by no means complete, but it indicates in a very general way the prominent tendencies at the periods indicated.

The second fact needing further elaboration is that of the complexity of the play activity. Take, for instance, a four-year-old playing with a doll. She fondles, cuddles, trundles it, and takes it to bed with her. It is jumped up and down and dragged about. It is put through many of the experiences that the child is having, especially the unpleasant ones. Its eyes and hair, its arms and legs, are examined. Questions are asked such as, "Where did it come from?" "Who made it?" "Has it a stomach?" "Will it die?" In many instances it is personified. The child is often perfectly content to play with it alone, without the presence of other children. This activity shows the presence of the nursing instinct, the tendency towards manipulation, physical activity, imitation and curiosity of the empirical type. The imagination is active but still undifferentiated from perception. The contentment in playing alone, or with an adult, shows the stage of development of the gregarious instinct. A girl of nine no longer cuddles or handles her doll just for the pleasure she gets out of that, nor is the doll put through such violent physical exercises. The child has passed beyond the aimless manipulation and physical activity that characterized the younger child. Instead she makes things for it, clothes, furniture, or jewelry, still manipulation, and still the nursing instincts, but modified and directed towards more practical ends. Imitation now shows itself in activities that are organized. The child plays Sunday, or calling, or traveling, or market day, in which the doll takes her part in a series of related activities. But in these activities constructive imagination appears as an element. Situations are not absolutely duplicated, occurrences are changed to suit the fancy of the player, as demanded by the dramatic interest. A fairy prince, or a godmother, may be participants, but at this age the constructive imagination is likely to work along more practical lines. Curiosity is also present, but now the questions asked are such as, "What makes her eyes work?" "Why can't she stand up?" or they often pertain to the things that are being made for the doll. They have to do with "How" or "Why" instead of the "What." The doll may still be talked to and even be supposed to talk back, but the child knows it is all play; it is no longer personified as in the earlier period. For the child fully to enjoy her play, she must now have companions of her own age, the older person no longer suffices.

The outdoor games of boys show the same kind of complexity,--for instance, take any of the running games. With little boys they are unorganized manifestations of mere physical activity. The running is more or less at random, arms and vocal organs are used as much as the legs and trunk. Imitation comes in-what one does others are likely to do. The mere "follow" instinct is strong, and they run after each other. The beginnings of the fighting instinct appear in the more or less friendly tussles they have. The stage of the gregarious instinct is shown by the fact that they all play together. Later with boys of nine or ten the play has become a game, with rules governing it. The general physical activity has been replaced by a specialized form. Imitation is less of a factor. The hunting instinct often appears unexpectedly, and in the midst of the play the elements of the chase interfere with the proper conduct of the game. The fighting instinct is strong, and is very easily aroused. The boys now play in gangs or groups, and the tendency towards leadership manifests itself within the group. The intellectual element appears again and again, in planning the game, in judging of the possibility of succeeding at different stages, or in settling disputes that are sure to arise. So it is with all the plays of children: they are complexes of the various tendencies present, and the controlling elements change as the inner development continues.

All activities when indulged in playfully have certain common characteristics. First, the activity is enjoyed for its own sake. The process is satisfying in itself. Results may come naturally, but they are not separated from the process; the reason for the enjoyment is not primarily the result, but rather the whole activity. Second, the activity is indulged in by the player because it satisfies some inner need, and only by indulging in it can the need be satisfied. It uses neurone tracts that were "ready." Growing out of these two major characteristics are several others. The attention is free and immediate; much energy is used with comparatively little fatigue; self-activity and initiative are freely displayed.

At the other extreme of activity is drudgery. Its characteristics are just the opposite of these. First, the activity is engaged in merely for the result--the process counting for nothing and the result being the only thing of value. Second, the process, instead of satisfying some need, is rather felt to be in violation of the nature of the one engaged. It uses neurone tracts that are not "ready" and at the same time prevents the action of tracts that are "ready." It becomes a task. The attention necessarily must be of the forced, derived type, in which fatigue comes quickly as a result of divided attention, results are poor, and there is no chance for initiative.

Between these two extremes lies work. It differs from play in that the results are usually of more value and in that the attention is therefore often of the derived type. It differs from drudgery in that there is not the sharp distinction between the process and the result and in that the attention may often be of the free spontaneous type. It was emphasized at the beginning of this chapter that the boundaries between the three were hazy and ill defined. This is especially true of work; it may be indistinguishable from play as it partakes of its characteristics, or it may swing to the other extreme and be almost drudgery. The difference between the three activities is a subjective matter--a difference largely in mood, in attitude of the person concerned, due to the readiness or unreadiness of the neurone tracts exercised. The same activity may be play for one person, work for another, and drudgery for still another. Further, for the same person the same activity may be play, work, or drudgery, at different times, even within the same day.

Which of the three is the most valuable for educational purposes? Certainly not drudgery. It is deadening, uneducative, undevelopmental. Any phase of education, though it may be a seemingly necessary one, that has the characteristics of drudgery is valueless in itself. As a means to an end it may serve--but with the antagonistic attitude, the annoyance aroused by drudgery, it seems a very questionable means. Education that can obtain the results required by a civilized community and yet use the play spirit is the ideal.

But to have children engaged in play, in the sense of free play, cannot be the only measure. There must be supervision and direction. The spirit that characterizes the activities which are not immediately useful must be incorporated into those that are useful by means of the shifting of association bonds. Nor can all parts of the process seem worth while to the learner. Sometimes the process or parts of it must become a means to an end, for the end is remote. But all this is true to some extent in free play--digging the worms in order to go fishing, finding the scissors and thread in order to make the doll's dress, making arrangements with the other team to play ball, finding the right pieces of wood for the hut, and so on, may not be satisfactory in and of themselves, but may be almost drudgery. They are *not* drudgery because they become fused in the whole process, they take over and are lost in the joy of the undertaking as a whole; they become a legitimate means to an end, and in so far take over in derived form the interest that is roused by the whole. It is this fusion of work and play that is desirable in education. This is the great lesson of play--it shows the value and encourages the logical combination of the two activities. Children learn to work as they play. They learn the meaning and value of work. Work becomes a means to an end, and that end not something remote and disconnected from the activity itself, but as part and parcel of it. Thus the activity as a whole imbued with the play spirit becomes motivated.

The play spirit is the spirit of art. No great result was achieved in any line of human activity without much work, and yet no great result was ever gained unless the play spirit controlled. It is to this interaction of work and play that each owes much of its value. Work in and of itself apart from play lacks educative power; it is only as it leads to and increases the power of play that it is of greatest value. Its logical place in education is as a means to an end, not as an end in itself. Play, on the other hand, that does not necessitate some work, that does not need work in order that it may function more fully, has lost most of its educational value. To work in play and to play while working is the ideal combination. Either by itself is dangerous.

Two misconceptions should be mentioned. First, the play spirit advocated as one of the greatest educational factors must not be limited to the merely physical activities, nor should it be considered synonymous with what is easy. This characterization of play as being the aimless trivial physical activities of a little child is a misconception of the whole play tendency. It has already been pointed out that any activity which in itself satisfies, whether that be physical, emotional, or intellectual, is play, and all these phases of human activity show themselves in play first. Also the fact that play does not mean ease of accomplishment has been noted. It is only in the play spirit that the full resources of child or adult are tested. It is only when the activity fully satisfies some need that the individual throws himself whole-souled into it. It is only under the stimulus of the play spirit that all one's energy is spent, and great results, clear, accurate, and far reaching, are obtained. Ease of performance often results in drudgery. To be play, the activity must be suited to the child's capacity, but leave chance for initiative and change and development.

The second misconception is that because present-day educators advocate play in education, they believe that the child should do nothing that he doesn't want to. This is wrong on two accounts. First, it is part of the business of an environment to stimulate--readiness depends partly on stimulation. The child may never play unless the stimulation is forcibly and continually applied. Second, after all it is the result we are most anxious for in education, and that result is an educated adult. By all means let us obtain this result by the most economical and effective method, and that is by use of the play spirit. But if the result cannot be obtained by this means because of the character of civilized ideals, or the difficulties of group education, or lack of capacity of the individual--then surely other methods, even that of drudgery, must be resorted to. The point is, with the goal in mind, adapt the material of education to the needs of the individual child; in other words, use the play spirit so far as is possible--after that gain the rest by any means whatsoever.

So far the discussion has been concerned with the characteristics of the play spirit and its use in connection with the more formal materials of education. However, the free plays of children are valuable in two ways--first, as sources of information as to the particular tendencies ready for exercise at different times, and second, as a means of education in themselves. A knowledge of just which tendencies are most prominent in the plays of a group of children, when they change from "play" to "games," the increase in complexity and organization, the predominance of the intellectual factors,--all this could be of direct service to a teacher in the schoolroom. But it means, to some extent, the observation by the teacher of his particular group of children. Such observation is extremely fruitful. The more vigorously, the more wholeheartedly, the more completely a child plays, other things being equal, the better. A deprivation of opportunity to play, or a loss of any particular type of play, means a loss of the development of certain traits or characteristics. An all-round, well-developed adult can grow only from a child developed in an all-round way because of many-sided play. Hence the value of public playgrounds and of time to play. Hence the danger of the isolated, lonely child, for many plays demand the group. Hence the opportunities and the dangers of supervision of play.

Supervision of play is valuable in so far as it furnishes opportunities and suggestions which develop the elements most worth while in play and which keep play at its highest level, and in so far as it concerns the nature of the individual child, protecting, admonishing, or encouraging, as the case may require. It is dangerous to the child's best good, in so far as it results in domination; for domination will mean, usually, the introduction of plays beyond the child's stage of development and the destruction of the independence and initiative which are two of the most valuable characteristics of free play. Valuable supervision of play is art that must be acquired. To influence, while effacing oneself, to guide, while being one of the players, to have an adult's understanding of the needs of child nature and yet to be one with the children--these are the essentials of the supervision of play.

QUESTIONS

1.   Distinguish between the fighting instinct and the instinctive basis of play.

2.   Under what conditions may an activity which we classify as play for a civilized child be called work for a child living under primitive conditions?

3.   What kinds of plays are characteristic of different age periods in the life of children?

4.   Trace the development of some game played by the older boys in your school from its simpler beginnings in the play of little children to its present complexity.

5.   Name the characteristics common to all playful activity.

6.   Distinguish between play and drudgery.

7.   What is the difference between work and play?

8.   To what degree may the activities of the school be made play?

9.   Explain why the same activity may be play for one individual, work for another, and drudgery for a third.

10.   Why should we seek to make the play element prominent in school activity?

11.   When is one most efficient in individual pursuits--when his activity is play, when he works, or when he is a drudge?

12.   Under what conditions should we compel children to work, or even to engage in an activity which may involve drudgery?

13.   Explain how play may involve the maximum of utilization of the abilities possessed by the individual, rather than a type of activity easy of accomplishment.

14.   In what does skill in the supervision of play consist?

X

The Significance of Individual Differences for the Teacher

It has been indicated here and there throughout the previous chapters that, despite the fact that there are certain laws governing the various mental traits and processes, still there is variation in the working of those laws. It was pointed out that people differ in kind of memory or imagination in which they excel, in their ability to appreciate, in the speed with which they form habits, and so on. In other words, that boys and girls are not exact duplicates of each other, but that they always differ from each other. Now a knowledge of these differences, their amounts, interrelations, and causes are very necessary for the planning of a school system or for the planning of the education of a particular child. What we plan and how we plan educational undertakings must always be influenced by our opinion as to inborn traits, sex differences, specialization of mental traits, speed of development, the respective power of nature and of nurture. The various plans of promotion and grouping of children found in different cities are in operation because of certain beliefs concerning differences in general mental ability. Coeducation is urged or deplored largely on the ground of belief in the differing abilities of the sexes.

Exact knowledge of just what differences do exist between people and the causes of these differences is important for two reasons. First, in order that the most efficient measures may be taken for the education of the individual, and second, in order that the race as a whole may be made better. Education can only become efficient and economical when we know which differences between people and which achievements of a given person are due to training, and which are due more largely to original equipment or maturity. It is a waste of time on the one hand for education to concern itself with trying to make all children good spellers--if spelling is a natural gift; and on the other hand, it is lack of efficiency for schools to be largely neglecting the moral development of the children, if morality is dependent primarily on education. Exact knowledge, not opinions, along all these lines is necessary if progress is to be made.

The principal causes for individual differences are sex, remote ancestry, near ancestry, maturity, and training. The question to be answered in the discussion of each of these causes is how important a factor is it in the production of differences and just what differences is it responsible for. That men differ from women has always been an accepted fact, but exact knowledge of how much and how they differ has, until recent years, been lacking. Recently quantitative measurement has been made by a number of investigators. In making these investigations two serious difficulties have to be met. First, that the tests measure only the differences brought about by differences in sex, and not by any other cause, such as family or training. This difficulty has been met by taking people of all ages, from all sorts of families, with all kinds of training, the constant factor being the difference in sex. The second difficulty is that of finding groups in which the selection agencies have been the same and equally operative. It would be obviously unfair to compare college men and women, and expect to get a fair result as to sex differences, because college women are a more highly selected group intellectually than the college men. It is the conventional and social demands that are primarily responsible for sending boys to college, while the intellectual impulse is responsible to a greater extent for sending girls. Examination of children in the elementary schools, then, gives a fairer result than of the older men and women. The general results of all the studies made point to the fact that the differences between the sexes are small. Sex is the cause of only a small fraction of the differences between individuals. The total difference of men from men and women from women is almost as great as the difference between men and women, for the distribution curve of woman's ability in any trait overlaps the men's curve to at least half its range. In detail the exact measurements of intellectual abilities show a slight superiority of the women in receptivity and memory, and a slight superiority of the men in control of movement and in thought about concrete mechanical situations. In interests which cannot be so definitely measured, women seem to be more interested in people and men in things. In instinctive equipment women excel in the nursing impulse and men in the fighting impulse. In physical equipment men are stronger and bigger than women. They excel in muscular tests in ability to "spurt," whereas women do better in endurance tests. The male sex seems on the whole to be slightly more variable than the female, i.e., its curve of distribution is somewhat flatter and extends both lower and higher than does that of the female; or, stated another way, men furnish more than their proportion of idiots and of geniuses.

Slight though these differences are, they are not to be disregarded, for sometimes the resulting habits are important. For instance, girls should be better spellers than boys. Boys should excel in physics and chemistry. Women should have more tact than men, whereas men should be more impartial in their judgments. With the same intellectual equipment as women, men should be found more often in positions of prominence because of the strength of the fighting instinct. The geniuses of the world, the leaders in any field, as well as the idiots, should more often be men than women. That these differences do exist, observation as well as experiment prove, but that they are entirely due to essential innate differences in sex is still open to question. Differences in treatment of the sexes in ideals and in training for generation after generation *may* account for some of the differences noted.

What these differences mean from the standpoint of practice is still another question. Difference in equipment need not mean difference in treatment, nor need identity of equipment necessarily mean identity of training. The kind of education given will have to be determined not only by the nature of the individual, but also by the ideals held for and the efficiency demanded from each sex.

Another cause of the differences existing between individuals is difference in race inheritance. In causing differences in physical traits this factor is prominent. The American Indians have physical traits in common which differentiate them from other races; the same thing is true of the Negroes and the Mongolians. It has always been taken for granted that the same kind of difference between the races existed in mental traits. To measure the mental differences caused by race is an extremely difficult problem. Training, environment, tradition, are such potent factors in confusing the issue. The difficulty is to measure inborn traits, not achievement. Hence the results from actual measurement are very few and are confined to the sensory and sensorimotor traits. Woodworth, in summing up the results of these tests, says, "On the whole, the keenness of the senses seems to be about on a par in the various races of mankind.... If the results could be taken at their face value, they would indicate differences in intelligence between races, giving such groups as the Pygmy and Negrito a low station as compared with most of mankind. The fairness of the test is not, however, beyond question."[14] The generality of this conclusion concerning the differences in intelligence reveals the lack of data. No tests of the higher intellectual processes, such as the ability to analyze, to associate in terms of elements, to formulate new principles, and the like, have, been given. Some anthropologists are skeptical of the existence of any great differences, while others believe that though there is much overlapping, still differences of considerable magnitude do exist. At present we do not know how much of the differences existing between individuals is due to differences in remote ancestry.

Maturity as a cause of differences between individuals gives quite as unsatisfactory results as remote ancestry. Every thoughtful student of children must realize that inner growth, apart from training, has something to do with the changes which take place in a child; that

___

14. Racial Differences in Mental Traits.

he differs from year to year because of a difference in maturity. This same cause, then, must account to some extent for the differences between individuals of different ages. But just how great a part it plays, what per cent of the difference it accounts for, and what particular traits it affects much or little, no one knows. We say in general that nine-year-old children are more suggestible than six-year-old, and than fourteen-year-old; that the point of view of the fifteen-year-old is different from that of the eleven-year-old; that the power of sense discrimination gradually increases up to about sixteen, and so on. That these facts are true, no one can question, but how far they are due to mere change in maturity and how far to training or to the increase in power of some particular capacity, such as understanding directions, or power of forced attention, is unknown. The studies which have been undertaken along this line have failed in two particulars: first, to distribute the actual changes found from year to year among the three possible causes, maturity, general powers of comprehension and the like, and training; second, to measure the same individuals from year to year. This last error is very common in studies of human nature. It is taken for granted that to examine ten year olds and then eleven year olds and then twelve year olds will give what ten year olds will become in one and two years' time respectively. To test a group of grammar grade children and then a group of high school and then a group of college students will not show the changes in maturity from grammar school to college. The method is quite wrong, for it tests only the ten year olds that stay in school long enough to become twelve year olds; it measures only the very small per cent of the grammar school children who get to college. In other words, it is measuring a more highly selected group and accepting the result obtained from them as true of the entire group. Because of these two serious errors in the investigations our knowledge of the influence of maturity as a cause of individual differences is no better than opinion. Two facts, however, such studies do make clear. First, the supposition that "the increases in ability due to a given amount of progress toward maturity are closely alike for all children save the so-called 'abnormally-precocious' or 'retarded' is false. The same fraction of the total inner development, from zero to adult ability, will produce very unequal results in different children. Inner growth acts differently according to the original nature that is growing. The notion that maturity is the main factor in the differences found amongst school children, so that grading and methods of teaching should be fitted closely to 'stage of growth,' is also false. It is by no means very hard to find seven year olds who can do intellectual work in which one in twenty seventeen year olds would fail."[15]

The question as to how far immediate heredity is a cause of differences found between individuals, can only be answered by measuring how much more alike members of the same family are in a given trait than people picked at random, and then making allowance for similarity in their training. The greater the likenesses between members of the same family, and the greater the differences between members of different families, despite similarities in training, the more can individual differences be traced to differences in ancestry as a controlling cause. The answer to this question has been obtained along four different lines: First, likenesses in physical traits; second, likenesses in particular abilities; third,

---

15. Thorndike, Educational Psychology, Briefer Course.

likenesses in achievement along intellectual and moral lines; fourth, greater likenesses between twins, than ordinary siblings. In physical traits, such as eye color, hair color, cephalic index, height, family resemblance is very strong (the coefficient of correlation being about .5), and here training can certainly have had no effect. In particular abilities, such as ability in spelling, the stage reached by an individual is due primarily to his inheritance, the ability being but little influenced by the differences in home or school training that commonly exist. In general achievement, Galton's results show that eminence runs in families, that one has more than three hundred times the chance of being eminent if one has a brother, father, or son eminent, than the individual picked at random. Wood's investigation in royal families points to the same influence of ancestry in determining achievement. The studies of the Edwards family on one hand and the so-called Kallikak family on the other, point to the same conclusion. Twins are found to be twice as much alike in the traits tested as other brothers and sisters. Though the difficulty of discounting the effect of training in all these studies has been great, yet in every case the investigators have taken pains to do so. The fact that the investigations along such different lines all bear out the same conclusion, namely, that intellectual differences are largely due to differences in family inheritance, weighs heavily in favor of its being a correct one.

The fifth factor that might account for individual differences is environment. By environment we mean any influence brought to bear on the individual. The same difficulty has been met in attempting to measure the effect of environment that was met in trying to measure the effect of inner nature--namely, that of testing one without interference from the other. The attempts to measure accurately the effect of any one element in the environment have not been successful. No adequate way of avoiding the complications involved by different natures has been found. One of the greatest errors in the method of working with this problem has been found just here. It has been customary when the effect of a certain element in the environment is to be ascertained to investigate people who have been subject to that training or who are in the process of training, thus ignoring the selective influence of the factor itself in original nature. For instance, to study the value of high school training we compare those in training with those who have never had any; if the question is the value of manual training or Latin, again the comparison is made between those who have had it and those who haven't. To find out the influence of squalor and misery, people living in the slums are compared with those from a better district. In each case the fact is ignored that the original natures of the two groups examined are different before the influence of the element in question was brought to bear. Why do some children go to high school and others not? Why do some choose classical courses and some manual training courses? Why are some people found in the slums for generations? The answer in each case is the same--the original natures are different. It isn't the slums make the people nearly so often as it is the people make the slums. It isn't training in Latin that makes the more capable man, but the more intellectual students, because of tradition and possibly enjoyment of language study, choose the Latin. It is unfair to measure a factor in the environment and give it credit or discredit for results, when those results are also due to original nature as well, which has not been allowed for. It must be recognized by all those working in this field that, after all, man to some extent selects his own environment. In the second place, it must be remembered that the environment will influence folks differently according as their natures are different. There can be no doubt that environment is accountable for some individual differences, but just which ones and to what extent are questions to which at present the answers are unsatisfactory.

The investigations which have been carried on agree that environment is not so influential a cause for individual differences in intellect as is near ancestry. One rather interesting line of evidence can be quoted as an illustration. If individual differences in achievement are due largely to lack of training or to poor training, then to give the same amount and kind of training to all the individuals in a group should reduce the differences. If such practice does not reduce the differences, then it is not reasonable to suppose that the differences were caused in the first place by differences in training. As a matter of fact, equalizing training *increases* the differences. The superior man becomes more superior, the inferior is left further behind than ever. A common occurrence in school administration bears out this conclusion reached by experimental means. The child who skips a grade is ready at the end of three years to skip again, and the child who fails a grade is likely at the end of three years to fail again. Though environment seems of little influence as compared with near ancestry in determining intellectual ability *per se*, yet it has considerable influence in determining the line along which this ability is to manifest itself. The fact that between 1840-44, 9.4 per cent of the college men went into teaching as a profession and 37.5 per cent into the ministry, while between 1890-94, 25.4

per cent chose the former and only 14 per cent the latter, can be accounted for only on the basis of environmental influence of some kind.[16]

Another fact concerning the influence of environment is that it is very much more effective in influencing morality than intellect. Morality is the outcome of the proper direction of capacities and tendencies possessed by the individual, and therefore is extremely susceptible to environmental influences. We are all familiar with the differences in moral standards of different social groups. One boy may become a bully and another considerate of the rights of others, one learns to steal and another to be honest, one to lie and another to be truthful, because of the influence of their environments rather than on account of differences in their original natures. We are beginning to recognize the importance of environment in moral training in the provisions made to protect children from immoral influences, in the opportunities afforded for the right sort of recreation, and even in the removal of children from the custody of their parents when the environment is extremely unfavorable.

Though changes in method and ideals cannot reduce the differences between individuals in the intellectual field to any marked extent, such changes can raise the level of achievement of the whole group. For instance, more emphasis on silent reading may make the reading ability of a whole school 20 per cent better, while leaving the distance between the best and worst reader in the school the same. Granting that heredity, original nature, is the primary cause of individual differences in intellect (aside from those sex differences mentioned) there remains for

---

16. Thorndike, Educational Psychology, Vol. III.

environment, education in all its forms, the tremendous task of: First, providing conditions favorable for nervous health and growth; second, providing conditions which stimulate useful capacities and inhibit futile or harmful capacities; third, providing conditions which continually raise the absolute achievement of the group and of the race; fourth, providing conditions that will meet the varying original equipments; fifth, assuming primary responsibility for development along moral and social lines.

Concerning those individual differences of which heredity is the controlling cause, two facts are worthy of note. First, that human nature is very highly specialized and that inheritance may be in terms of special abilities or capacities. For instance, artistic, musical, or linguistic ability, statesmanship, power in the field of poetry, may be handed down from one generation to the next. This also means that two brothers may be extremely alike along some lines and extremely different along others. Second, that there seems to be positive combinations between certain mental traits, whereby the presence of one insures the presence of the other to a greater degree than chance would explain. For instance, the quick learner is slow in forgetting, imagery in one field implies power to image in others, a high degree of concentration goes with superior breadth, efficiency in artistic lines is more often correlated with superiority in politics or generalship or science than the reverse, ability to deal with abstract data implies unusual power to deal with the concrete situation. In fact, as far as exact measures go, negative correlations between capacities, powers, efficiencies, are extremely rare, and, when they occur, can be traced to the influence of some environmental factor.

Individuals differ from each other to a much greater degree than has been allowed for in our public education. The common school system is constructed on the theory that children are closely similar in their abilities, type of mental make-up, and capacities in any given line. Experimentation shows each one of these presuppositions to be false. So far as general ability goes, children vary from the genius to the feeble-minded with all the grades between, even in the same school class. This gradation is a continuous one--there are no breaks in the human race. Children cannot be grouped into the very bright, bright, mediocre, poor, very poor, failures--each group being distinct from any other. The shading from one to the other of these classes is gradual, there is no sharp break. Not only is this true, but a child may be considered very bright along one line and mediocre along another. Brilliancy or poverty in intellect does not act as a unit and apply to all lives equally. The high specialization of mental powers makes unevenness in achievement the common occurrence. Within any school grade that has been tested, even when the gradings are as close as those secured by term promotions, it has been found in any subject there are children who do from two to five times as well as others, and from two to five times as much as others. Of course this great variation means an overlapping of grades on each side. In Dr. Bonser's test of 757 children in reasoning he found that 90 per cent of the 6A pupils were below the best pupils of 4A grade and that 4 per cent of 6A pupils were below the mid-pupils of the 4A, and that the best of the 4A pupils made a score three times as high as the worst pupils of 6A. Not only is this tremendous difference in ability found among children of the same class, but the same difference exists in rate of development. Some children can cover the same ground in one half or one third the time as others and do it better. Witness the children already quoted who, skipping a grade, were ready at the end of three years to skip again. Variability, not uniformity, is what characterizes the abilities and rate of intellectual growth of children in the schools, and these differences, as has already been pointed out, are caused primarily by a difference in original nature.

There is also great difference between the general mental make-up of children--a difference in type. There is the child who excels in dealing with abstract ideas. He usually has power also in dealing with the concrete, but his chief interest is in the abstract. He is the one who does splendid work in mathematics, formal grammar, the abstract phases of the sciences. Then there is the child who is a thinker too, but his best work is done when he is dealing with a concrete situation. Unusual or involved applications of principles disturb him. So long as his work is couched in terms of the concrete, he can succeed, but if that is replaced by the x, y, z elements, he is prone to fail. There is another type of child--the one who has the executive ability, the child of action. True, he thinks, too, but his forte is in control of people and of things. He is the one who manages the athletic team, runs the school paper, takes charge of the elections, and so on. For principles to be grasped he must be able to put them into practice. The fourth type is the feeling type, the child who excels in appreciative power. As has been urged so many times before, these types have boundaries that are hazy and ill defined; they overlap in many cases. Some children are of a well-defined mixed type, and most children have something of each of the four abilities characteristic of the types. Still it is true that in looking over a class of children these types emerge, not pure, but controlled by the dominant characteristics mentioned.

The same variation is found among any group of children if they are tested along one line, such as memory. Some have desultory, some rote, some logical memories; some have immediate memories, others the permanent type. In imagery, some have principally productive imagination, others the matter-of-fact reproductive; some deal largely with object images that are vivid and clear-cut, others fail almost entirely with this type, but use word images with great facility. In conduct, some are hesitating and uncertain, others just the reverse; some very open to suggestions, others scarcely touched at all by it; some can act in accordance with principle, others only in terms of particular associations with a definite situation. So one might run the whole gamut of human traits, and in each one any group of individuals will vary: in attention, in thinking, in ideals, in habits, in interests, in sense discrimination, in emotions, and so on. This is one of the greatest contributions of experimental psychology of the past ten years, the tremendous differences between people along all lines, physical as well as mental.

It is lack of recognition of such differences that makes possible such a list of histories of misfits as Swift quotes in his chapter on Standards of Human Power in "Mind in the Making." Individual differences exist, education cannot eliminate them, they are innate, due to original nature. Education that does not recognize them and plan for them is wasteful and, what is worse, is criminal.

The range of ability possessed by children of the same grade in the subjects commonly taught seems not always to be clear in the minds of teachers. It will be discussed at greater length in another chapter, but it is important for the consideration of individual differences to present some data at this time. If we rate the quality of work done in English composition from 10 to 100 per cent, being careful to evaluate as accurately as possible the merit of the composition written, we will find for a seventh and an eighth grade a condition indicated by the following table:

Quality of Composition	Grades	
	7	8
	No. of Pupils	
Rated At 10	2	1
Rated At 20	6	6
Rated At 30	8	8
Rated At 40	7	8
Rated At 50	2	4
Rated At 60	1	1
Rated At 70	1	1
Rated At 80	1	1
Rated At 90	1	1

The table reads as follows: two pupils in the seventh grade and one in the eighth wrote compositions rated at 10; six seventh-grade and six eighth-grade pupils wrote compositions rated at 20, and so on for the whole table.

A similar condition of affairs is indicated if we ask how many of a given type of addition problems are solved correctly in eight minutes by a fifth- and a sixth-grade class.

Number of Problems	Grades	
	5	**6**
	No. of Pupils	
0	2	3
1	6	6
2	6	6
3	6	6
4	4	5
5	4	5
6	3	4
7	1	2
8	1	1
9	1	1

In like manner, if we measure the quality of work done in penmanship for a fifth and sixth grade, with a system of scoring that ranks the penmanship in equal steps from a quality which, is ranked four up to a quality which is ranked eighteen, we find the following results:

Quality of Penmanship	Grades	
	5	**6**
	No. of Pupils	
Rated at 4	5	6
Rated at 5	1	1
Rated at 6	0	0
Rated at 7	2	4

Quality of Penmanship	Grades	
	5	6
	No. of Pupils	
Rated at 8	10	4
Rated at 9	12	1
Rated at 10	3	6
Rated at 11	3	8
Rated at 12	3	3
Rated at 13	1	2
Rated at 14	1	1
Rated at 15	0	1
Rated at 16	1	1
Rated at 17	0	0
Rated at 18	0	0

Results similar to those recorded above will be found if any accurate measurement is made of the knowledge possessed by children in history or in geography, or of the ability to apply or derive principles in physics or in chemistry, or of the knowledge of vocabulary in Latin or in German, and the like.

All such facts indicate clearly the necessity for differentiating our work for the group of children who are classified as belonging to one grade. Under the older and simpler form of school organization, the one-room rural school, it was not uncommon for children to recite in one class in arithmetic, in another in geography or history, and in possibly still another in English. In our more highly organized school systems, with the attempt to have children pass regularly from grade to grade at each promotion period, we have in some measure provided for individual differences through allowing children to skip a grade, or not infrequently by having them repeat the work of a grade. In still other cases an attempt has been made to adapt the work of the class to the needs and capacities of the children by dividing any class group into two or more groups, especially in those subjects in which children seem to have greatest difficulty. Teachers who are alive to the problem presented have striven to adjust their work to different members of the class by varying the assignments, and in some cases by excusing from the exercises in which they are already proficient the abler pupils.

Whatever adjustment the school may be able to make in terms of providing special classes for those who are mentally or physically deficient, or for those who are especially capable, there will always be found in any given group a wide variation in achievement and in capacity. Group teaching and individual instruction will always be required of teachers who would adapt their work to the varying capacities of children. A period devoted to supervised study during which those children who are less able may receive special help, and those who are of exceptional ability be expected to make unusual preparation both in extent and in quality of work done, may contribute much to the efficiency of the school. As paradoxical as the statement may seem, it is true that the most retarded children in our school systems are the brightest. Expressed in another way, it can be proved that the more capable children have already achieved in the subjects in which they are taught more than those who are tow or three grades farther advanced. Possibly the greatest contribution which teachers can make to the development of efficiency upon the part of the children with whom they work is to be found in special attention which is given to capable children with respect to both the quantity and quality of work demanded of them, together with provision for having them segregated in special classes or passed through the school system with greater rapidity than is now common. In an elementary school with which the writer is acquainted, and in which there were four fifth grades, it was discovered during the past year that in one of these fifth grades in which the brighter children had been put they had achieved more in terms of ability to solve problems in arithmetic, in their knowledge of history and geography, in the quality of English composition they wrote, and the like, than did the children in any one of the sixth grades. In this school this particular fifth grade was promoted to the seventh grade for the following year. Many such examples could be found in schools organized with more than one grade at work on the same part of the school course, if care were taken to segregate children in terms of their capacity. And even where there is only one teacher per grade, or where one teacher teaches two or three grades, it should be found possible constantly to accelerate the progress of children of more than ordinary ability.

The movement throughout the United States for the organization of junior high schools (these schools commonly include the seventh, eighth, and ninth school years) is to be looked upon primarily as an attempt to adjust the work of our schools to the individual capacities of boys and girls and to their varying vocational outlook. Such a school, if it is to meet this demand for adjustment to individual differences, must offer a variety of courses. Among the courses offered in a typical junior high school is one which leads directly to the high school. In this course provision is made for the beginning of a foreign language, of algebra, and, in some cases, of some other high school subject during the seventh and eighth years. In another course emphasis is placed upon work in industrial or household arts in the expectation that work in these fields may lead to a higher degree of efficiency in later vocational training, and possibly to the retention of children during this period who might otherwise see little or no meaning in the traditional school course. The best junior high schools are offering in the industrial course a variety of shop work. In some cases machine shop practice, sheet metal working, woodworking, forging, printing, painting, electrical wiring, and the like are offered for boys; and cooking, sewing, including dressmaking and designing, millinery, drawing, with emphasis upon design and interior decoration, music, machine operating, pasting, and the like are provided for girls. Another type of course has provided for training which looks toward commercial work, even though it is recognized that the most adequate commercial training may require a longer period of preparation. In some schools special work in agriculture is offered.

Our schools cannot be considered as satisfactorily organized until we make provision for every boy or girl to work up to the maximum of his capacity. The one thing that a teacher cannot do is to make all of his pupils equal in achievement. Whatever adjustment may have been made in terms of special classes or segregation in terms of ability, the teacher must always face the problem of varying the assignment to meet the capacities of individual children, and she ought, wherever it is possible, especially to encourage the abler children to do work commensurate with their ability, and to provide, as far as is possible, for the rapid advancement of these children through the various stages of the school system.

QUESTIONS

1.   What are the principal causes of differences in abilities or in achievement among school children?

2.   What, if any, of the differences noticed among children may be attributed to sex?

3.   Are any of the sex differences noticeable in the achievements of the school children with whom you are acquainted?

4.   To what extent is maturity a cause of individual differences?

5.   What evidence is available to show the fallacy of the common idea that children of the same age are equal in ability?

6.   How important is heredity in determining the achievement of men and women?

7.   To what extent, if any, would you be interested in the immediate heredity of the children in your class? Why?

8.   To what extent is the environment in which children live responsible for their achievements in school studies?

9.   What may be expected in the way of achievement from two children of widely different heredity but of equal training?

10. For what factor in education is the environment most responsible? Why?

11. If you grant that original nature is the primary cause of individual differences in intellectual achievements, how would you define the work of the school?

12. Why are you not justified in grouping children as bright, ordinary, and stupid?

13. Will a boy who has unusual ability in music certainly be superior in all other subjects?

14. Why are children who skip a grade apt to be able to skip again at the end of two or three years?

15. Are you able to distinguish differences in type of mind (or general mental make-up) among the children in your classes? Give illustrations.

16. What changes in school organization would you advocate for the sake of adjusting the teaching done to the varying capacities of children?

17. How should a teacher adjust his work to the individual differences in capacity or in achievement represented by the usual class group?

XI

The Development of Moral Social Conduct

Morality has been defined in many ways. It has been called "a regulation and control of immediate promptings of impulses in conformity with some prescribed conduct"; as "the organization of activity with reference to a system of fundamental values." Dewey says, "Interest in community welfare, an interest that is intellectual and practical, as well as emotional--an interest, that is to say, in perceiving whatever makes for social order and progress, and in carrying these principles into execution--is the moral habit."[17] Palmer defines it as "the choice by the individual of habits of conduct that are for the good of the race." All these definitions point to control on the part of the individual as one essential of morality.

Morality is not, then, a matter primarily of mere conduct. It involves conduct, but the essence of morality lies deeper than the act itself; motive, choice, are involved as well. Mere law-abiding is not morality in the strict sense of the word. One may keep the laws merely as a matter of blind habit. A prisoner in jail keeps the laws. A baby of four keeps the laws, but in neither case could such conduct be called moral. In neither of these cases do we find "control" by the individual of impulses, nor

---

17. Moral Principles in Education.

"conscious choice" of conduct. In the former compulsion was the controlling force, and in the second blind habit based on personal satisfaction. Conduct which outwardly conforms to social law and social progress is unmoral rather than moral. A moment's consideration will suffice to convince any one that the major part of conduct is of this non-moral type. This is true of adults and necessarily true of children. As Hall says, most of the supposedly moral conduct of the majority of men is blind habit, not thoughtful choosing. In so far as we are ruled by custom, by tradition, in so far as we do as the books or the preacher says, or do as we see others do, without principles to guide us, without thinking, to that extent the conduct is likely to be non-moral. This is the characteristic reaction of the majority of people. We believe as our fathers believed, we vote the same ticket, hold in horror the same practices, look askance on the same doctrines, cling to the same traditions. Morality, on the other hand, is rationalized conduct. Now this non-moral conduct is valuable so far as it goes. It is a conservative force, making for stability, but it has its dangers. It is antagonistic to progress. So long as the conditions surrounding the non-moral individual remain unchanged, he will be successful in dealing with them, but if conditions change, if he is confronted by a new situation, if strong temptation comes, he has nothing with which to meet it, for his conduct was blind. It is the person whose conduct is non-moral that suffers collapse on the one hand, or becomes a bigot on the other, when criticism attacks what he held as true or right. Morality requires that men have a reason for the faith that is in them.

In the second place, morality is conduct. Ideals, ideas, wishes, desires, all may lead to morality, but in so far as they are not expressed in conduct, to that extent they do not come under the head of morality. One may express the sublimest idea, may claim the highest ideals, and be immoral. Conduct is the only test of morality, just as it is the ultimate test of character. Not only is morality judged in terms of conduct, but it is judged according as the conduct is consistent. "Habits of conduct" make for morality or immorality. It is not the isolated act of heroism that makes a man moral, or the single unsocial act that makes a man immoral. The particular act may be moral or immoral, and the person be just the reverse. It is the organization of activity, it is the habits a man has that places him in one category or the other.

In the third place, morality is a matter of individual responsibility. It is "choice by the individual," the "perceiving whatever makes for social order and progress." No one can choose for another, no one can perceive for another. The burden of choosing for the good of the group rests on the individual, it cannot be shifted to society or the Church, or any other institution. Each individual is moral or not according as he lives up to the light that he has, according as he carries into execution principles that are for the good of his race. A particular act, then, may be moral for one individual and immoral for another, and non-moral for still another.

In the third place, morality is a matter of individual responsibility. It is "choice be the individual," the "perceiving whatever makes for social order and progress." No one can choose for another, no one can perceive for another. The burden of Choosing for the good of the group rests on the individual, it cannot be shifted to society or the Church, or any other institution. Each individual is moral or not according as he lives up to the light that he has, according as he carries into execution principles that are for the good of his race. A particular act, then, may be moral for one individual and immoral for another, and non-moral for still another.

To go off into the forest to die if one is diseased may be a moral act for a savage in central Africa; but for a civilized man to do so would probably be immoral because of his greater knowledge. To give liquor to babies to quiet them may be a non-moral act on the part of ignorant immigrants from Russia; but for a trained physician to do so would be immoral. Morality, then, is a personal matter, and the responsibility for it rests on the individual.

Of course this makes possible the setting up of individual opinion as to what is for the good of the group in opposition to tradition and custom. This is, of course, dangerous if it is mere opinion or if it is carried to an extreme. Few men have the gift of seeing what makes for social well-being beyond that of the society of thoughtful people of their time. And yet if a man has the insight, if his investigations point to a greater good for the group from doing something which is different from the standards held by his peers, then morality requires that he do his utmost to bring about such changes. If it is borne in mind that every man is the product of his age and that it is evolution, not revolution, that is constructive, this essential of true morality will not seem so dangerous. All the reformers the world has ever seen, all the pioneers in social service, have been men who, living up to their individual responsibility, have acted as they believed for society's best good in ways that were not in accord with the beliefs of the majority of their time. Shirking responsibility, not living up to what one believes is right, is immoral just as truly as stealing from one's neighbor.

The fourth essential in moral conduct is that it be for the social good. It is the governing of impulses, the inhibition of desires that violate the good of the group, and the choice of conduct that forwards its interests. This does not mean that the group and the individual are set over against each other, and the individual must give way. It means, rather, that certain impulses, tendencies, motives, of the individual are chosen instead of others; it means that the individual only becomes his fullest self as he becomes a social being; it means that what is for the good of the group in the long run is for the good of the units that make up that group. Morality, then, is a relative term. What is of highest moral value in one age may be immoral in another because of change in social conditions. As society progresses, as different elements come to the front because of the march of civilization, so the acts that are detrimental to the good of the whole must change. To-day slander and stealing a man's good name are quite as immoral as stealing his property. Acts that injure the mental and spiritual development of the group are even more immoral than those which interfere with the physical well-being.

A strong will is not necessarily indicative of a good character. A strong will may be directed towards getting what gives pleasure to oneself, irrespective of the effect on other people. It is the goal, the purpose with which it is exercised, that makes a man with a strong will a moral man or an immoral man. Only when one's will is used to put into execution those principles that will bring about social progress is it productive of a good character.

Thus it is seen that morality can be discussed only in connection with group activity. It is the individual as a part of a group, acting in connection with it, that makes the situation a moral one. Individual morality is discussed by some authors, but common opinion limits the term to the use that has been discussed in the preceding paragraphs.

If social well-being is taken in its broadest sense, then all moral behavior is social, and all social behavior comes under one of the three types of morality. Training for citizenship, for social efficiency, for earning a livelihood, all have a moral aspect. It is only as the individual is trained to live a complete life as one of a group that he can be trained to be fully moral, and training for complete social living must include training in morality. Hence for the remainder of this discussion the two terms will be considered as synonymous. We hear it sometimes said, "training in morals and manners," as if the two were distinct, and yet a full, realization of what is for social betterment along emotional and intellectual lines must include a realization of the need of manners. Of course there are degrees of morality or immorality according as the act influences society much or little--all crimes are not equally odious, nor all virtues equally commendable, but any act that touches the well-being of the group must come under this category.

From the foregoing paragraph, the logical conclusion would be that there is no instinct or inborn tendency that is primarily and distinctly moral as over against those that are social. That is the commonly accepted belief to-day. There is no moral instinct. Morality finds its root in the original nature of man, but not in a single moral instinct. It is, on the other hand, the outgrowth of a number of instincts all of which have been listed under the head of the social instinct. Man has in his original equipment tendencies that will make him a moral individual *if*they are developed, but they are complex, not simple. Some of these social tendencies which are at the root of moral conduct are gregariousness, desire for approval, dislike of scorn, kindliness, attention to human beings, imitation, and others. Now, although man possesses these tendencies as a matter of original equipment, he also possesses tendencies which are opposed to these, tendencies which lead to the advancement of self, rather than the well-being of the group. Some of these are fighting, mastery, rivalry, jealousy, ownership. Which of these sets of tendencies is developed and controls the life of the individual is a matter of training and environment. In the last chapter it was pointed out that morality was much more susceptible to environmental influences than intellectual achievement, because it was much more a direction and guidance of capacities and tendencies possessed by every one. One's character is largely a product of one's environment. In proof of this, read the reports of reform schools, and the like. Children of criminal parents, removed from the environment of crime, grow up into moral persons. The pair of Jukes who left the Juke clan lost their criminal habits and brought up a family of children who were not immoral. Education cannot produce geniuses, but it can produce men and women whose chief concern is the well-being of the group.

From a psychological point of view the "choice by the individual of habits of conduct that are for the good of the group" involves three considerations: First, the elements implied in such conduct; second, the stages of development; third, the laws governing this development. First, moral conduct involves the use of habits, but these must be rational habits, so it involves the power to think and judge in order to choose. But thinking that shall result in the choice of habits that are for the well-being of the group must use knowledge. The individual must have facts and standards at his disposal by means of which he may evaluate the possible lines of action presented. Further, an individual may know intellectually what is right and moral and yet not care. The interest, the emotional appeal, may be lacking, hence he must have ideals to which he has given his allegiance, which will force him to put into practice what his knowledge tells him is right. And then, having decided what is for the social good and having the desire to carry it out, the moral man must be able to put it into execution. He must have the "will power." Morality, then, is an extremely complex matter, involving all the powers of the human being, intellectual, emotional, and volitional--involving the coöperation of heredity and environment. It is evident that conduct that is at so high a level, involving experience, powers of judgment, and control, cannot be characteristic of the immature individual, but must come after years of growth, if at all. Therefore we find stages of development towards moral conduct.

The first stage of development, which lasts up into the pre-adolescent years, is the non-moral stage. The time when a child may conform outwardly to moral law, but only as a result of blind habit--not as a result of rational choice. It is then that the little child conforms to his environment, reflecting the characters of the people by whom he is surrounded. Right to him means what those about him approve and what brings him satisfaction. If stealing and lying meet with approval from the people about him, they are right to him. To steal and be caught is wrong to the average child of the streets, because that brings punishment and annoyance. He has no standards of judging other than the example of others and his own satisfaction and annoyance. The non-moral period, then, is characterized by the formation of habits--which outwardly conform to moral law, or are contrary to it, according as his environment directs.

The need to form habits that do conform, that are for the social good, is evident. By having many habits of this kind formed in early childhood, truthfulness, consideration for others, respect for poverty, promptness, regularity, taking responsibility, and so on, the dice are weighted in favor of the continuation of such conduct when reason controls. The child has then only to enlarge his view, build up his principles in accord with conduct already in operation--he needs only to rationalize what he already possesses. On the other hand, if during early years his conduct violates moral law, he is in the grip of habits of great strength which will result in two dangers. He may be blind to the other side, he may not realize how his conduct violates the laws of social progress; or, knowing, he may not care enough to put forth the tremendous effort necessary to break these habits and build up the opposite. From the standpoint of conduct this non-moral period is the most important one in the life of the child. In it the twig is bent. To urge that a child cannot understand and therefore should be excused for all sorts of conduct simply evades the issue. He is forming habits--that cannot be prevented; the question is, Are those habits in line with the demands of social efficiency or are they in violation of it?

But character depends primarily on deliberate choice. We dare not rely on blind habit alone to carry us through the crises of social and spiritual adjustment. There will arise the insistent question as to whether the habitual presupposition is right. Occasions will occur when several possible lines of conduct suggest themselves; what kind of success will one choose, what kind of pleasure? Choice, personal choice, will be forced upon the individual. This problem does not usually grow acute until early adolescence, although it may along some lines present itself earlier. When it appears will depend to a large extent on the environment. For some people in some directions it never comes. It should come gradually and spontaneously. This period is the period of transition, when old habits are being scrutinized, when standards are being formulated and personal responsibility is being realized, when ideals are made vital and controlling. It may be a period of storm and stress when the youth is in emotional unrest; when conduct is erratic and not to be depended on; when there is reaction against authority of all kinds. These characteristics are unfortunate and are usually the result of unwise treatment during the first period. If, on the other hand, the period of transition is prepared for during the preadolescent years by giving knowledge, opportunities for self-direction and choice, the change should come normally and quietly. The transition period should be characterized by emphasis upon personal responsibility for conduct, by the development of social ideals, and by the cementing of theory and practice. This period is an ever recurring one.

The transition period is followed by the period of true morality during which the conduct chosen becomes habit. The habits characteristic of this final period are different from the habits of the non-moral period, in that they have their source in reason, whereas those of the early period grew out of instincts. This is the period of most value, the period of steady living in accordance with standards and ideals which have been tested by reason and found to be right. The transition period is wasteful and uncertain. True morality is the opposite. But so long as growth in moral matters goes on there is a continuous change from transition period to truly moral conduct and back again to a fresh transition period and again a change to morality of a still higher order. Each rationalized habit but paves the way for one still higher. Morality, then, should be a continual evolution from level to level. Only so is progress in the individual life maintained.

Morality, then, requires the inhibition of some instincts and the perpetuation of others, the formation of habits and ideals, the development of the power to think and judge, the power to react to certain abstractions such as ought, right, duty, and so on, the power to carry into execution values accepted. The general laws of instinct, of habit, the response by piecemeal association, the laws of attention and appreciation, are active in securing these responses that we call moral, just as they are operative in securing other responses that do not come under this category. It is only as these general psychological laws are carried out sufficiently that stable moral conduct is secured. Any violation of these laws invalidates the result in the moral field just as it would in any other. There is not one set of principles governing moral conduct and another set governing all other types of conduct. The same general laws govern both. This being true, there is no need of discussing in detail the operation of laws controlling moral conduct--that has all been covered in

the previous chapters. However, there are some suggestions which should be borne in mind in the application
of these laws to this field.

First, it is a general principle that habits, to be fixed
and stable, must be followed by satisfactory results and
that working along the opposite line, that of having annoyance follow a lapse in the conduct, is uneconomical
and unreliable. This principle applies particularly to moral habits. Truth telling, bravery, obedience, generosity,
thought for others, church going, and so on must be followed by positive satisfaction, if they are to be part of the
warp and woof of life. Punishing falsehood, selfishness,
cowardice, and so on is not enough, for freedom from
supervision will usually mean rejection of such forced
habits. A child must find that it pays to be generous; that
he is happier when he coöperates with others than when
he does not. Positive satisfaction should follow moral
conduct. Of course this satisfaction must vary in type
with the age and development of the child, from physical
pleasure occasioned by an apple as a reward for self-control at table to the satisfaction which the consciousness
of duty well done brings to the adolescent.

Second, the part played by suggestion in bringing
about moral habits and ideals must be recognized. The
human personalities surrounding the child are his most
influential teachers in this line. This influence of personalities begins when the child is yet a baby. Reflex imitation first, and later conscious imitation plus the feeling of dependence which a little child has for the adults
in his environment, results in the child reflecting to a
large extent the characters of those about him. Good
temper, stability, care for others, self-control, and many

other habits; respect for truth, for the opinion of others, and many other ideals, are unconsciously absorbed by the child in his early years. Example not precept, actions not words, are the controlling forces in moral education. Hence the great importance of the characters of a child's companions, friends, and teachers, to say nothing of his parents. Next to personalities, theaters, moving pictures, and books, all have great suggestive power.

Third, there is always a danger that theory become divorced from practice, and this is particularly true here because morality is conduct. Knowing what is right is one thing, doing it is another, and knowing does not result in doing unless definite connections are made between the two. Instruction in morals may have but little effect on conduct. It is only as the knowledge of what is right and good comes in connection with social situations when there is the call for action that true morality can be gained. Mere classroom instruction cannot insure conduct. It is only as the family and the school become more truly social institutions, where group activity such as one finds in life is the dominant note, that we can hope to have morality and not ethics, ideals and not passive appreciation, as a result of our teaching.

Fourth, it is without question true that in so far as the habits fixed are "school habits" or "Sunday habits," or any other special type of habits, formed only in connection with special situations, to that extent we have no reason to expect moral conduct in the broader life situations. The habits formed are those that will be put into practice, and they are the only ones we are sure of. Because a child is truthful in school, prompt in attendance, polite to his teacher, and so on is no warrant that he will be the same on the playground or on the street. Because a child can think out a problem in history or mathematics is no warrant that he will therefore think out moral problems. The only sure way is to see to it that he forms many useful habits out of school as well as in, that he has opportunity to think out moral problems as well as problems in school subjects.[18]

Fifth, individual differences must not be forgotten in moral training. Individual differences in suggestibility will influence the use of this factor in habit formation. Individual differences in power of appreciation will influence the formation of ideals. Differences in interest in books will result in differing degrees of knowledge. Differences in maturity will mean that certain children in a class are ready for facts concerning sex, labor and capital, crime, and so on, long before other children in the same class should have such knowledge. Differences in thinking power will determine efficiency in moral situations just as in others.

The more carefully we consider the problem of moral social conduct, the more apparent it becomes that the work of the school can be modified so as to produce more significant results than are commonly now secured. Indeed, it may be contended that in some respects the activities of the school operate to develop an attitude which is largely individualistic, competitive, and, if not anti-social, at least non-social. Although we may not expect that the habits and attitudes which are developed in the school will entirely determine the life led outside, yet one may not forget that a large part of the life of children is spent under school supervision. As children work in an

---

18. For a fuller discussion of this topic see next chapter.

atmosphere of coöperation, and as they form habits of helpfulness and openmindedness, we may expect that in some degree these types of activity will persist, especially in their association with each other. In a school which is organized to bring about the right sort of moral social conduct we ought to expect that children would grow in their power to accept responsibility for each other. The writer knows of a fourth grade in which during the past year a boy was absent from the room after recess. The teacher, instead of sending the janitor, or she herself going to find the boy, asked the class what they were going to do about it, and suggested to them their responsibility for maintaining the good name which they had always borne as a group. Two of the more mature boys volunteered to go and find the boy who was absent. When they brought him into the room a little while later, they remarked to the teacher in a most matter-of-fact way, "We do not think that he will stay out after recess again." In the corridor of an elementary school the writer saw during the past year two boys sitting on a table before school hours in the morning. The one was teaching the multiplication tables to the other. They were both sixth-grade pupils,--the one a boy who had for some reason or other never quite thoroughly learned his tables. The teacher had suggested that somebody might help him, and a boy had volunteered to come early to school in order that he might teach the boy who was backward. A great many teachers have discovered that the strongest motive which they can find for good work in the field of English is to be found in providing an audience, both for the reading or story-telling, and for the English composition. The idea which prevails is that if one is to read, he ought to read well enough to entertain others. If one has enjoyed a story, he may, if he prepares himself sufficiently well, tell it to the class or to some other group.

Much more emphasis on the undertakings in the attempt to have children accept responsibility, and to engage in a type of activity which has a definite moral social value, is to be found in the schools in which children are responsible for the morning exercises, or for publishing a school paper, or for preparing a school festival. One of the most notable achievements in this type of activity which the writer has ever known occurred in a school in which a group of seventh-grade children were thought to be particularly incompetent. The teachers had almost despaired of having them show normal development, either intellectually or socially. After a conference of all of the teachers who knew the members of this group, it was decided to allow them to prepare a patriot's day festival. The idea among those teachers who had failed with this group was that if the children had a large responsibility, they would show a correspondingly significant development. The children responded to the motive which was provided, became earnest students of history in order that they might find a dramatic situation, and worked at their composition when they came to write their play, some of them exercising a critical as well as a creative faculty which no one had known that they possessed. But possibly the best thing about the whole situation was that every member of the class found something to do in their coöperative enterprise. Some members of the class were engaged in building and in decorating the stage scenery; others were responsible for costumes; those who were strong in music devoted themselves to this field. The search for a proper dramatic situation in history and the writing of the play have already been suggested. The staging of the play and its presentation to a large group of parents and other interested patrons of the school required still further specialization and ability. Out of it all came a realization of the possibility of accomplishing great things when all worked together for the success of a common enterprise. When the festival day came, the most common statement heard in the room on the part of the parents and others interested in the work of the children was expressed by one who said: "This is the most wonderful group of seventh-grade children that I have ever seen. They are as capable as most high school boys and girls." It is to be recalled that this was the group in whom the teachers originally had little faith, and who had sometimes been called in their school a group of misfits.

Some schools have found, especially in the upper grades, an opportunity for a type of social activity which is entirely comparable with the demand made upon the older members of our communities. This work for social improvement or betterment is carried on frequently in connection with a course in civics. In some schools there is organized what is known as the junior police. This organization has been in some cases coordinated with the police department. The boys who belong pledge themselves to maintain, in so far as they are able, proper conditions on the streets with respect to play, to abstain from the illegal use of tobacco or other narcotics, and to be responsible for the correct handling of garbage, especially to see that paper, ashes, and other refuse are placed in separate receptacles, and that these receptacles are removed from the street promptly after they are emptied by the department concerned. In one city with which the writer is acquainted, the children in the upper grades, according to the common testimony of the citizens of their community, have been responsible for the cleaning up of the street cars. In other cities they have become interested, and have interested their parents, in the question of milk and water supply. In some cases they have studied many different departments of the city government, and have, in so far as it was possible, lent their coöperation. In one case a group of children became very much excited concerning a dead horse that was allowed to remain on a street near the school, and they learned before they were through just whose responsibility it was, and how to secure the action that should have been taken earlier.

Still another type of activity which may have significance for the moral social development of children is found in the study of the life activities in the communities in which they live. There is no reason why children, especially in the upper grades or in the high school, should not think about working conditions, especially as they involve sweat-shops or work under unsanitary conditions. They may very properly become interested in the problems of relief, and of the measures taken to eliminate crime. Indeed, from the standpoint of the development of socially efficient children, it would seem to be more important that some elementary treatment of industrial and social conditions might be found to be more important in the upper grades and in the high school than any single subject which we now teach.

Another attempt to develop a reasonable attitude concerning moral situations is found in the schools which have organized pupils for the participation in school government. There is no particular value to be attached to any such form of organization. It may be true that there is considerable advantage in dramatizing the form of government in which the children live, and for that purpose policemen, councilmen or aldermen, mayors, and other officials, together with their election, may help in the understanding of the social obligations which they will have to meet later on. But the main thing is to have these children come to accept responsibility for each other, and to seek to make the school a place where each respects the rights of others and where every one is working together for the common good. In this connection it is important to suggest that schemes of self-government have succeeded only where there has been a leader in the position of principal or other supervisory officer concerned. Children's judgments are apt to be too severe when they are allowed to discipline members of their group. There will always be need, whatever attempt we may make to have them accept responsibility, for the guidance and direction of the more mature mind.

We seek in all of these activities, as has already been suggested, to have children come to take, in so far as they are able, the rational attitude toward the problems of conduct which they have to face. It is important for teachers to realize the fallacy of making a set of rules by which all children are to be controlled. It is only with respect to those types of activity in which the response, in order to further the good of the group, must be invariable that we should expect to have pupils become automatic. It is important in the case of a fire drill, or in the passing of materials, and the like, that the response, although it does involve social obligation, should be reduced to the level of mechanized routine. Most school situations involve, or may involve, judgment, and it is only as pupils grow in power of self-control and in their willingness to think through a situation before acting, that we may expect significant moral development. In the case of offenses which seem to demand punishment, that teacher is wise who is able to place responsibility with the pupil who has offended. The question ought to be common, "What can I do to help you?" The question which the teacher should ask herself is not, "What can I do to punish the pupil?" but rather, "How can I have him realize the significance of his action and place upon him the responsibility of reinstating himself with the social group?" The high school principal who solved the problem of a teacher who said that she would not teach unless a particular pupil were removed from her class, and of the pupil who said that she would not stay in school if she had to go to that teacher, by telling them both to take time to think it through and decide how they would reconcile their differences, is a case in point. What we need is not the punishment which follows rapidly upon our feeling of resentment, but rather the wisdom of waiting and accepting the mistake or offense of the pupil as an opportunity for careful consideration upon his part and as a possible means of growth for him.

There has been considerable discussion during recent years concerning the obligation of the school to teach children concerning matters of sex. Traditionally, our policy has been one of almost entire neglect. The consequence has been, on the whole, the acquisition upon the part of boys and girls of a large body of misinformation, which has for the most part been vicious. It is not probable that we can ever expect most teachers to have the training necessary to give adequate instruction in this field. For children in the upper grades, during the preadolescent period especially, some such instruction given by the men and women trained in biology, or possibly by men and women doctors who have made a specialty of this field, promises a large contribution to the development of the right attitudes with respect to the sex life and the elimination of much of the immorality which has been due to ignorance or to the vicious misinformation which has commonly been spread among children. The policy of secrecy and ignorance cannot well be maintained if we accept the idea of responsibility and the exercise of judgment as the basis of moral social activity. In no other field are the results of a lack of training or a lack of morality more certain to be disastrous both for the individual and for the social group.

QUESTIONS

1. How satisfactory is the morality of the man who claims that he does no wrong?

2. How is it possible for a child to be unmoral and not immoral?

3. Are children who observe school rules and regulations necessarily growing in morality?

4. Why is it important, from the standpoint of growth in morality, to have children form socially desirable habits, even though we may not speak of this kind of activity as moral conduct?

5. What constitutes growth in morality for the adult?

6. In what sense is it possible for the same act to be immoral, unmoral, and moral for individuals living under differing circumstances and in different social groups? Give an example.

7. Why have moral reformers sometimes been considered immoral by their associates?

8.   What is the moral significance of earning a living? Of being prompt? Of being courteous?

9.   What are the instincts upon which we may hope to build in moral training? What instinctive basis is there for immoral conduct?

10.   To what extent is intellectual activity involved in moral conduct? What is the significance of one's emotional response?

11.   What stages of development are distinguishable in the moral development of children? Is it possible to classify children as belonging to one stage or the other by their ages?

12.   Why is it true that one's character depends upon the deliberate choices which he makes among several possible modes or types of action?

13.   Why is it important to have positive satisfaction follow moral conduct?

14.   How may the conduct of parents and teachers influence conduct of children?

15.   What is the weakness of direct moral instruction, e.g. the telling of stories of truthfulness, the teaching of moral precepts, and the like?

16.   What opportunities can you provide in your class for moral social conduct?

17.   Children will do what is right because of their desire to please, their respect for authority, their fear of unpleasant consequences, their careful, thoughtful analysis of the situation and choice of that form of action which they consider right. Arrange these motives in order of their desirability. Would you be

satisfied to utilize the motive which brings results most quickly and most surely?

18. In what sense is it true that lapses from moral conduct are the teacher's best opportunity for moral teaching?

19. How may children contribute to the social welfare of the school community? Of the larger social group outside of the school?

20. How may pupil participation in school government be made significant in the development of social moral conduct?

XII

Transfer of Training

Formal discipline or transfer of training concerns itself with the question as to how far training in one subject, along one line, influences other lines. How far, for instance, training in reasoning in mathematics helps a child to reason in history, in morals, in household administration; how far memorizing gems of poetry or dates in history aids memory when it is applied to learning stenography or botany; how far giving attention to the gymnasium will insure attention to sermons and one's social engagements. The question is, How far does the special training one gets in home and school fit him to react to the environment of life with its new and complex situations? Put in another way, the question is what effect upon other bonds does forming this particular situation response series of bonds have. The practical import of the question and its answer is tremendous. Most of our present school system, both in subject matter and method, is built upon the assumption that one answer is correct--if it is false, much work remains to be done by the present-day education.

The point of view which was held until recent years is best made clear by a series of quotations.

"Since the mind is a unit and the faculties are simply phases or manifestations of its activity, whatever strengthens one faculty indirectly strengthens all the others. The *verbal* memory seems to be an exception to this statement, however, for it may be abnormally cultivated without involving to any profitable extent the other faculties. But only things that are rightly perceived and rightly understood can be *rightly* remembered. Hence whatever develops the acquisitive and assimilative powers will also strengthen memory; and, conversely, rightly strengthening the memory necessitates the developing and training of the other powers." (R.N. Roark, Method in Education.)

"It is as a means of training the faculties of perception and generalization that the study of such a language as Latin in comparison with English is so valuable." (C.L. Morgan, Psychology for Teachers.)

"Arithmetic, if judiciously taught, forms in the pupil habits of mental attention, argumentative sequence, absolute accuracy, and satisfaction in truth as a result, that do not seem to spring equally from the study of any other subject suitable to this elementary stage of instruction." (Joseph Payne, Lectures on Education, Vol. I.)

"By means of experimental and observational work in science, not only will his attention be excited, the power of observation, previously awakened, much strengthened, and the senses exercised and disciplined, but the very important habit of doing homage to the authority of facts rather than to the authority of men, be initiated." (*Ibid.*)

The view maintained by these writers is that the mind is made up of certain elemental powers such as attention, reasoning, observation, imagination, and the like, each of which acts as a unit. Training any one of these powers means simply its exercise irrespective of the material used. The facility gained through this exercise may then be transferred to other subjects or situations, which are quite different. The present point of view with regard to this question is very different, as is shown by the following quotations:

"We may conclude, then, that there is something which may be called formal discipline, and that it may be more or less general in character. It consists in the establishment of habitual reactions that correspond to the form of situations. These reactions foster adjustments, attitudes, and ideas that favor the successful dealing with the emergencies that arouse them. On the other hand, both the form that we can learn to deal with more effectively, and the reactions that we associate with it, are definite. There is no general training of the powers or faculties, so far as we can determine." (Henderson, 10, f.)

"One mental function or activity improves others in so far as and because they are in part identical with it, because it contains elements common to them. Addition improves multiplication because multiplication is largely addition; knowledge of Latin gives increased ability to learn French because many of the facts learned in the one case are needed in the other. The study of geometry may lead a pupil to be more logical in all respects, for one element of being logical in all respects is to realize that facts can be absolutely proven and to admire and desire this certain and unquestionable sort of demonstration...." (Thorndike, '06, *passim*.)

"Mental discipline is the most important thing in education, but it is specific, not general. The ability developed by means of one subject can be transferred to another subject only in so far as the latter has elements in common with the former. Abilities should be developed in school only by means of those elements of subject-matter and of method that are common to the most valuable phases of the outside environment. In the high school there should also be an effort to work out general concepts of method from the specific methods used." (Heck, '09, Edition of '11.)

"... No study should have a place in the curriculum for which this general disciplinary characteristic is the chief recommendation. Such advantage can probably be gotten in some degree from every study, and the intrinsic values of each study afford at present a far safer criterion of educational work than any which we can derive from the theory of formal discipline." (Angell, '08.)

These writers also believe in transfer of training, but they believe the transfer to be never complete, to be in general a very small percentage of the special improvement gained and at times to be negative and to interfere with responses in other fields instead of being a help. They also emphasize the belief that when the transfer does occur, it is for some perfectly valid reason and under certain very definite conditions. They reject utterly the machine-like idea of the mind and its elemental faculties held by the writers first quoted. They hold the view of mental activity which has been emphasized in the discussion of original tendencies and inheritance from near ancestry, *i.e.*, that the physical correlate of all types of mental activity is a definite forming of connections between particular bonds-these connections, of course, according to the laws of readiness exercise, and effect, would be determined by the situation acting as a stimulus and would, therefore, vary as the total situation varied. They believe in a highly specialized human brain, which reacts in small groups of nerve tracts--not in gross wholes. They would express each of the "elemental" powers in the plural and not in the singular.

The basis of this change of view within the last fifteen or twenty years is to be found in experimental work. The question has definitely been put to the test as to how far training in one line did influence others. For a full description of the various types of experiments performed the reader is referred to Thorndike's "Psychology of Learning," Chapter 12. Only an indication of the type of work done and the general character of the results can be given here. Experiments in the effect of cross education, in memorizing, in observing and judging sensory and perceptual data, and in forming sensori-motor association habits have been conducted in considerable numbers. A few experiments in special school functions have also been carried out. Investigations in the correlation between various parts of the same subject and between different subjects supposed to be closely allied also throw light upon this subject. The results from these different lines of experiment, although confusing and sometimes contradictory, seem to warrant the belief stated above. They have made it very clear that the question of transfer is not a simple one, but, on the contrary, that it is extremely complex. They make plain that in some cases where large transfer was confidently expected, that little resulted, while, on the other hand, in some cases when little was expected, much more occurred. It is evident that the old idea of a large transfer in some subtle and unexplained way of special improvements to a general faculty is false. But, on the other hand, it would be equally false to say that no transfer occurred. The general principle seems to be that transfer occurs when the same bonds are used in the second situation to the extent that the alteration in these particular connections affects the second response. Both the knowledge of what bonds are used in various responses and to what extent alteration in them will affect different total responses is lacking. Therefore, all that is at present possible is a statement of conditions under which transfer is probable.

In general, then, transfer of training will occur to the extent that the two responses use the same bonds- -to the extent, then, that there is identity of some sort. This identity which makes transfer possible may be of all degrees of generality and of several different types. First, there may be identity of content. For instance, forming useful connections with six, island, and, red, habit, Africa, square root, triangle, gender, percentage, and so on, in this or that particular context should be of use in other contexts and therefore allow of transfer of training. The more common the particular responses are to all sorts of life situations, the greater the possibility of transfer. Second, the identity may be that of method or procedure. To be able to add, to carry, to know the method of classifying an unknown flower, to have a definite method of meeting a new situation in hand-work, to know how to use source material in history, to have gained the technique of laboratory skill in chemistry, to know how to study in geography, should be useful in other departments where the same method would serve. Some of these methods are, of course, of much more general service than others.

In establishing skill in the use of these various procedures, two types of responses are needed. The learner must form connections of a positive nature, such as analyzing, collecting material, criticizing according to standard, picking out the essential and so on, and he must also form connections of a negative character which will cause him to neglect certain tendencies. He must learn not to accept the first idea offered, to neglect suggestions, to hurry or to leave half finished, to ignore interruptions, to prevent personal bias to influence criticism, and so on. These connections which result in neglecting certain elements are quite as important as the positive element, both in the production of the particular procedure and in the transfer to other fields. Third, the identity may be of still more general character and be in terms of attitude or ideal. To learn to be thorough in connection with history, accurate in handwork, open-minded in science, persistent in Latin, critical in geometry, thorough in class and school activities, to form habits of allegiance to ideals of truth, coöperation, fair play, tolerance, courage, and so on, *may* help the learner to exhibit these same attitudes in other situations in life. Here again the connections of neglect are important. To neglect selfish suggestions, to ignore the escape from consequences that falsehood might make possible, to be dead to fear, to ignore bodily aches and pains, are quite as necessary in producing conduct that is generous, truthful, and courageous as are the positive connections made in building up the ideal.

In the discussion of transfer because of identity, it was emphasised that the presence of identity of various types explained cases of transfer that exist and made transfer possible. In no case must it be understood, however, that the presence of these identical elements is a warrant of transfer. Transfer *may* take place under such conditions, but it need not do so. Transfer is most sure to occur in cases of identity of substance and least likely in cases of identity of attitude or ideals. To have useful responses to six, above, city, quart, and so on, in one situation will very likely mean responses of a useful nature in almost all situations which have such elements present. It is very different with the ideals. A child may be very accurate in handwork, and yet almost nothing of it show elsewhere; he may be truthful to his teacher and lie to his parents; he may be generous to his classmates and the reverse to his brothers and sisters. Persistence in Latin may not influence his work in the shop, and the critical attitude of geometry be lacking in his science. Transfer in methods holds a middle ground. It seems that the more complex and the more subtle the connections involved, the less is the amount and the surety of the transfer.

In order to increase the probability of transfer when connections of method or attitudes are being formed, first, it should be made conscious, and second, it should be put into practice in several types of situations. There is grave danger that the method will not be differentiated from the subject, the ideal from the context of the situation. To many children learning how to study in connection with history, or to be critical in geometry, or to be scientific in the laboratory, has never been separated from the particular situation. The method or the ideal and the situation in which they have been acquired are one--one response. The general elements of method or attitude have never been made conscious, they are submerged in the particular subject or situation, and therefore the probability of transfer is lessened. If, on the other hand, the question of method, as an idea by itself, apart from any particular subject, is brought to the child's attention; if truth as an ideal, independent of context, is made conscious, it is much more likely to be reacted to in a different situation, for it has become a free idea and therefore crystallized. Then having freed the general somewhat from its particular setting, the learner should be given opportunity to put it in practice in other settings. To simply form the method connections or the attitude responses in Latin and then blindly trust that they will be of general use is unsafe. It is the business of the educator to make as sure as he can of the transfer, and that can only be done by practicing in several fields. These two procedures which make transfer more sure, i.e., making the element conscious and giving practice in several fields, are not sharply divided, but interact. Practice makes the idea clearer and freer, and this in turn makes fresh practice profitable. It is simply the application of the law of analysis by varying concomitants.

In all this matter of transfer it must be borne in mind that a very slight amount of transfer of some of these more general responses may be of tremendous value educationally, provided it is over a very wide field. If a boy's study of high school science made him at all more scientific in his attitude towards such life situations as politics, morals, city sanitation, and the like, it would be of much more value than the particular habit formed. If a girl's work in home economics resulted in but a slight transfer of vital interest to the actual problems of home-making, it would mean much to the homes of America. If a boy's training in connection with the athletics of his school fosters in him an ideal of fair play which influences him at all in his dealings with men in business, with his family, with himself, the training would have been worth while. To discount training simply because the transfer is slight is manifestly unfair. The kind of responses which transfer are quite as important as the amount of the transfer.

The idea that every subject will furnish the same amount of discipline provided they are equally well taught is evidently false. Every school subject must now be weighed from two points of view,--first, as to the worth of the particular facts, responses, habits, which it forms, and second, as to the opportunity it offers for the formation of connections which are of general application. The training which educators are sure of is the particular training offered by the subject; the general training is more problematic. Hence no subject should be retained in our present curriculum whose only value is a claim to disciplinary training. Such general training as the subject affords could probably be gained from some other subject whose content is also valuable. Just because a subject is difficult, or is distasteful, is no sign that its pursuit will result in disciplinary training. In fact, the psychology of play and drudgery make it apparent that the presence of annoyance, of distaste, will lessen the disciplinary value. Only those subjects and activities which are characterized by the play spirit can offer true educational development. The more the play spirit enters in, the greater the possibility of securing not only special training, but general discipline as well. Thorndike sums up the present attitude towards special subjects by saying, "An impartial inventory of the facts in the ordinary pupil of ten to eighteen would find the general training from English composition greater than that from formal logic, the training from physics and chemistry greater than that from geometry, and the training from a year's study of the laws and institutions of the Romans greater than that from equal study of their language. The grammatical studies which have been considered the chief depositories of disciplinary magic would be found in general inferior to scientific treatments of human nature as a whole. The superiority for discipline of pure overapplied science would be referred in large measure to the fact that pure science could be so widely applied. The disciplinary value of geometry would appear to be due, not to the simplicity of its conditions, but to the rigor of its proofs; the greatest disciplinary value of Latin would appear in the case, not of those who disliked it and found it hard, but of those to whom it was a charming game."

QUESTIONS

1. It has been experimentally determined that the ease with which one memorizes one set of facts may be very greatly improved without a corresponding improvement in ability to memorize in some other field. How would you use this fact to refute the argument that we possess a general faculty of memory?

2. How is it possible for a man to reason accurately in the field of engineering and yet make very grave mistakes in his reasoning about government or education?

3. What assurance have we that skill or capacity for successful work developed in one situation will be transferred to another situation involving the same mental processes of habit formation, reasoning, imagination, and the like?

4. What are the different types of identity which make possible transfer of training?

5. How can we make the identity of methods of work most significant for transfer of training and for the education of the individual?

6. Why do ideals which seem to control in one situation fail to affect other activities in which the same ideal is called for?

7. Under what conditions may a very slight amount of transfer of training become of the very greatest importance for education?

8. Why may we not hope for the largest results in training by compelling children to study that which is distasteful? Do children (or adults) work hardest when they are forced to attend to that from which they derive little or no satisfaction?

9. Which student gets the most significant training from his algebra, the boy who enjoys work in this field or the boy who worries through it because algebra is required for graduation from the high school?

10. Why may we hope to secure more significant training in junior high schools which offer a great variety of courses than was accomplished by the seventh and eighth grades in which all pupils were compelled to study the same subjects?

11. Why is Latin a good subject from the standpoint of training for one student and a very poor subject with which to seek to educate another student?

XIII

Types of Classroom Exercises

The exercises which teachers conduct in their classrooms do not commonly involve a single type of mental activity. It is true, however, that certain lessons tend to involve one type of activity predominantly. There are lessons which seek primarily to fix habits, others in which thinking of the inductive type is primarily involved, and still others in which deductive thinking or appreciation are the ends sought. As has already been indicated in the discussion of habit, thinking, and appreciation in the previous chapters, these types of mental activity are not to be thought of as separate and distinct. Habit formation may involve thinking. In a lesson predominantly inductive or deductive, some element of drill may enter, or appreciation may be sought with respect to some particular part of the situation presented. These different kinds of exercises, drills, thinking (inductive or deductive), and appreciation are fairly distinct psychological types.

In addition to the psychological types of exercises mentioned above, exercises are conducted in the classroom which may be designated under the following heads: lecturing, the recitation lesson, examination and review lessons. In any one of these the mental process involved may be any of those mentioned above as belonging to the purely psychological types of lessons or a combination of any two or more of them. It has seemed worth while to treat briefly of both sorts of lesson types, and to discuss at some length, lecturing, about which there is considerable disagreement, and the additional topic of questioning, which is the means employed in all of these different types of classroom exercises.

The Inductive Lesson. It has been common in the discussion of the inductive development lesson to classify the stages through which one passes from his recognition of a problem to his conclusion in five steps. These divisions have commonly been spoken of as

(1)   preparation;

(2)   presentation;

(3)   comparison and abstraction;

(4)   generalization; and

(5)   application. It has even been suggested that all lessons should conform to this order of procedure.

From the discussions in the previous chapters, the reader will understand that such a formal method of procedure would not conform to what we know about mental activity and its normal exercise and development. There is some advantage, however, in thinking of the general order of procedure in the inductive lesson as outlined by these steps.

The step of preparation has to do with making clear to the pupil the aim or purpose of the problem with which he is to deal. It is not always possible in the classroom to have children at work upon just such problems as may occur to them. The orderly development of a subject to be taught requires that the teacher discover to children problems or purposes which may result in thinking. The skill of the teacher depends upon his knowledge of the previous experiences of the children in the class and his skill in having them word the problem which remains unsolved in their experience in such a way as to make it attractive to them. Indeed, it may be said that children never have a worthy aim unless it is one which is intellectually stimulating. A problem exists only when we desire to find the answer.

The term "presentation" suggests a method of procedure which we would not want to follow too frequently; that is, we may hope not simply to present facts for acceptance or rejection, but, rather, we want children to search for the data which they may need in solving their problem. From the very beginning of their school career children need, in the light of a problem stated, to learn to utilize all of the possible sources of information available. Their own experience, the questions which they may put to other people, observations which they may undertake with considerable care, books or other sources of information which they may consult, all are to be thought of as tools to be used or sources of information available for the solution of problems. It cannot be too often reiterated that it is not simply getting facts, reading books, performing experiments, which is significant, but, rather, which of these operations is conducted in the light of a problem clearly conceived by children.

The step of presentation, as above described, is not one that may be begun and completed before other parts of the inductive lesson are carried on. As soon as any facts are available they are either accepted or rejected, as they may help in the solution of the problem; comparisons are instituted, the essential elements of likeness are noticed, and even a partial solution of the problem may be suggested in terms of a new generalization. The student may then begin to gather further facts, to pass through further steps of comparison, and to make still further modifications of his generalization as he proceeds in his work. At any stage of the process the student may stop to apply or test the validity of a generalization which has been formed. It is even true that the statement of the problem with which one starts may be modified in the light of new facts found, or new analyses instituted, or new elements of likeness which have been discovered.

In the conduct of an inductive lesson it is of primary importance that the teacher discover to children problems, the solutions of which are important for them, that he guide them in so far as it is possible for them to find all of the facts necessary in their search for data, that he encourage them to discuss with each other, even to the extent of disagreeing, with respect to comparisons which are instituted or generalizations which are premature, and above all, that he develop, in so far as it is possible, the habit of verifying conclusions.

THE DEDUCTIVE LESSON

The interdependence of induction and deduction has been discussed in the chapter devoted to thinking. The procedure in a deductive lesson is from a clear recognition of the problem involved, through the analysis of the situation and abstraction of the essential elements, to a search for the laws or principles in which to classify the particular element or individual with which we are dealing, to a careful comparison of this particular with the general that we have found, to our conclusion, which is established by a process of verification. Briefly stated, the normal order of procedure might be indicated as follows:

(1)   finding the problem;

(2)   finding the generalization or principles;

(3)   inference;

(4)   verification.

It is important in this type of exercise, as has been indicated in the discussion of the inductive lesson, that the problem be made clear. So long as children indulge in random guesses as to the process which is involved in the solution of a problem in arithmetic, or the principle which is to be invoked in science, or the rule which is to be called to mind in explaining a grammatical construction, we may take it for granted that they have no very clear conception of the process through which they must pass, nor of the issues which are involved. In the search for the generalization or principle which will explain the problem, a process of acceptance and rejection is involved. It helps children to state definitely, with respect to a problem in arithmetic, that they know that this particular principle is not the one which they need. It is often by a process of elimination that a child can best explain a grammatical construction, either in English or in a foreign language. Of course the elimination of the principle or law which is not the right one means simply that we are reducing the number of chances of making a mistake. If out of four possibilities we can immediately eliminate two of them, there are only two left to be considered. After children have discovered the generalization or principle involved, it is well to have them state definitely the inference which they make. Just as in the inductive process we pass almost immediately from the step of comparison and abstraction to the statement of generalization, so in the deductive lesson, when once we have related the particular case under consideration to the principle which explains it, we are ready to state our inference. Verification involves the trying out of our inference to see that it certainly will hold. This may be done by proposing some other inference which we find to be invalid, or by seeking to find any other law or principle which will explain our particular situation. Here again, as in the inductive lesson, the skillful teacher makes his greatest contribution by having children become increasingly careful in this step of verification. Almost any one can pass through the several stages involved in deductive thinking and arrive at a wrong conclusion. That which distinguishes the careful thinker from the careless student is the sincerity of the former in his unwillingness to accept his conclusions until they are verified.

THE DRILL LESSON

The drill lesson is so clearly a matter of fixing habits that little needs to be added to the chapter dealing with this subject. If one were to attempt to give in order the steps of the process involved, they might be stated as follows:

> (1)   establishing a motive for forming the habit;
>
> (2)   knowing exactly what we wish to do, or the habit or skill to be acquired;

(3)   recognition of the importance of the focusing of attention during the period devoted to repetitions;

(4)   variation in practice in order to lessen fatigue and to help to fix attention;

(5)   a recognition of the danger of making mistakes, with consequent provision against lapses;

(6)   the principle of review, which may be stated best by suggesting that the period between practice exercises may only gradually be lengthened.

Possibly the greatest deficiency in drill work, as commonly conducted, is found in the tendency upon the part of some teachers to depend upon repetition involving many mistakes. This is due quite frequently to the assignment of too much to be accomplished. Twenty-five words in spelling, a whole multiplication table, a complete conjugation in Latin, all suggest the danger of mistakes which will be difficult to eliminate later on. The wise teacher is the one who provides very carefully against mistakes upon the part of pupils. He assigns a minimum number of words, or a number of combinations, or a part of a conjugation, and takes care to discover that children are sure of themselves before indulging in that practice which is to fix the habit.

In much of the drill work there is, of course, the desirability of gaining in speed. In this field successful teachers have discovered that much is gained by more or less artificial stimuli which seem to be altogether outside of the work required to form a habit. In drill on column addition successful work is done by placing the problem on the board and following through the combinations by pointing the pointer and making a tap on the board as one proceeds through the column. Concert work of this sort seems to have the effect of speeding up those who would ordinarily lag, even though they might get the right result. The most skillful teachers of typewriting count or clap their hands or use the phonograph for the sake of speeding up their students. They have discovered that the same amount of time devoted to typewriting practice will produce anywhere from twenty-five to one hundred per cent more speed under such artificial stimulation as they were in the habit of getting merely by asking the students to practice. These experiences, of course, suggest that drill work will require an expenditure of energy and an alertness upon the part of teachers, and not merely an assignment of work to be done by pupils.

APPRECIATION LESSON

The work which the teacher does in securing appreciation has been suggested in a previous chapter. It will suffice here briefly to state what may be thought of as the order of procedure in securing appreciation. It is not as easy in this case to state the development in terms of particular steps or processes, since, as has already been indicated in the chapter on appreciation, the student is passive rather than active, is contemplating and enjoying, rather than attacking and working to secure a particular result. The work of the teacher may, however, be organized around the following heads:

(1) it is of primary importance that the teacher bring to the class an enthusiasm and joy for the picture, music, poetry, person, or achievement which he wishes to present;

(2) children must not be forced to accept nor even encouraged to repeat the evaluation determined by teachers;

(3) spontaneous and sincere response upon the part of children should be accepted, even though it may not conform to the teacher's estimate;

(4) children should be encouraged to choose from among many of the forms or situations presented for their approval those which they like best;

(5) the technique involved in the creation of the artistic form should be subordinated to enjoyment in the field of the fine arts;

(6) throughout, the play spirit should be predominant, for if the element of drudgery enters, appreciation disappears.

Teachers who get good results in appreciation secure them mainly by virtue of the fact that they have large capacity for enjoyment in the fields which they present to children. A teacher who is enthusiastic, and who really finds great joy in music, will awaken and develop power of appreciation upon the part of his pupils. The teacher who can enter into the spirit of the child poetry, or of the fairy tale, will get a type of appreciation not enjoyed by the teacher who finds delight only in adult literature.

It is of the utmost importance to recognize the fact that children only gradually grow from an appreciation or joy in that which is crude to that which represents the highest type of artistic production. It is important to have children try themselves out in creative work; but the influence of a teacher may be far greater than that of the attempts of the children to produce in these fields.

LECTURING

Among the various types of methods used in teaching there is probably no one which has received such severe criticism as the so-called lecture method. The result of this criticism has been, theoretically at least, to abolish lecturing from the elementary school and to diminish the use of this method in the high school, although in the colleges and universities it is still the most popular method. Although it is true that the lecture method is not the best one for continual use in elementary and high school, still its entire disuse is unfortunate. So is its blind use by those who still adhere to the old ways of doing things.

The chief criticisms of the method are, first, that it makes of the learner a mere recipient instead of a thinker; second, that the material so gained does not become part of the mental life of the hearers and so is not so well remembered nor so easily applied as material gained in other ways; third, that the instructor has no means of determining whether his class is getting the right ideas or wholly false ones; fourth, the method lacks interest in the majority of cases. Despite the truth of these criticisms, there are occasions when the lecture or telling method is the best one--in fact the only one that can accomplish the desired result.

First, the lecture method may sometimes take the place of books. Often, even in the elementary school, there is need for the children to get facts,--information in history or geography or literature,--and the getting of these facts from books would be too difficult or too wasteful. In such a case telling the facts is certainly the best way to give them. A teacher in half a period can give material that it might take the children hours to find. By telling them the facts, he not only saves waste of time, but also retains the interest. Very often discouragement and even dislike results from a prolonged search for a few facts. Of course in the higher schools, when the material to be given is not in print, when the professor is the source of certain theories, methods, and explanations, lecturing is the only way for students to get the material. It must be borne in mind that human beings are naturally a source of interest, particularly to children, and therefore having the teacher tell, other things being equal, will make a greater impression than reading it in a book.

Second, the lecture method is valuable as a means of explanation. Despite the fact that the material given may be adapted to the child's level of development, still it often happens that it is not clear. Then, instead of sending the child to the same material again, an explanation by teacher or fellow pupil is much better. It may be just the inflection used, or the choice of different words, that will clear up the difficulty.

Third, the telling method should be used for illustration. Very often when illustration is necessary the lecture method is supplemented by illustrative material of various types--objects, experiments, pictures, models, diagrams, and so on. None of this material, however, is used to its best advantage unless it is accompanied by the telling method. It is through the telling that the essentials of the illustrative material gain the proper perspective. Without such explanation some unimportant detail may focus the attention and the value of the material be lost. It has been customary to emphasize the need for and the value of this concrete illustrative material. Teachers have felt that if it was possible to have the actual object, it should be obtained; if that was not possible, why then have pictures, but diagrams and words should only be used as a last resort. There can be no doubt as to the value of the concrete material, especially with little children--but its use has been carried to an extreme because it has been used blindly. For instance, sometimes the concrete material because of its general inherent interest, or because of its special appeal to some instinct, attracts the attention of the child in such a way that the point which was to be illustrated is lost sight of. Witness work in nature study in the lower grades, and in chemistry in the high school. The concrete material may be so complex that again the essential point is lost in the mass of detail. No perspective can be obtained because of the complexity--witness work with principles of machines in physics and the circulation of the blood in biology. Sometimes the diagram or word explanation with nothing of the more concrete material is the best type of illustration. A fresh application of the principle or lesson by the teacher is another means of illustration and one of the best, for it not only broadens the student's point of view and gives another cue to the material, but it may also make direct connection with his own experience. Illustrations in the book often fail to do this, but the teacher knowing his particular class can make the application that will mean most. Telling a story or incident is another way of illustration. The personal element is nearly always present in this means, and is a valuable spur to interest.

Illustrations of all kinds, from the concrete to the story form, have been grossly misused in teaching, so that to-day teachers are almost afraid to use any. The difficulty has been that illustrations have been used as a means of regaining wandering attention. It has been the sugar-coating. The illustration, then, has become the important thing and the material nonimportant. The class has watched the experiment or listened to the story, but when that was over the attention was gone again. Illustrations should not be the means of holding the attention; that is the function of the material itself. If the lesson cannot hold the interest, illustrations are worse than useless. Illustrations, then, of all kinds must be subordinated to the material--they are only a means to an end, and that end is a better understanding of the material. Illustrations, further, should have a vital, necessary connection with the point they are used to make clearer. Illustrations that are dragged in, that are not vitally connected with the point, are entirely out of place. If illustrations always truly illustrated, then children would not remember the illustration and forget the point, for remembering the illustration they would be led directly to the point because of the closeness of the connection.

Fourth, telling or lecturing is the best way to get appreciation. This was discussed in the chapter on appreciation, so need only be mentioned here. The interpretation by the teacher of the character, the picture, the poem, the policy, or what not, not only increases the understanding of the listener, but also calls up feeling responses. It is in this telling that the personality of the teacher, his experiences, his ideals, make themselves felt. One can often win appreciation of and allegiance to the best in life by the use of the telling method in the appropriate situations.

Fifth, the lecture method should sometimes be used as a means of getting the desired mental attitude. The general laws of learning emphasize the importance of the mind's set as a condition to readiness of neurone tracts. Five or ten minutes spent at the beginning of a subject, or a new section of work, in introducing the class to it, may give the keynote for the whole course. A whole period may be profitably be spent this way. Not only will the telling method used on such occasions give the right emotional attitude towards a subject, but also the right intellectual set as well.

It is evident then that the lecture or telling method has its place in all parts of the educational system, but its place should be clearly and definitely recognized. The danger is not in using it, but in using it at the wrong time, and in overusing it. Bearing in mind the dangers that adhere to its use, it is always well, whether the method is used in grades or in college, to mix it with other methods or to follow it by another method that will do the things that the lecture method may have left undone.

THE RECITATION LESSON

As has been suggested in the opening of this chapter, the recitation lesson is not a type involving any particular psychological process. It is, rather, a method of procedure which may involve any of the other types of work already discussed. When the recitation lesson means merely reciting paragraphs from the book with little or no reference to problems to be solved or skill to be developed, it has no place in a schoolroom. When, however, the teacher uses the recitation lesson as an exercise in which he assures himself that facts needed for further progress in thinking have been secured, or that habits have been established, or verbatim memorization accomplished, this type of exercise is justified. It is well to remember that the thought process involved in the development of a subject, or the solution even of a single problem, may extend over many class periods. The recitation lesson may be important in organizing the material which is to be used in the larger thought whole. Again, this type of exercise may involve the presentation of material which is to be used as a basis for appreciation in literature, in music, in art, in history, and the like. The organization of experiences of children, whether secured through observations, discussions, or from books, around certain topics may furnish a most satisfactory basis for the development of problems or of the gathering of the material essential for their solution. A better understanding of the conditions which make for success in habit formation, in thinking, and the development of appreciation, will tend to eliminate from our schools that type of exercise in which teachers ask merely that children recite to them what they have been able to remember from the books which they have read or the lectures which they have heard.

THE EXAMINATION AND REVIEW LESSONS

In the establishment of habits, the development of appreciation, or the growth in understanding which we seek to secure through thinking, there will be many occasions for checking up our work. Successful teaching requires that the habit that we think we have established be called for and additional practice given from time to time in order to be certain that it is fixed. In like manner, the development of our thought in any field is not something which is accomplished without respect to later neglect. We, rather, build a system of thought with reference to a particular field or subject as a result of thinking, and re-thinking through the many different situations which are involved. In like manner, in the field of appreciation the very essence of our enjoyment is to be found in the fact that that which we have enjoyed we recall, and strength-en our appreciation through the revival of the experience. The review is, of course, most successful when it is not simply going over the whole material in exactly the same way. In habit formation it is often advisable to arrange in a different order the stimuli which are to bring the desired responses, for the very essence of habit formation is found in the fact that the particular response can be secured regardless of the order in which they are called for. In thinking, as a subject is developed, our control is measured by the better perspective which we secure. This means, of course, that in review we will not be con-cerned with reviving all of the processes through which we have passed, but, rather, in a reorganization quite dif-ferent from that which was originally provided.

The examination lesson is classified here as of the same type as the review because a good examination in-volves all that has been suggested by review. The writer has no sympathy with those who argue against examina-tions. The only proof that we can get of the success or failure of our work is to be found in the achievement of pupils. It is not desirable to set aside a particular period of a week devoted entirely to examinations, because examinations in all subjects cannot to best advantage be given during the same period. There are stages in the development of our thinking, or in the acquiring of skill, or in our understanding and appreciation which occur at irregular intervals and which call for a summing up of what has gone before, in order that we may be sure of success in the work which is to follow. It is, of course, undesirable to devote a whole week to examinations on account of the strain and excitement under which children labor. It is entirely possible to know of the achievements of children through examinations which have been given at irregular intervals throughout the term. It would be best, probably, never to give more than one examination on any one day, and, as a rule, to devote only the regular class period to such work. In another chapter the discussion of more exact methods of measuring the achievements of children will be discussed at some length.

In all of the lesson types mentioned above, one of the most important means employed by teachers for the stimulation of pupils is the question. It seems wise, therefore, to devote some paragraphs to a consideration of questioning as determining skill in teaching.

QUESTIONING

The purpose of a question is to serve as a situation which shall arouse to activity certain nerve connections and thus bring a response. Questions, oral or written, are the chief tools used in schools to gain responses. In some situations it is the only means a teacher may have of arousing the response. Psychologically, then, the value of the question must be judged by the response.

Questions may be considered from the point of view of the kind of response they call for. Probably the most common kind of question is the one that calls for facts as answers. It involves memory--but memory of a rote type. It does not require thinking. All drill questions are of this type. The connections aroused are definitely final in a certain order, and the question simply sets off the train of bonds that leads directly to the answer. Another type of question involving the memory process is the one which initiates recall, but here thought is active. The answer cannot be gained in a mechanical way, but selection and rejection are involved. The answer is to be found by examining past experience, but only in a thoughtful way. Questions which call for comparison form another type. These may vary from those which involve the comparison of sense material to those which involve the comparison of policies or epochs. Words, characters, plots, definitions, plans, subjects--everything with which intellectual life deals is open to comparison. Comparison is one of the steps in the process of reasoning, and hence questions of this type are extremely important. Then there are the questions which arouse the response of analysis. These questions vary among themselves according to the type of analysis needed, whether piecemeal attention or analysis due to varying concomitants. The former drives the thinker through gradual recognition and elimination of the known elements to a consciousness of the only partly known. The latter, by attracting the attention to unvarying factors in the changing situations, forces out the new and until then unknown element. Some questions require judgment as a response. The judgment may be one concerning relationships, or concerning worth or value, or be merely a matter of definition--all questions calling for criticism are of this type. In any case this type of question involves the thought element at its best. The question requiring organization forms another type. There is no sharp line of division between these types of questions. No one of them should be used exclusively. Some of them imply operations of a simple type as well as the particular response demanded by that form. For instance, some of the questions involving analysis imply comparison and recalling. A judgment question might call for all the simple processes noted above and others as well. The responses then vary in complexity and difficulty. The order of advance in both complexity and difficulty of the response is from the mere drill question to the judgment question.

Another type of question is the one which desires appreciation as a response. This question is one of the most difficult to frame, for it must tend to inhibit the critical attitude and by means of the associations it arouses or its own suggestive power get the appreciative response. Questions of this type often call for constructive imagery as a means to the desired end. Some questions are directive in their tendency. They require as response an attitude or set of the mind. They set the child thinking in this direction rather than that. In a sense they are suggestive, but they suggest the line of search rather than the response. A final type of question is akin to the one just discussed--the question whose response is further questions. Here again the response desired is an attitude, but in this case it is more than an attitude, it is also a definite response that shall come in the form of questions. The questions of a good teacher should result in students asking questions both of people and of books. These last three types of questions are perhaps the most difficult of all. Because of their complexity and subtlety they often miss fire and fail of their purpose. Properly handled they are among the most powerful tools a teacher has. The type of question used must vary, not only with the particular group of children, and the type of lesson, but also with the subject. Questions that would be the best type in mathematics might not be so good for an art lesson. The kinds of questions used must be adapted to the particular situation.

Psychologically a question is valuable not only in accordance with the kind of response it gets, but also in proportion to the readiness of the response. A question that is of such a character that the response is hazy, stumbling, hesitating--a question that brings no clear-cut response because the child does not understand what is wanted, is a poor question. This does not at all mean that the right response must always come immediately. Some of the best questions are put with the intention of forcing the child to realize that he can't answer--that he doesn't know. If that type of response comes to that question, it is the best possible answer. Nor need the whole answer come immediately. For instance, in many of the judgment questions the thinking process aroused may take some time before the judgment is reached, and meanwhile several partial answers may be given. But if the question asked started the process, without waste of time in trying to find out what it meant, the question is good. With these explanations, then, the second qualification of a good question is that it secures the appropriate response readily. In order to do this, these factors must be considered: First, the principle of apperception must be recognized. Every question must deal with material that is on a level with the stage of development of the one questioned. Not only so, but the question must connect somewhere with the learner's experience. This means a recognition also of individual differences. The question must also be couched in language that can be understood easily by the one questioned. To have to try to understand the language of the question as well as the question, results in divided attention and delayed responses. Second, the question should be clear and definite. A question that has these characteristics will challenge the attention of the class. It is directed straight at the point at issue, and no time will be lost in wondering what the question means, or in trying two or three tentative answers. Third, the younger the child, the simpler the question must be. With little children, to be good a question may involve only one idea, or relationship. The amount involved in the question, its scope and content, must be adapted to the mental development of the learner. It is only a mature thinker who can carry simultaneously two or three points of issue, or possibilities. Fourth, the question to gain a ready response must be interesting. Not only must the lesson as a whole be interesting, but the questions themselves must have the same quality. Dull questions can kill an otherwise good lesson. The form of the question is thus a big factor in gaining a ready response. All the qualities which gain involuntary attention can be used in framing an interesting question--novelty, exaggeration, contrast, life, color, and so on.

The third point to be considered in determining a good question is whether or not it satisfies the demands of economy. This demand is a fair one both from the standpoint of the best use of the time at the disposal of the learner, and also from the standpoint of the best means of gaining the greatest development on the part of the learner in a given time. The number of questions asked thus enters in as a factor. When a teacher asks four or five questions when one would serve the same purpose, she is not only wasting time, but the child is not getting the opportunity to do any thinking and therefore is not developing. Recent studies on the actual number of questions asked in a recitation point to the conclusion that economy both of time and in development is being seriously overlooked. Economy in response may also be brightened by preserving a logical sequence between questions. It is a matter of fact in psychology that associations are systematized about central ideas; it is also a fact that the set of the mind, in this direction rather than that, is characteristic of all work. Logical sequence, then, makes use of both these facts--both of the systematization of ideas and of the mental attitude.

The fourth test of good questioning is the universality of its appeal. Some questions which are otherwise good appeal but to comparatively few in the class. This, of course, means that responses are being gained but from few. The best questioning stimulates most of the class; all members of the class are working. In order to secure this result the questions must be properly distributed over the class. The bright pupils must not be allowed to do all the work; or, on the other hand, all the attention of the teachers must not be given to the dull pupils. Not only should the questions be well distributed, but they must vary according to the individual ability of the particular child. This has already been emphasized in dealing with readiness of response. Many a lesson has been unsuccessful because the teacher gave too difficult a question to a dull child, and while she was struggling with him, she lost the rest of the class. The reverse is also true, to give a bright child a question that requires almost no thinking means that a mechanical answer will be given and no further activity stimulated. The extent to which all the class are mentally active is one measure of a good question.

QUESTIONS

1. Give an example of a lesson which you have taught which was predominantly inductive. Show how you proceeded from the discovery of the problem to your pupils to the solution attained.

2. What is involved in the "step" of presentation?

3. Why may we not consider the several "steps" of the inductive lesson as occurring in a definite and mutually exclusive sequence?

4. In what respect is the procedure in a deductive lesson like that which you follow in an inductive lesson?

5. Show how verification is an important element in both inductive and deductive lessons.

6. Give illustrations of successful drill lessons and make clear the reason for the degree of success achieved.

7. What measures have you found most advantageous in securing speed in drill work?

8. What are the elements which make for success in an appreciation lesson?

9. Upon what grounds and to what extent can lecturing be defended as a method of instruction?

10.   What may be the relation between a good recitation lesson and the solution of a problem? Growth in power of appreciation?

11.   For what purposes should examinations be given? When should examinations be given?

12.   When are questions which call for facts justified?

13.   Why are questions which call for comparisons to be considered important?

14.   Why is it important to phrase questions carefully?

15.   Why should a teacher ask some questions which cannot be answered immediately?

16.   What criteria would you apply in testing the questions which you put to your class?

17.   Write five questions which in your judgment will demand thinking upon some topic which you plan to teach to your class.

XIV

How to Study

The term study has been used very loosely by both teachers and children. As used by teachers it frequently meant something very different from what children had in mind when they used it. Further, teachers themselves have often used the term in connection with mental activities which, technically speaking, could not possibly come under that head. Much confusion and lack of efficient work has been the result. Recently various attempts have been made to give the term study a more exact meaning. McMurry defines it as "the work that is necessary in the assimilation of ideas"--"the vigorous application of the mind to a subject for the satisfaction of a felt need." In other words, study is thinking. Psychologically, what makes for good thinking makes for good study. Study is controlled mental activity working towards the realization of a goal. It is the adaptation of means to end, in the attempt to satisfy a felt need. It involves a definite purpose or goal, which is problematic, the selection and rejection of suggestions, tentative judgments, and conclusion. The mind of the one who studies is active, vigorously active, not in an aimless fashion, but along sharply defined lines. This is the essential characteristic of all study.

There are, however, various types of study which differ materially from each other according to the subject matter or to the type of response required. Some study involves comparatively little thinking. The directed activity must be present, but the choice, the judgment, may need to be exercised only in the beginning when methods of procedure need to be selected, and later on, perhaps, when successes or failures need to be noted and changes made in the methods accordingly. Another type of study needs continual thinking of the most active sort all the way through the period. Just the proportion of the various factors involved in thinking which is present at any given study period must be determined by the response. A type of study which would be completely satisfactory for one subject needing one response, would be entirely inadequate for another subject needing another response. To illustrate, in some cases the study must deal with habit formation. The need felt is to learn a mechanical response of a very definite nature to this situation; the problem is to get that response. The thinking would come in in deciding upon the method, in watching for successes, in criticizing progress, and in judging when the end was obtained. A large part of the time spent in study would, however, need to be spent in repetition, in drill. Of such character is study of spelling, of vocabularies, of dates; study in order to gain skill in adding, or speed in reading, or to improve in writing or sewing. Much of habit formation goes on without study--in fact, to some it may seem to be ludicrous to use the word "study" in connection with the formation of habits. It is just because the study elements in connection with responses of this type have been omitted that there has been such a tremendous waste of time in teaching children to form right habits. This omission also explains the poor results, for the process has been mechanical and blind on the part of the student. At the other extreme in types of study is that which can be used in science and mathematics, in geography and history, when the major part of the time is given to selecting and rejecting suggestions and seems required by the goal. In this type the habituation, the fixing of the material, comes largely as a by-product of the factors used in the thinking.

Study may, then, be classified according as the response required is physical habit, memory, appreciation, or judgment. These types overlap, no one of them can exist absolutely alone, but it is possible to name them according to the response. Study may also be classified into supervised study, or unsupervised study, into individual or group study. We might also classify study as it has to do with books, with people, or with materials. The term has been rather arbitrarily applied to activities that dealt with books, but surely much study is accomplished when people are consulted instead of books, and also when the sources of information or the standards are flowers, or rocks, or textiles.

Study, then, is a big term, including many different varieties of activities, of varying degrees of difficulty and responsibility. It cannot possibly be taught all at once, according to one method, at one spot in the school curriculum. Power to study is of very gradual growth. It must proceed slowly, from simple to complex types. From easy to difficult problems, from situations where there is close supervision and direction to situations where the student assumes full responsibility. Knowing how to study is not an inborn gift--it does not come as a matter of intuition, nor does it come in some mysterious way when the child is of high school age. It is governed by the laws of learning, or readiness, exercise, and effect, just as truly as any other ability is. If adults are to know how to study, if they are to use the technique of the various kinds of study efficiently, children must be taught how. Nor can we expect the upper grammar grade or the high school teachers to do this. Habits of study must be formed just as soon as the responses to which it leads are needed. Beginning down in the kindergarten with study in connection with physical and mental habits, the child should be taught how to study. The type must gradually become more complex; he must pass from group to individual study, from supervised to unsupervised, but it must all come logically, from step to step. True, it is not easy to teach how to study. A careful analysis of the various types with their peculiar elements should be a help. First, however, there are some general principles that underlie all study which must be discussed.

Study must have, as has already been stated, a purpose. The individual, in order to exercise his mind in a controlled way, must have an aim. The clearer and more definite the aim, whether it be little or big, the better the study will be. From the beginning, then, children must be taught to make sure they know what they are going to do before beginning to study. It may be necessary to teach them in the early grades to say to themselves or to the class just what they are going to accomplish in the study. Teach them when the lesson is assigned to write down in their books just what the problem for study is. Warn them never to begin study without definitely knowing the aim--if they don't know it, make them realize that the first thing to do is to find out the purpose by asking some one else. Better no study at all than aimless or mis-directed activity, because of lack of purpose.

No study worthy of the name can be carried on without interest. The child who studies well must be brought to realize this. The value of interest can be brought home to him by having him compare the work he does, the time he spends, and how he feels when studying something in which he has a vital interest with the results when the topic is uninteresting. Of course, as will be pointed out later, much of the gaining of interest lies in the hands of the teacher necessarily, but if the child realizes the need of it in efficient study, some responsibility will rest on him to find an interest if it is not already there. No matter how expert the teacher may be, because of individual differences no problem will be equally interesting to all pupils in itself, and no incentive will have an equal appeal to all children. Therefore children should be taught to find interest for themselves. Certain devices can be suggested, such as working with another child and competing with him, "making believe" in study, and finding some connection with something in which he is interested, working against his own score, and the like.

Not only do the demands of economy require that the topic of study receive concentrated attention, but the results themselves are better when such is the case. Half an hour of concentrated work gives much better results than an hour of study with scattered attention. An hour spent when half an hour would do is thus not only wasteful of time, but is productive of poorer results and bad habits of study as well. Children need to be taught this from the beginning. Much time is wasted even by mature university students when they suppose themselves to be studying. Children can be taught to ignore distractions--to train themselves to keep their eyes on the book, despite the fact that the door is opened, or a seat mate is looking for a book. They should be encouraged to set themselves time limits in various subjects and adhere to them. It is economical to follow a regular schedule in study--either in the school or at home. Let each child make out his study schedule and keep to it. Teach children that the best work is done when they are calm and steady. That either excitement or worry is a hindrance. Therefore they should avoid doing their studying under those conditions, and should do all they can to remove such conditions. Training children to do their best and then not to worry would not only improve the health of many upper grammar grade and high school children, but would also improve their work.

Study requires a certain critical attitude, a checking up of results against the problem set. In order to be efficient in study a child should know when he has reached the solution, when the means have been adapted to the end, when he has reached the goal. This checking up, of course, means habits of self-criticism and standards. Sometimes all that is necessary is for the child to be made conscious of this fact so that he can test himself, for instance, in memory work, or in solving a problem in mathematics. On the other hand, sometimes he will have to compare his work with definite standards, such as the Thorndike Handwriting Scale, or the Hillegas Composition Scale.[19] In other instances, he will have to search for standards. He will need to know what his classmates have accomplished, what other people think, what other text-books say, and so on. Gradually he must be made conscious that study is a controlled activity, and unless it reaches the goal, and the correct one, it is useless. He

---

19. For a discussion of these scales see Chapter XV

must be made to feel that the responsibility to see that such results are reached rests on him.

These, then, are the general factors involved in all types of study, and therefore are fundamental to good habits of study: a clear purpose; vital interest of some kind; concentrated attention, and a critical attitude. There are further additional suggestions which are peculiar to the special type of study.

In study which is directed to habit formation, the student should be taught the danger of allowing exceptions. He should know the possibility of undoing much good work through a little carelessness. Preaching won't bring this home to him--it must come through having his attention attracted to such an occurrence in his own work or in that of his mates. After that knowledge of the actual experiences of others, athletes, musicians, and others will help to intensify the impression. The value of repetition as one of the chief factors in habit formation must be emphasized. The child should be encouraged to make opportunities for practice both in free minutes during the school program, and outside of school. He must be taught in habit formation to practice the new habit in the way it is to be used: practicing the sounds of letters in words, the writing movements in writing words, swimming movements in the water, and so on. Practicing the whole movements, not trying to gain perfection in parts of it and then putting it together. It is important also that the learner be taught to keep his attention on the result to be obtained, instead of the movements. He should attend to the swing of the club, the lightness of the song, the cut the saw is making, the words he is writing, instead of the muscle movements involved.

In breaking up bad habits it is sometimes necessary to concentrate on a part or a movement, when that is the crux of the error, but in general it is a bad practice when forming a new habit. The child must also learn to watch the habit of skill he is forming for signs of improvement and then to try to find out the reason for it. It has been proved experimentally that much of the improvement in habits of skill comes unconsciously to the learner, and necessarily so, but that in order for the improvement to continue and be effective, it must become conscious. Of course, at the beginning and for a long time it must be the teacher's duty to point out the improvement and to help the child to think out the reasons for it, but if he is to learn to study by himself the child must finally come to habits of self-criticism which will enable him to recognize success or failure in his own work. In all this discussion of teaching children to study it must be constantly borne in mind that it is a gradual process--and only very slowly does the child become conscious of the technique. Which elements can be made conscious, how much he can be left to himself, must depend on his maturity and previous training. In time, however, he should be able to apply them all--for only by so doing will he become capable of independent study.

When the study is primarily concerned with memory responses, all the elements which have just been discussed in connection with habit apply, for, after all, memory is but mental habit. There are other factors which enter into and which should be used in this type of study. First, the child should realize the need for understanding the material that is to be learned, before beginning to memorize it. He will then be taught to read the entire assignment through--look up difficult words and references, master the content, whether prose or poetry, whether the learning is to be verbatim or not, before doing anything further. Second, he will need to know the value of the modified whole method of learning, as well as its difficulties. If in the supervised periods of study and in class work, this method has been followed, it is very easy to make him conscious of it and willing to adopt it when he comes to do independent study. Third, he must be taught to distribute his time so that he does not devote too long a stretch to one subject. The value of going over work in the morning, after having studied the night or two nights before, should be emphasized. Also the value of beginning on assignments some time ahead, even if there is not time to finish them. Fourth, the child should be taught not to stop his work the minute he can give it perfectly. The need for overlearning, for permanent retention, must be made clear. How much overlearning is necessary, each child should find out for himself. Fifth, the value of outlining material as a means of aiding memory must be stressed. Sixth, the child should be taught to search for associations, connections of all types, in order to help himself remember facts. He might even be encouraged to make up some mnemonic device as an aid if these measures fail. If instead of simply trying to hammer material in by mere repetition children had been taught in their study to consciously make use of the other elements in a good memory, much time would be saved. But the responsibility should rest finally on the child to make use of these helps. The teacher must make him conscious of them, sometimes from their value by experiment, and then teach him to use them himself.

Much less can be done as a matter of conscious technique when the occasion of study is to further appreciation. A few suggestions might be offered. First, the child should be taught the value of associating with those who do appreciate in the line in which he is striving for improvement. He should be encouraged to consciously associate with them when opportunities for appreciation come. Second, he should know the need for coming in contact with the objects of appreciation if true feeling is to be developed. It is only by mingling with people, reading books, listening to music, that appreciation in those fields can be developed. Third, the value of concrete imagery and of connections with personal experience in arousing emotional tone should be emphasized. The child might be encouraged to consciously call up images and make connections with his own experience during study.

Study, when the object is to arrive at responses of judgment, is the type which has received most attention. This type of study includes within itself several possibilities. Although judgment is the only response that can solve the problem, still the problem may be one of giving the best expression in art or music or drama. It may be the analysis of a course of action or of a chemical compound. It may be the comparison of various opinions. It may be the arriving at a new law or principle. It is to one of these types of thinking that the term "study" is usually applied. Important as it is, the other three types already discussed cannot be neglected. If children are taught to study in connection with the simpler situations provided by the first two types, they will be the better prepared to deal with this complex type, for this highest type of study involves habit formation often and memory work always.

In the type of study involving reasoning, because of its complexity, and because the individual must work more independently, the child must learn the danger of following the first suggestion which offers itself. He must learn to weigh each suggestion offered with reference to the goal aimed at. Each step in the process must be tested and weighed in this manner. To go blindly ahead, following out a line of suggestions until the end is reached, which is then found to be the wrong one, wastes much time and is extremely discouraging. No suggestion of the way to adapt means to end should be accepted without careful criticism. The pupil should gradually be made conscious of the technique of reasoning, analysis, comparison, and abstraction. He must know that the first thing to do is to analyze the problem and see just what it requires. He must know that the abstraction depends upon the goal. The learner should be taught the sources of some of the commonest mistakes in judgment. For instance, if he knows of the tendency to respond in terms of analogy, and sees some of the errors to which accepting a minor likeness between two situations as identity lead, he will be much more apt to avoid such mistakes than would otherwise be true. If he knows how unsafe it is to form a judgment on limited data,--if from his own and his classmates' thinking first, and later from the history of science, illustrations are drawn of the disastrous effect of such thinking, he will see the value of seeking sources of information and several points of view before forming his own judgment. In his study the child should be taught not to be satisfied until he has tested the correctness of his judgment by verifying the result. This is a very necessary part of studying. He should check up his own thinking by finding out through appeal to facts if it is so; by putting the judgment into execution; by consulting the opinion of others, and so on.

Study may be considered from the point of view of the type of material which is used in the process. The student may be engaged on a problem which involves the use of apparatus or specimens of various kinds, or he may need to consult people, or he may have to use books. So far as the first type is concerned, it is obviously unwise to have a student at work on a problem which involves the use of material, unless the technique of method of use is well known. Until he can handle the material with some degree of facility it is waste of time for him to be struggling with problems which necessitate such use. Such practice results in divided attention, poor results from the study, and often bad habits in technique as well. Gaining the technique must be in itself a problem for separate study.

Children should be taught to ask questions which bear directly on the point they wish to know. If they in working out some problem are dependent on getting some information from the janitor, or the postman, or a mason, they must be able to ask questions which will bring them what they want to know. Much practice in framing questions, having them criticized, having them answered just as they are asked, is necessary. Children should be aware of the question as a tool in their study and therefore they must know how to handle it. In connection with this second type of material, the problem of the best source of information will arise. Children must then be made conscious of the relative values of various persons as sources of a particular piece of information. Training in choice of the source of information is very important both when that source is people and also when it is books.

Teaching children to use books in their study is one of the big tasks of the teacher. They must learn that books are written in answer to questions. In order to thoroughly understand a book, students must seek to frame the questions which it answers. They must also know how to use books to answer their own questions. This means they must know how to turn from part to part, gleaning here or there what they need. It means training in the ability to skim, omitting unessentials and picking out essentials. It means the ability to recognize major points, minor points, and illustrative material. Children must be taught to use the table of contents, the index, and paragraph headings. They must, in their search for fuller information or criticism, be able to interpret different authors, use different language, and attack from different angles, even when treating the same object. Children must in their studying be taught to use books as a means to an end--not an infallible means, but one which needs continual criticism, modification, and amplification.

Study may be supervised study, or unsupervised study. To some people the requirements in learning to study may seem too difficult to be possible, but it should be remembered that the process is gradual--that one by one these elements in study are taught to the children in their supervised study periods. These periods should begin in the primary grades, and require from the teacher quite as much preparation as any other period. Many teachers have taught subjects, but not how to study subjects. The latter is the more important. The matter of distributed learning periods, of search for motive, of asking questions, of criticizing achievement, of use of books; each element is a topic for class discussion before it is accepted as an element in study. Even after it is accepted, it may be raised by some child as a source of particular difficulty and fresh suggestions added. Very often with little children it is necessary for the teacher to study the lesson with them. Teachers need much more practice in doing this, for one of the best ways to teach a child to study is to study with him. Not to tell him, and do the work for him, but to really study with him. Later on the supervised study period is one in which each child is silently engaged upon his own work and the teacher passes from one to the other. In order to do this well, the teacher needs to be able to do two things. First, to find out when the child is in difficulty and to locate it, and second, to help him over the trouble without giving too much assistance. Adequate questioning is needed in both cases. It is probably true that comparatively little new work should be given for unsupervised study. There is too much danger of error as well as lack of interest unless a start is given under supervision.

Studying, especially unsupervised, may be done in groups or individually. The former is a stepping-stone to the latter. There is a greater chance for suggestions, for getting the problem worded, for arousing interest and checking results, when a group of children are working together than when a child is by himself. Two things must be looked after. First, that the children in the group be taught not to waste time, and second, that the personnel of the group be right. It is not very helpful if one child does all the work, nor if one is so far below the level of the group that he is always tagging along behind. More opportunities for group study in the grammar grades would be advantageous.

When it comes to individual study, the student then assumes all responsibility for his methods of study. He should be taught the influence of physical conditions or mental reactions. He will therefore be responsible for choosing in the home and in the school the best possible conditions for his study. He will see to it that, in so far as possible, the air and light are good, that there are no unnecessary distractions, and that he is as comfortable bodily as can be. He must think not only in terms of the goal to be reached, but also with respect to the methods to be employed. He should be asked by the teacher to report his methods of work as well as his results.

QUESTIONS

1. Are children always primarily engaged in thinking when they study?

2. What type of study is involved in learning a multiplication table, a list of words in spelling, a conjugation in French?

3. How would you teach a pupil to study his spelling lesson?

4. In what sense may one study in learning to write? In acquiring skill in swimming?

5. How would you teach your pupils to memorize?

6. Show how ability to study may be developed over a period of years in some subject with which you are familiar. Reading? Geography? History? Latin translation?

7. Is the boy who reads over and over again his lesson necessarily studying?

8. Can one study a subject even though he may dislike it? Can one study without interest?

9. How can you teach children what is meant by concentration of attention?

10. How have you found it possible to develop a critical attitude toward their work upon the part of children?

11. Of what factors in habit formation must children become conscious, if they are to study to best advantage in this field?

12. How may we hope to have children learn to study in the fields requiring judgment? Why will not consciousness of the technique of study make pupils equally able in studying?

13. What exercises can you conduct which will help children to learn how to use books?

14. How can a teacher study with a pupil and yet help him to develop independence in this field?

15. How may small groups of children work together advantageously in studying?

XV

Measuring the Achievements of Children

The success or failure of the teacher in applying the principles which have been discussed in the preceding chapters is measured by the achievements of the children. Of course, it is also possible that the validity of the principle which we have sought to establish may be called in question by the same sort of measurement. We cannot be sure that our methods of work are sound, or that we are making the best use of the time during which we work with children, except as we discover the results of our instruction. Teaching is after all the adaptation of our methods to the normal development of boys and girls, and their education can be measured only in terms of the changes which we are able to bring about in knowledge, skill, appreciation, reasoning, and the like.

Any attempt to measure the achievements of children should result in a discovery of the progress which is being made from week to week, or month to month, or year to year. It would often be found quite advantageous to note the deficiencies as well as the achievements at one period as compared with the work done two or three months later. It will always be profitable to get as clearly in mind as is possible the variation among members of the same class, and for those who are interested in the supervision of schools, the variation from class to class, from school to school, or from school system to school system. For the teacher a study of the variability in achievement among the members of his own class ought to result in special attention to those who need special help, especially a kind of teaching which will remove particular difficulties. There should also be offered unusual opportunity and more than the ordinary demand be made of those who show themselves to be more capable than the ordinary pupils.

The type of measurement which we wish to discuss is something more than the ordinary examination. The difficulties with examinations, as we have commonly organized them, has been their unreliability, either from the standpoint of discovering to us the deficiencies of children, or their achievements. Of ten problems in arithmetic or of twenty words in spelling given in the ordinary examination, there are very great differences in difficulty. We do not have an adequate measure of the achievements of children when we assign to each of the problems or words a value of ten or of five per cent and proceed to determine the mark to be given on the examination paper. If we are wise in setting our examinations, we usually give one problem or one word which we expect practically everybody to be able to get right. On the other hand, if we really measure the achievements of children, we must give some problems or some words that are too hard for any one to get right. Otherwise, we do not know the limit or extent of ability possessed by the abler pupils. It is safe to say that in many examinations one question may actually be four or five times as hard as some other to which an equal value is assigned.

Another difficulty that we have to meet in the ordinary examination is the variability among teachers in marking papers. We do not commonly assign the same values to the same result. Indeed, if a set of papers is given to a group of capable teachers and marked as conscientiously as may be by each of them, it is not uncommon to find a variation among the marks assigned to the same paper which may be as great as twenty-five per cent of the highest mark given. Even more interesting is the fact that upon re-marking these same papers individual teachers will vary from their own first mark by almost as great an amount.

Still another difficulty with the ordinary examination is the tendency among teachers to derive their standards of achievement from the group itself, rather than from any objective standard by which all are measured. It is possible, for example, for children in English composition to write very poorly for their grade and still to find the teacher giving relatively high marks to those who happen to belong to the upper group in the class. As a result of the establishment of such a standard, the teacher may not be conscious of the fact that children should be spurred to greater effort, and that possibly he himself should seek to improve his methods of work.

Out of the situation described above, which includes on the one hand the necessity for measurement as a means of testing the success of our theories and of our practice, and on the other hand of having objective standards, has grown the movement for measurement by means of standard tests and scales. A standard test which has been given to some thousands of children classified by grades or by ages, if given to another group of children of the same grade or age group will enable the teacher to compare the achievement of his children with that which is found elsewhere. For example, the Courtis tests in arithmetic, which consist of series of problems of equal difficulty in addition, subtraction, multiplication, and division may be used to discover how far facility in these fields has been accomplished by children of any particular group as compared with the achievements of children in other school systems throughout the country. In these tests each of the problems is of equal difficulty. The measure is made by discovering how many of these separate problems can be solved in a given number of minutes.[20]

A scale for measuring the achievements of children in the fundamental operations of addition, subtraction, multiplication, and division has been derived by Dr. Clifford Woody,[21] which differs from the Courtis tests in that it affords opportunity to discover what children can achieve from the simplest problem in each of these fields to a problem which is in each case approximately twice as difficult as the problems appearing on the Courtis tests. The great value of this type of test is in discovering to teachers and to pupils, as well, their particular difficulties. A pupil must be able to do fairly acceptable work in addition before he can solve one problem on the Courtis tests. Considerable facility can be measured on the Woody tests before an ability sufficient to be registered on the Courtis tests has been acquired. In his mono-

20. The Courtis Tests, Series B, for Measuring the Achievements of Children in the Fundamentals of Arithmetic, can be secured from Mr. S.A. Curtis, 82 Eliot Street, Detroit, Mich.
21. Measurements of Some Achievements in Arithmetic, by Clifford Woody, published by the Teachers College Bureau of Publications, Columbia University, 1916.

graph on the derivation of these tests Mr. Woody gives results which will enable the teacher to compare his class with children already tested in other school systems. In the case of all of these standard tests, school surveys and superintendents' reports are available which will make it possible to institute comparisons among different classes and different school systems. One form of the Woody tests is as follows:

SERIES A
Addition Scale

By Clifford Woody

Name...

When is your next birthday?........................   How old will you be?...............................

Are you a boy or girl?.................................   In what grade are you?.............................

(1)	(3)	(5)	(7)		(9)	(10)	(11)	(12)	(13)	(15)	(16)
2	17	72	3+1=		20	21	32	43	23	100	9
3	2	26			10	33	59	1	25	33	24
--	--	--			2	35	17	2	16	45	12
					30	--	--	13	--	201	15

(2)	(4)	(6)	(8)		(9)			(12)		(15)	(16)
2	53	60	2+5+1=		25			--		46	19
4	45	37			--					--	--
3	--	--									
--											

(14)

25+42=

(17)
199
194
295
156
----

(18)
2563
1387
4954
2065
-----

(3)
$ .75
1.25
.49
------

(20)
$ 12.50
16.75
15.75

(21)
$ 8.00
5.75
2.33
4.16
.94
6.32
------

(22)
547
197
685
678
456
393
525
240
152
---

(23)
1/3−1/3=

(24)
4.0125
1.5907
4.10
8.573
------

(25)
3/8+5/8+7/8+1/8

(26)
121/2
621/2
121/2
371/2
------

(27)
1/8+1/4+1/2=

(28)
3/4+1/4=

(29)
4   3/4
2   1/4
5   1/4
-----

(30)
2   1/2
6   3/8
3   3/4
------

(31)	(33)	(34)	(35)	(36)	(37)	
113.46	.49	1/6+3/8=	2ft. 6in.	2yr. 5mo.	16	1/3
49.6097	.28		3ft. 5in.	3yr. 6mo.	12	1/8
19.9	.63		4ft. 9in.	4yr. 9mo.	21	1/2
9.87	.95		---------	5yr. 2mo.	32	3/4
.0086	1.69			6yr. 7mo.	--------	
18.253	.22			----------		
6.04	.33					
	.36					
	1.01					
(32)	.56					
3/4+1/2+1/4=	.88					
	.75					
	.56					
	1.10					
	.18					
	.56					
	-----					

(38)

25.091+100.4+25+98.28+19.3614=

SERIES A

Subtraction Scale

By Clifford Woody

Name..

When is your next birthday?........................ How old will you be?..............................

Are you a boy or girl?.................................. In what grade are you?..............................

(1)	(2)	(3)	(4)	(5)	(6)	(7)	(8)	(9)	(10)	(11)
8	6	2	9	4	11	13	59	78	7–4=	76
5	0	1	3	4	7	8	12	37		
--	--	--	--	--	--	--	--	--		--

(12)	(13)	(14)	(15)	(16)	(17)	(18)	(19)	(20)	
27	16	50	21	270	393	1000	567482	2	3/4–1=
3	9	25	9	190	178	537	106493		
--	--	--	--	---	---	----	-------		

(21)   (22)   (23)   (24)   (30)
10.00   3   1/2–1/2=   80836465   8   7/8   9.8063–9.019=
3.49   49178036   5   3/4
----   ----   ----

        (27)   (28)   (29)   (30)
5yd.   1ft.   4in.   10–6.25   75   3/4   9.8063–9.019=
2yd.   2ft.   8in.   52   1/4
        ----   ----

        (31)   (32)   (33)   (34)   (35)
7.3–3.00081=   1912   6mo.   8da.   5/12–2/10=   6   1/8   3   7/8–1   5/8–
                        1910   7mo.   15da.   2   7/8
        ----   ----

SERIES A

Division Scale

By Clifford Woody

Name..

When is your next birthday?.........................   How old will you be?.................................

Are you a boy or girl?.................................   In what grade are you?.................................

(1)	(2)	(3)	(4)	(5)	(6)
$3\overline{)6}$	$9\overline{)27}$	$4\overline{)28}$	$1\overline{)5}$	$9\overline{)36}$	$3\overline{)39}$

(7)	(8)	(9)	(10)	(11)	(12)
$4 \div 2 =$	$9\overline{)10}$	$1\overline{)1}$	$6 \times \underline{} = 30$	$2\overline{)13}$	$2 \div 2 =$

(13)	(14)	(15)	(16)	(17)
$4\overline{)24}$ lbs. 8 oz.	$8\overline{)5856}$	1/4 of 128 =	$68\overline{)2108}$	$50 \div 7 =$

(18)
$13\overline{)65065}$

(19)
$248 \div 7 =$

(20)
$2.1\overline{)25.2}$

(21)
$25\overline{)9750}$

(22)
$2\overline{)13.50}$

(23)
$23\overline{)469}$

(24)
$75\overline{)2250300}$

(25)
$2400\overline{)504000}$

(26)
$12\overline{)2.76}$

(27)
7/8 of 624 =

(28)
$.003\overline{).0936}$

(29)
3 1/2 ÷ 9 =

(30)
3/4 ÷ 5 =

(31)
5/4 ÷ 3/5 =

(32)
9 5/8 ÷ 3 3/4

(33)
$52\overline{)3756}$

(34)
62.50 ÷ 1 1/4 =

(35)
$531\overline{)37722}$

(36)
$9\overline{)69}$ lbs. 9 oz.

SERIES A

Multiplication Scale

By Clifford Woody

Name..

When is your next birthday?..........................   How old will you be?...............................

Are you a boy or girl?...................................   In what grade are you?............................

(1)	(2)	(3)	(4)	(5)	(6)	(7)
				23	310	
$3 \times 7 =$	$5 \times 1 =$	$2 \times 3 =$	$4 \times 8 =$	3	4	$7 \times 9 =$
				--	--	

(8)	(9)	(10)	11	(12)	(13)	(14)	(15)
50	254	623	1036	5096	8754	165	235
3	6	7	8	6	8	40	23
--	--	--	----	---	-----	----	----

(16)	(17)	(18)	(19)	(20)	(21)	(22)
7898	145	24	9.6	287	24	
9	206	234	4	.05	21/2	8 × 53/4
---	---	---	---	---	---	

(23)	(24)	(25)	(26)	(27)	(28)	(29)
	16		9742	6.25	.0123	
11/4 × 8 =	2 5/8	7/8 × 3/4 =	59	3.2	9.8	1/8 × 2 =
	----		------	----	----	

(30)	(31)	(32)	(33)	(34)
2.49	12 15	6 dollars 49 cents		
36	--- ---	8	21/2 × 31/2 =	1/2 × 1/2 =
-----	25 32	-----------------------		

(35)	(36)	(37)	(38)	(39)
9873/4	3ft. 5in.			.0963 1/8 8ft. 91/2in.
25	5	21/4 × 41/2	× 11/2 = .084	9
-----	---------			----------

A series of problems in reasoning in arithmetic which were given in twenty-six school systems by Dr. C.W. Stone furnish a valuable test in this field, as well as an opportunity for comparison with other schools in which these problems have been used.[22] A list of problems follows.

Solve as many of the following problems as you have time for; work them in order as numbered:

1. If you buy 2 tablets at 7 cents each and a book for 65 cents, how much change should you receive from a two-dollar bill?

2. John sold 4 Saturday Evening Posts at 5 cents each. He kept 1/2 the money and with the other 1/2 he bought Sunday papers at 2 cents each. How many did he buy?

3. If James had 4 times as much money as George, he would have $16. How much money has George?

4. How many pencils can you buy for 50 cents at the rate of 2 for 5 cents?

5. The uniforms for a baseball nine cost $2.50 each. The shoes cost $2 a pair. What was the total cost of uniforms and shoes for the nine?

6. In the schools of a certain city there are 2200 pupils; 1/2 are in the primary grades, 1/4 in the grammar grades, 1/8 in the High School, and the rest in the night school. How many pupils are there in the night school?

---

22. Reasoning Test in Arithmetic, by C.W. Stone, published by the Bureau of Publications, Teachers College, Columbia University, 1916.

7. If 3-1/2 tons of coal cost $21, what will 5-1/2 tons cost?

8. A news dealer bought some magazines for $1. He sold them for $1.20, gaining 5 cents on each magazine. How many magazines were there?

9. A girl spent 1/8 of her money for car fare, and three times as much for clothes. Half of what she had left was 80 cents. How much money did she have at first?

10. Two girls receive $2.10 for making button-holes. One makes 42, the other 28. How shall they divide the money?

11. Mr. Brown paid one third of the cost of a building; Mr. Johnson paid 1/2 the cost. Mr. Johnson received $500 more annual rent than Mr. Brown. How much did each receive?

12. A freight train left Albany for New York at 6 o'clock. An express left on the same track at 8 o'clock. It went at the rate of 40 miles an hour. At what time of day will it overtake the freight train if the freight train stops after it has gone 56 miles?

A different type of measurement is accomplished by using Thorndike's scale for measuring the quality of handwriting.[23] A typical distribution of the scores which children receive on the handwriting scale reads as follows: For a fourth grade one child writes quality four, two quality six, five quality seven, seven quality eight, eight

---

23. A Scale for Handwriting of Children, by E.L. Thorndike, published by the Bureau of Publications, Teachers College, Columbia University.

quality nine, three quality ten, two quality eleven, two quality twelve, one quality thirteen, one quality fourteen. In a table the distributions of scores in penmanship for a large number of papers selected at random show the following results:

Scores	Grades						
	2	**3**	**4**	**5**	**6**	**7**	**8**
0	--	--	--	--	--	--	--
1	--	--	--	--	--	--	--
2	--	--	--	--	--	--	--
3	--	--	--	--	--	--	--
4	5	2	--	--	--	--	--
5	22	2	3	3	--	1	--
6	21	21	16	3	2	--	1
7	29	44	24	12	1	3	3
8	28	86	42	56	20	15	7
9	42	41	55	61	25	29	11
10	7	8	20	16	9	11	1
11	29	13	21	17	32	25	23
12	5	2	15	15	44	12	21
13	7	2	2	6	17	19	9
14	--	--	3	4	10	16	9
15	--	--	1	--	9	6	15
16	1	--	--	1	10	12	17
17	--	--	--	--	6	2	3
18	--	--	--	--	3	1	--
Total papers	**196**	**221**	**202**	**194**	**188**	**152**	**124**

A SCALE FOR HANDWRITING OF CHILDREN IN GRADES 5-8

The Unit of the Scale Equals approximately One-Tenth of the Difference between the Best and Worst of the Formal Writings of 1,000 Children in Grades 5-8. The Differences 16-15, 15-14, 14-13, etc., represent Equal Fractions of the Combined Mental Scale of Merit of from 23-55 Competent Judges.

Sample 140, representing zero merit in handwriting. Zero merit is arbitrarily defined as that of a handwriting, recognizable as such, but yet not legible at all and possessed of no beauty.

Quality 0

Quality 0

Quality 4

Quality 4

Quality 5

bushes and the carriage
swayed along down the
driveway. The audie

Quality 5

Quality 6

gathering about them mel-
ted away in an instant leaving
only a poor old lady

Quality 6

Quality 7

card, John vanished behind the
bushes and the carriage moved

Quality 7

Quality 8

moved along down the driveway. The
audience of passers by which had been
gathering about them melted away

Quality 8

> Then the carelessly gentleman step-
> ped lightly into Warrens carriage and
> held out a small card, John vanished be-
> hind the bushes and the carriage moved

Quality 8

Quality 9

> Then the carelessly dressed gentleman
> stepped lightly into Warren's carriage
> and held out a small card, J

Quality 9

> Then the carelessly dressed gentleman
> stepped lightly into Warrens carriage and
> held out a small card, John vanished behind

Quality 9

> Then the carelessly dressed gentleman stepped
> lightly into Warren's carriage and held out a small
> card, John vanished behind the bushes and the

Quality 9

Quality 10

> driveway. The audience of passers-by, which
> had been gathering about them melted away
> in an instant leaving only a poor old lady on
> the curb. Abert was sadly stricking

Quality 10

Quality 11

rage moved along down the driveway. The audience of passers-by which had been gathering about them melted away

Quality 11

along the down the driveway The audience of passers-by which had been gathering about them

Quality 11

John vanished behind the bushes and the carriage moved along down the driveway The audience

Quality 11

Quality 12

lightly into Warren's carriage and held out a small card, John vanished behind the bushes and the carriage moved along down the drive-

Quality 12

behind the bushes and the carriage moved along down the driveway. The audience of passers-by

Quality 12

Then the carelessly dressed gentlemen stepped lightly into Warren's carriage and held out a small card, John vanished behind the bushes and the

Quality 12

Quality 13

Then the carelessly dressed gentleman stepped lightly into Warren's carriage and held out a

Quality 13

ished behind the bushes and the carriage moved along down the driveway The audience of passers-by which had

Quality 13

Then the carelessly dressed gentleman stepped lightly into Warren's carriage and

Quality 13

Then the carelessly dresse gentlemen stepped lightl into Warren's carriage and

Quality 13

Quality 14

Then the carelessly dressed gentleman
stepped lightly into Warren's carriage
and held out a small card, J

Quality 14

Then the carelessly dressed gentleman
stepped lightly into Warrens carriage and
held out a small card, John vanished behind

Quality 14

Quality 15

lightly into Warren's carriage and held out a
small card, John vanished behind the bushes
and the carriage moved along down the drive

Quality 15

held out a small card, John vanished behind
the bushes and the carriage moved along
down the driveway The audience of passers.

Quality 15

John vanished behind the bushes
and the carriage moved along
down the driveway. The audience

Quality 15

> Then the carelessly dressed gentle-
> man stepped lightly into Warrens
> carriage and held out a small white

Quality 15

Quality 16

> Then the carelessly dressed gentle-
> man stepped lightly into Warren's
> carriage and held out a small

Quality 16

Quality 17

> Then the carelessly dressed gentleman
> stepped lightly into Warren's carriage and
> held out a small card, John vanished be-

Quality 17

Quality 18

> showed that the rise and fall of the tides
> the attraction of the moon and sun upon

Quality 18

This table reads as follows: Quality four was written by five children in the second grade and two in the third grade, quality five was written by twenty-two children in the second grade, two children in the third grade, three in the fourth grade, three in the fifth grade, none in the sixth grade, one in the seventh grade, and none in the eighth grade, and so on for the whole table.[24]

A scale for measuring ability in spelling prepared by Dr. Leonard P. Ayres arranges the thousand words most commonly used in the order of their difficulty. From this sheet it is possible to discover words of approximately the same difficulty for each grade. A test could therefore be derived from this scale for each of the grades with the expectation that they would all do about equally well. There would also be the possibility of determining how well the spelling was done in the particular school system in which these words were given as compared with the ability of children as measured by an aggregate of more than a million spellings by seventy thousand children in eighty-four cities throughout the United States. Such a list could be taken from the scale for the second grade, which includes words which have proved to be of a difficulty represented by a seventy-three percent correct spelling for the class. Such a list might be composed of the following words: north, white, spent, block, river, winter, Sunday, letter, thank, and best. A similar list could be taken from the scale for a third, fourth, fifth, sixth, seventh, or eighth grade. For example, the words which have approximately the same difficulty,--seventy-three percent to be spelled correctly by the class for the sixth grade,-- read as follows: often, stopped, motion, theater, improvement, century, total, mansion, arrive, supply. The great value of such a measuring scale, including as it does the thousand words most commonly used, is to be found not only in the opportunity for comparing the achievements

---

24. A scale derived by Dr. Leonard P. Ayres of the Russell Sage Foundation is also valuable for measuring penmanship, and can be purchased from the Russell Sage Foundation.

of children in one class or school with another, but also in the focusing of the attention of teachers and pupils upon the words most commonly used.[25]

One of the fields in which there is greatest need for measurement is English composition. Teachers have too often thought of English composition as consisting of spelling, punctuation, capitalization, and the like, and have ignored the quality of the composition itself in their attention to these formal elements. A scale for measuring English composition derived by Dr. M.B. Hillegas,[26] consisting of sample compositions of values ranging from 0 to 9.37, will enable the teacher to tell just how many pupils in the class are writing each different quality of composition. The use of such a scale will tend to make both teacher and pupil critical of the work which is being done not only with respect to the formal elements, but also with respect to the style or adequacy of the expression of the ideas which the writer seeks to convey. Probably in no other field has the teacher been so apt to derive his standard from the performance of the class as in work in composition. Even though some teachers find it difficult to evaluate the work of their pupils in terms of the sample compositions given on the scale, much good must come, it seems to the writer, from the attempt to grade compositions by such an objective scale. If such measurements are made two or three times during the year, the performance of individual pupils and of the class will be indicated much more certainly than is the case when

---

25. Copies of the Spelling Scale can be secured from the Russell Sage Foundation, New York, for five cents a copy.
26. A Scale for the Measurement of Quality in English Composition, by Milo B. Hillegas, published by the Bureau of Publications, Teachers College, Columbia University.

teachers feel that they are getting along well without any definite assurance of the amount of their improvement.

In one large school system in which the writer was permitted to have the principals measure compositions collected from the sixth and the eighth grades, it was discovered that almost no progress in the quality of composition had been accomplished during these two years. This lack of achievement upon the part of children was not, in the opinion of the writer, due to any lack of conscientious work upon the part of teachers, but, rather, developed out of a situation in which the whole of composition was thought of in terms of the formal elements mentioned above. The Hillegas scale, together with the values assigned to each of the samples, is given below.

A SCALE FOR THE MEASUREMENT OF THE QUALITY OF ENGLISH COMPOSITION

By Milo B. Hillegas

Value 0   Artificial sample

Letter

Dear Sir:

I write to say that it aint a square deal Schools is I say they is I went to a school. red and gree green and brown aint it hito bit I say he don't know his business not today nor yeaterday and you know it and I want Jennie to get me out.

Value 183   Artificial sample

My Favorite Book

The book I refer to read is Ichabod Crane, it is an grate book and I like to rede it. Ichabod Crame was a man and a man wrote a book and it is called Ichabod Crane i like it because the man called it ichabod crane when I read it for it is such a great book.

Value 260   Artificial sample

The Advantage of Tyranny

Advantage evils are things of tyranny and there are many advantage evils. One thing is that when they opress the people they suffer awful I think it is a terrible thing when they say that you can be hanged down or trodden down without mercy and the tyranny does what they want there was tyrans in the revolutionary war and so they throwed off the yok.

Value 369   Written by a boy in the second year of the high school, aged 14 years

Sulla as a Tyrant

When Sulla came back from his conquest Marius had put himself consul so sulla with the army he had with him in his conquest siezed the government from Marius and put himself in consul and had a list of his enemys printy and the men whoes names were on this list we beheaded.

Value 474   Written by a girl in the third year of the high school, aged 17 years

De Quincy

First: De Quincys mother was a beautiful women and through her De Quincy inhereted much of his genius.

His running away from school enfluenced him much as he roamed through the woods, valleys and his mind became very meditative.

The greatest enfluence of De Quincy's life was the opium habit. If it was not for this habit it is doubtful whether we would now be reading his writings.

His companions during his college course and even before that time were great enfluences. The surroundings of De Quincy were enfluences. Not only De Quincy's habit of opium but other habits which were peculiar to his life.

His marriage to the woman which he did not especially care for.

The many well educated and noteworthy friends of De Quincy.

Value 585   Written by a boy in the fourth year of the high school, aged 16 years

Fluellen

The passages given show the following characteristic of Fluellen: his inclination to brag, his professed knowledge of History, his complaining character, his great patriotism, pride of his leader, admired honesty, revengeful, love of fun and punishment of those who deserve it.

Value 675   Written by a girl in the first year of the high
school, aged 18 years

Ichabod Crane

Ichabod Crane was a schoolmaster in a place called
Sleepy Hollow. He was tall and slim with broad
shoulders, long arms that dangled far below his coat
sleeves. His feet looked as if they might easily have
been used for shovels. His nose was long and his entire frame was most loosely hung to-gether.

Value 772   Written by a boy in the third year of the high
school, aged 16 years

Going Down with Victory

As we road down Lombard Street, we saw flags waving
from nearly every window. I surely felt proud that day
to be the driver of the gaily decorated coach. Again and
again we were cheered as we drove slowly to the postmas-
ters, to await the coming of his majestie's mail. There
wasn't one of the gaily bedecked coaches that could have
compared with ours, in my estimation. So with waving
flags and fluttering hearts we waited for the coming of
the mail and the expected tidings of victory.

When at last it did arrive the postmaster began to
quickly sort the bundles, we waited anxiously. Immediately upon receiving our bundles, I lashed the horses and they
responded with a jump. Out into the country we drove
at reckless speed--everywhere spreading like wildfire the
news, "Victory!" The exileration that we all felt was shared
with the horses. Up and down grade and over bridges, we
drove at breakneck speed and spreading the news at every

hamlet with that one cry "Victory!" When at last we were back home again, it was with the hope that we should have another ride some day with "Victory."

Value 838   Written by a boy in the Freshman class in college

Venus of Melos

In looking at this statue we think, not of wisdom, or power, or force, but just of beauty. She stands resting the weight of her body on one foot, and advancing the other (left) with knee bent. The posture causes the figure to sway slightly to one side, describing a fine curved line. The lower limbs are draped but the upper part of the body is uncovered. (The unfortunate loss of the statue's arms prevents a positive knowledge of its original attitude.) The eyes are partly closed, having something of a dreamy langour. The nose is perfectly cut, the mouth and chin are moulded in adorable curves. Yet to say that every feature is of faultless perfection is but cold praise. No analysis can convey the sense of her peerless beauty.

Value 937   Written by a boy in the Freshman class in college

A Foreigner's Tribute to Joan of Arc

Joan of Arc, worn out by the suffering that was thrust upon her, nevertheless appeared with a brave mien before the Bishop of Beauvais. She knew, had always known that she must die when her mission was fulfilled and death held no terrors for her. To all the bishop's questions she answered firmly and without hesitation. The bishop failed to confuse her and at last condemned her to death for heresy, bidding her recant if she would live. She refused and was lead to prison, from there to death.

While the flames were writhing around her she bade the old bishop who stood by her to move away or he would be injured. Her last thought was of others and De Quincy says, that recant was no more in her mind than on her lips. She died as she lived, with a prayer on her lips and listening to the voices that had whispered to her so often.

The heroism of Joan of Arc was wonderful. We do not know what form her great patriotism took or how far it really led her. She spoke of hearing voices and of seeing visions. We only know that she resolved to save her country, knowing though she did so, it would cost her her life. Yet she never hesitated. She was uneducated save for the lessons taught her by nature. Yet she led armies and crowned the dauphin, king of France. She was only a girl, yet she could silence a great bishop by words that came from her heart and from her faith. She was only a woman, yet she could die as bravely as any martyr who had gone before.

The following compositions have been evaluated by Professor Thorndike, and may be used to supplement the scale given above.

Value 13

Last Monday the house on the corner of Jay street was burned down to the ground and right down by Mrs. brons house there is a little child all alone and there is a bad man sleeping in the seller, but we have a wise old monkey in the coal ben so the parents are thankful that they don't have to pay any reward.

Value 20

Some of the house burned and the children were in bed and there were four children and the lady next store broke the door in and went up stars and woke the peple up and whent out of the house when they moved and and the girl was skard to look out of the window and all the time thouhth that she saw a flame.

And the wise monkey reward from going to the firehouse and jumping all round and was thankful from his reward and was thankful for what he got. $15. was his reward.

Value 30

A long time ago, I do not know, how long but a man and a woman and a little boy lived together also a monkey a pet for the little boy it happened that the man and the woman were out, and the monkey and little boy, and the house started to burn, and the monkcy took the little boys hand, and, went out.

The father had come home and was glad that the monkey had saved his little boy.

And that, monkey got a reward.

Value 40

Once upon a time a woman went into a dark room and lit a match. She dropped it on the floor and it of course set the house afire.

She jumped out of the window and called her husband to come out too.

They both forgot all about the baby. All of a sudden he appeared in the window calling his mother.

His father had gone next door to tel afone to the fire house.

They had a monkey in the house at the time and he heard the child calling his mother.

He had a plan to save the baby.

He ran to the window where he was standing. He put his tail about his waist and jumped off the window sill with the baby in his tail.

When the people were settled again they gave him a silver collar as a reward.

Value 50

A University out west, I cannot remember the name, is noted for its hazing, and this is what the story is about. It is the hazing of a freshman. There was a freshman there who had been acting as if he didn't respect his upper class men so they decided to teach him a lesson. The student brought before the Black Avenger's which is a society in all college to keep the freshman under there rules so they desided to take him to the rail-rode track and tie him to the rails about two hours before a train was suspected and leave him there for about an hour, which was a hour before the 9.20 train was expected. The date came that they planned this hazing for so the captured the fellow blindfolded him and lead him to the rail rode tracks, where they tied him.

Value 60

I should like to see a picture, illustrating a part of L'alle-gro. Where the godesses of Mirth and Liberty trip along hand in hand. Two beautiful girls dressed in flowing garments, dancing along a flower-strewn path, through a pretty garden. Their hair flowing down in long curls. Their countenances showing their perfect freedom and happiness. Their arms extended gracefully smelling some sweet flower. In my mind this would make a beautiful picture.

Value 70

It was between the dark and the daylight when far away could be seen the treacherous wolves skulking over the hills. We sat beside our campfires and watched them for awhile. Sometimes a few of them would howl as if they wanted to get in our camp. Then, half discouraged, they would walk away and soon there would be others doing the same thing. They were afraid to come near because of the fires, which were burning brightly. I noticed that they howled more between the dark and the daylight than at any time of the night.

Value 80

The sun was setting, giving a rosy glow to all the trees standing tall black against the faintly tinted sky. Blue, pink, green, yellow, like a conglomeration of paints dropped carelessly onto a pale blue background. The trees were in such great number that they looked like a mass of black crepe, each with its individual, graceful form in view. The lake lay smooth and unruffled, dimly reflecting the beautiful coloring of the sky. The wind started madly up and blew over the lake's glassy surface making mysterious murmurings blending in with the chirping songs of the birds blew through the tree tops setting the leaves rustling and whispering to one another. A squirrel ran from his perch chattering, to the lofty branches--a far and distant hoot echoed in the silence, and soon night, over all came stealing, blotting out the scenery and wrapping all in restful, mysterious darkness.

Value 90

Oh that I had never heard of Niagara till I beheld it! Blessed were the wanderers of old, who heard its deep roar, sounding through the woods, as the summons to an unknown wonder, and approached its awful brink, in all the freshness of native feeling. Had its own mysterious voice been the first to warn me of its existence, then, indeed, I might have knelt down and worshipped. But I had come thither, haunted with a vision of foam and fury, and dizzy cliffs, and an ocean tumbling down out of the sky--a scene, in short, which nature had too much good taste and calm simplicity to realize. My mind had struggled to adapt these false conceptions to the reality, and finding the effort vain, a wretched sense of disappointment weighed me down. I climbed the precipice, and threw myself on the earth feeling that I was unworthy to look at the Great Falls, and careless about beholding them again.

A scale for measuring English composition in the eighth grade, which takes account of different types of composition, such as narration, description, and the like, has been developed by Dr. Frank W. Ballou, of Boston.[27] For those interested in the following up of the

---

27. The Harvard-Newton Scale for the Measurement of English Composition, published by the Harvard University Press, Cambridge, Mass.

problem of English composition this scale will prove interesting and valuable.

Several scales have been developed for the measurement of the ability of children in reading. Among them may be mentioned the scale derived by Professor Thorndike for measuring the understanding of sentences.[28] This scale calls attention to that element in reading which is possibly the most important of them all, that is, the attempt to get meanings. We are all of us, for the most part, concerned not primarily with giving expression through oral reading, but, rather, in getting ideas from the printed page. A sample of this scale is given on the following page.

SCALE ALPHA. FOR MEASURING THE UNDERSTANDING OF SENTENCES

Write your name here...

Write your age.....................years.....................months.

SET *a*

Read this and then write the answers. Read it again as often as you need to.

---

28. Scale Alpha. For Measuring the Understanding of Sentences, by E.L. Thorndike, published by the Bureau of Publications, Teachers College, Columbia University.

    Scales for measuring the rate of silent reading and oral reading have been derived by Dr. W.S. Gray, of the Univeristy of Chicago, and by Dr. F.J. Kelly, of the University of Kansas. Reference to the use of Dr. Gray's scale will be found in Judd's Measuring Work of the Schools, one of the volumes of the Cleveland survey, published by the Russell Sage Foundation. Dr. Kelly's test, called The Kansas Silent Reading Test, can be had from the Emporia, Kansas, State Normal School.

John had two brothers who were both tall. Their names were Will and Fred. John's sister, who was short, was named Mary. John liked Fred better than either of the others. All of these children except Will had red hair. He had brown hair.

1.   Was John's sister tall or short?

    ....

2.   How many brothers had John?

    ....

3.   What was his sister's name?

    ....

SET *b*

Read this and then write the answers. Read it again as often as you need to.

Long after the sun had set, Tom was still waiting for Jim and Dick to come. "If they do not come before nine o'clock," he said to himself, "I will go on to Boston alone." At half past eight they came bringing two other boys with them. Tom was very glad to see them and gave each of them one of the apples he had kept. They ate these and he ate one too. Then all went on down the road.

1.   When did Jim and Dick come?

    ....

2.   What did they do after eating the apples?

    ....

3.   Who else came besides Jim and Dick?

....

4.   How long did Tom say he would wait for them?

....

5.   What happened after the boys ate the apples?

....

Read this and then write the answers. Read it again as often as you need to.

It may seem at first thought that every boy and girl who goes to school ought to do all the work that the teacher wishes done. But sometimes other duties prevent even the best boy or girl from doing so. If a boy's or girl's father died and he had to work afternoons and evenings to earn money to help his mother, such might be the case. A good girl might let her lessons go undone in order to help her mother by taking care of the baby.

1.   What are some conditions that might make even the best boy leave school work unfinished?

....

2.   What might a boy do in the evenings to help his family?

....

3.   How could a girl be of use to her mother?

....

4. Look at these words: *idle, tribe, inch, it, ice, ivy, tide, true, tip, top, tit, tat, toe.*

Cross out every one of them that has an *i* and has not any *t* (T) in it.

SET *d*

Read this and then write the answers. Read it again as often as you need to.

It may seem at first thought that every boy and girl who goes to school ought to do all the work that the teacher wishes done. But sometimes other duties prevent even the best boy or girl from doing so. If a boy's or girl's father died and he had to work afternoons and evenings to earn money to help his mother, such might be the case. A good girl might let her lessons go undone in order to help her mother by taking care of the baby.

1. What is it that might seem at first thought to be true, but really is false?

   ....

2. What might be the effect of his father's death upon the way a boy spent his time?

   ....

3. Who is mentioned in the paragraph as the person who desires to have all lessons completely done?

   ....

4. In these two lines draw a line under every 5 that comes just after a 2, unless the 2 comes just after a 9. If that is the case, draw a line under the next figure after the 5:

5 3 6 2 5 4 1 7 4 2 5 7 6 5 4 9 2 5 3 8 6 1 2 5
4 7 3 5 2 3 9 2 5 8 4 7 9 2 5 6

1 2 5 7 4 8 5 6

Many tests have been devised which have been thought to have more general application than those which have been mentioned above for the particular subjects. One of the most valuable of these tests, called technically a completion test, is that derived by Dr. M.R. Trabue.[29] In these tests the pupil is asked to supply words which are omitted from the printed sentences. It is really a test of his ability to complete the thought when only part of it is given. Dr. Trabue calls his scales language scales. It has been found, however, that ability of this sort is closely related to many of the traits which we consider desirable in school children. It would therefore be valuable, provided always that children have some ability in reading, to test them on the language scale as one of the means of differentiating among those who have more or less ability. The scores which may be expected from different grades appear in Dr. Trabue's monograph. Three separate scales follow.

---

29. Completion Test Language Scales, by M.R. Trabue, published by the Bureau of Publications, Teachers College, Columbia University.

Write only one word on each blank

Time Limit: Seven minutes

NAME ....

TRABUE

LANGUAGE SCALE B

1.   We like good boys................girls.

6.   The................is barking at the cat.

8.   The stars and the................will shine tonight.

22.   Time................often   more   valuable................
money.

23.   The poor baby................as if it....................sick.

31.   She................if she will.

35.   Brothers and sisters .... always ....
to help.............other and should................quar-
rel.

38.   .... weather usually................ a good effect
.... one's spirits.

48.   It is very annoying to...........................tooth-
ache, ...often comes at the most................
time imaginable.

54.   To................friends is always................the........ it
takes.

Write only one word on each blank

Time Limit: Seven minutes

NAME..............................

TRABUE

LANGUAGE SCALE D

4.   We are going...............school.

76.   I...............to school each day.

11.   The...............plays...............her dolls all day.

21.   The rude child does not...............many friends.

63.   Hard...............makes...............tired.

27.   It is good to hear...............voice......................
..........friend.

71.   The happiest and...............contented man is the one...............lives a busy and useful.................

42.   The best advice...............usually...............ob-tained...............one's parents.

51.   ....things are............... satisfying to an or-dinary...............than congenial friends.

84.   ....a rule one...............association..........friends.

Write only one word on each blank

Time Limit: Five minutes

NAME ....

TRABUE

LANGUAGE SCALE J

20.   Boys and................soon   become................and women.

61.   The................are often more contented.............. the rich.

64.   The rose is a favorite................. because of................ fragrance and.................

41.   It is very................ to become................acquainted ....persons who...............timid.

93.   Extremely old................sometimes.................al-most as................. care as ....

87.   One's................in life................upon so............ factors .... it is not .... to state any single................for................ failure.

89.   The future................of the stars and the facts of............history   are................now   once   for all,................I like them................not.

Other standard tests and scales of measurement have been derived and are being developed. The examples given above will, however, suffice to make clear the distinction between the ordinary type of examination and the more careful study of the achievements of children which may be accomplished by using these measuring sticks. It is important for any one who would attempt to apply these tests to know something of the technique of recording results.

In the first place, the measurement of a group is not expressed satisfactorily by giving the average score or rate of achievement of the class. It is true that this is one measure, but it is not one which tells enough, and it is not the one which is most significant for the teacher. It is important whenever we measure children to get as clear a view as we can of the whole situation. For this purpose we want not primarily to know what the average performance is, but, rather, how many children there are at each level of achievement. In arithmetic, for example, we want to know how many there are who can do none of the Courtis problems in addition, or how many there are who can do the first six on the Woody test, how many can do seven, eight, and so on. In penmanship we want to know how many children there are who write quality eight, or nine, or ten, or sixteen, or seventeen, as the case may be. The work of the teacher can never be accomplished economically except as he gives more attention to those who are less proficient, and provides more and harder work for those who are capable, or else relieves the able members of the class from further work in the field. It will be well, therefore, to prepare, for the sake of comparing grades within the same school or school system, or for the sake of preparing the work of a class at two different times during the year, a table which shows just how many children there are in the group who have reached each level of achievement. Such tables for work in composition for a class at two different times, six months apart, appear as follows:

Distribution of Composition Scores for a Seventh Grade

	Number of Children	
	November	February
Rated at 0	0	0
1.83	1	1
2.60	6	4
3.69	12	6
4.74	8	11
5.85	3	4
6.75	1	3
7.72	1	2
8.38	0	1
9.37	0	0

A study of such a distribution would show not only that the average performance of the class has been raised, but also that those in the lower levels have, in considerable measure, been brought up; that is, that the teacher has been working with those who showed less ability, and not simply pushing ahead a few who had more than ordinary capacity. It would be possible to increase the average performance by working wholly with the upper half of the class while neglecting those who showed less ability. From a complete distribution, as has been given above, it has become evident that this has not been the method of the teacher. He has sought apparently to do everything that he could to improve the quality of work upon the part of all of the children in the class.

It is very interesting to note, when such complete distributions are given, how the achievement of children in various classes overlaps. For example, the distribution of the number of examples on the Courtis tests, correctly finished in a given time by pupils in the seventh grades, makes it clear that there are children in the fifth grade who do better than many in the eighth.

The Distribution of the Number of Examples Correctly Finished in the Given Time by Pupils in the Several Grades

Addition					Subtraction				
No. of Examples Finished	Grades				No. of Examples Finished	Grades			
	5	6	7	8		5	6	7	8
0	12	15	5	4	0	6	2	2	--
1	26	23	14	9	1	5	6	2	1
2	27	31	8	6	2	7	8	1	--
3	31	27	27	9	3	13	21	3	1
4	25	28	19	16	4	21	18	13	2
5	16	23	16	15	5	26	30	12	7
6	15	22	12	12	6	17	27	15	9
7	1	11	8	9	7	15	27	18	9
8	3	4	6	11	8	15	20	12	12
9	1	2	3	8	9	10	13	9	12
10	--	--	--	6	10	8	6	13	11
11	--	--	1	--	11	6	2	3	12
12	--	--	1	2	12	3	1	7	9
13	--	--	--	--	13	2	2	3	5
14	--	--	--	--	14	1	1	3	7
15	--	--	--	2	15	--	--	2	3
16	--	--	--	1	16	--	--	1	2

Addition					Subtraction				
No. of Exam-ples Finished	Grades				No. of Exam-ples Finished	Grades			
	5	6	7	8		5	6	7	8
17	--	--	--	--	17	--	1	--	1
18	--	--	--	--	18	--	--	--	1
19	--	--	--	--	19	--	--	--	4
20	--	--	--	--	20	--	--	--	2
21	--	--	--	--	21	--	--	--	1
22	--	--	--	--	22	--	--	--	--
Total papers	157	86	119	111	Total papers	155	185	119	111

The Distribution of the Number of Examples Correctly Finished in the Given Time by Pupils in the Several Grades

Multiplication					Division				
No. of Exam-ples Finished	Grades				No. of Exam-ples Finished	Grades			
	5	6	7	8		5	6	7	8
0 . . .	10	4	--	--	0 . . .	17	7	1	--
1 . . .	10	4	3	--	1 . . .	19	17	2	1
2 . . .	19	20	5	1	2 . . .	18	22	8	4
3 . . .	21	17	11	5	3 . . .	21	26	6	2
4 . . .	28	31	16	3	4 . . .	25	27	8	6
5 . . .	26	34	12	13	5 . . .	21	27	11	7
6 . . .	24	27	13	13	6 . . .	9	15	12	4
7 . . .	9	20	16	10	7 . . .	10	15	16	18
8 . . .	5	14	21	19	8 . . .	6	7	20	9

	Multiplication					Division			
No. of Examples Finished	Grades				No. of Examples Finished	Grades			
	5	6	7	8		5	6	7	8
9 . . .	3	9	11	13	9 . . .	4	7	11	6
10 . . .	--	4	6	10	10 . . .	4	9	7	13
11 . . .	1	--	2	9	11 . . .	1	3	3	7
12 . . .	--	--	2	6	12 . . .	--	2	10	10
13 . . .	--	--	1	3	13 . . .	--	2	--	10
14 . . .	--	--	--	3	14 . . .	1	--	1	4
15 . . .	--	--	--	--	15 . . .	--	1	2	9
16 . . .	--	--	--	1	16 . . .	--	--	--	2
17 . . .	--	--	--	--	17 . . .	--	--	--	4
18 . . .	--	--	--	1	18 . . .	--	--	--	2
19 . . .	--	--	--	1	19 . . .	--	--	--	1
20 . . .	--	--	--	--	20 . . .	--	--	--	1
21 . . .	--	--	--	--	21 . . .	--	--	--	1
22 . . .	--	--	--	--	22 . . .	--	--	--	--
Total Papers	156	184	119	111	Total Papers	156	187	118	111

If the tests had been given in the fourth or the third grade, it would have been found that there were children, even as low as the third grade, who could do as well or better than some of the children in the eighth grade. Such comparisons of achievements among children in various subjects ought to lead at times to reorganizations of classes, to the grouping of children for special instruction, and to the rapid promotion of the more capable pupils.

In many of these measurements it will be found helpful to describe the group by naming the point above and below which half of the cases fall. This is called the median. Because of the very common use of this measure in the current literature of education, it may be worth while to discuss carefully the method of its derivation.[30]

[31]The *median point* of any distribution of measures is that point on the scale which divides the distribution into two exactly equal parts, one half of the measures being greater than this point on the scale, and the other half being smaller. When the scales are very crude, or when small numbers of measurements are being considered, it is not worth while to locate this median point any more accurately than by indicating on what step of the scale it falls. If the measuring instrument has been carefully derived and accurately scaled, however, it is often desirable, especially where the group being considered is reasonably large, to locate the exact point within the step on which the median falls. If the unit of the scale is some measure of the variability of a defined group, as it is in the majority of our present educational scales, this median point may well be calculated to the nearest tenth of a unit, or, if there are two hundred or more individual measurements in the distribution, it may be found interesting to calculate the median point to the nearest hundredth of a scale unit. Very seldom will anything be gained by carrying the calculation beyond the second decimal place.

The best rule for locating the median point of a distribution is to *take as the median that point on the scale which is reached by counting out one half of the measures*, the measures being taken in the order of their

---

30. The student who is not interested in the statistical methods involved in measuring with precision the achievements of pupils may omit the remainder of this chapter.
31. This explanation of the method of finding the median was prepared for one of the classes in Teachers College by Dr. M.R. Trabue.

magnitude. If we let *n* stand for the number of measures in the distribution, we may express the rule as follows: Count into the distribution, from either end of the scale, a distance covered by *⋆n/2* measures. For example, if the distribution contains 20 measures, the median is that point on the scale which marks the end of the 10th and the beginning of the 11th measure. If there are 39 measures in the distribution, the median point is reached by counting out 19-1/2 of the measures; in other words, the median of such a distribution is at the mid-point of that fraction of the scale assigned to the 20th measure.

The *median step* of a distribution is the step which contains within it the median point. Similarly, the *median measure* in any distribution is the measure which contains the median point. In a distribution containing 25 measures, the 13th measure is the median measure, because 12 measures are greater and 12 are less than the 13th, while the 13th measure is itself divided into halves by the median point. Where a distribution contains an even number of measures, there is in reality no median measure but only a median point between the two halves of the distribution. Where a distribution contains an uneven number of measures, the median measure is the $(n+1)/2$ measurement, at the mid-point of which measure is the median point of the distribution.

Much inaccurate calculation has resulted from misguided attempts to secure a *median point* with the formula just given, which is applicable only to the location of the *median measure*. It will be found much more advantageous in dealing with educational statistics to consider only the median point, and to use only the *n/2* formula given in a previous paragraph, for practically all educational scales are or may be thought of as continuous scales rather than scales composed of discrete steps.

The greatest danger to be guarded against in considering all scales as continuous rather than discrete, is that careless thinkers may refine their calculations far beyond the accuracy which their original measurements would warrant. One should be very careful not to make such unjustifiable refinements in his statement of results as are often made by young pupils when they multiply the diameter of a circle, which has been measured only to the nearest inch, by 3.1416 in order to find the circumference. Even in the ordinary calculation of the average point of a series of measures of length, the amateur is sometimes tempted, when the number of measures in the series is not contained an even number of times in the sum of their values, to carry the quotient out to a larger number of decimal places than the original measures would justify. Final results should usually not be refined far beyond the accuracy of the original measures.

It is of utmost importance in calculating medians and other measures of a distribution to keep constantly in mind the significance of each step on the scale. If the scale consists of tasks to be done or problems to be solved, then "doing 1 task correctly" means, when considered as part of a continuous scale, anywhere from doing 1.0 up to doing 2.0 tasks. A child receives credit for "2 problems correct" whether he has just barely solved 2.0 problems or has just barely fallen short of solving 3.0 problems. If, however, the scale consists of a series of productions graduated in quality from very poor to very good, with which series other productions of the same sort are to be compared, then each sample on the scale stands at the middle of its "step" rather than at the beginning.

The second kind of scale described in the foregoing paragraph may be designated as "scales for the *quality* of products," while the other variety may be called "scales for *magnitude* of achievement." In the one case, the child makes the best production he can and measures its quality by comparing it with similar products of known quality on the scale. Composition, handwriting, and drawing scales are good examples of scales for quality of products. In the other case, the scales are placed in the hands of the child at the very beginning, and the magnitude of his achievement is measured by the difficulty or number of tasks accomplished successfully in a given time. Spelling, arithmetic, reading, language, geography, and history tests are examples of scales for quantity of achievement.

Scores tend to be more accurate on the scales for magnitude of achievement, because the judgment of the examiner is likely to be more accurate in deciding whether a response is correct or incorrect than it is in deciding how much quality a given product contains. This does not furnish an excuse for failing to employ the quality-of-products scales, however, for the qualities they measure are not measurable in terms of the magnitude of tasks performed. The fact appears, however, that the method of employing the quality-of-products scales is "by comparison" (of child's production with samples reproduced on the scale), while the method of employing the magnitude-of-achievement scales is "by performance" (of child on tasks of known difficulty).

In this connection it may be well to take one of the scales for quality of products and outline the steps to be followed in assigning scores, making tabulations, and finding the medians of distributions of scores.

When the Hillegas scale is employed in measuring the quality of English composition, it will be advisable to assign to each composition the score of that sample on the scale to which it is nearest in merit or quality. While some individuals may feel able to assign values intermediate to those appearing on the Hillegas scale, the majority of those persons who use this scale will not thereby obtain a more accurate result, and the assignment of such intermediate values will make it extremely difficult for any other person to make accurate use of the results. To be exactly comparable, values should be assigned in exactly the same manner.

The best result will probably be obtained by having each composition rated several times, and if possible, by a number of different judges, the paper being given each time that value on the Hillegas scale to which it seems nearest in quality. The final mark for the paper should be the median score or step (not the median point or the average point) of all the scores assigned. For example, if a paper is rated five times, once as in step number five (5.85), twice as in step number six (6.75), and twice as in step number seven (7.72), it should be given a final mark indicating that it is a number six (6.75) paper.

After each composition has been assigned a final mark indicating to what sample on the Hillegas scale it is most nearly equal in quality, proceed as follows:

Make a distribution of the final marks given to the individual papers, showing how many papers were assigned to the zero step on the scale, how many to step number one, how many to step number two, and so on for each step of the scale. We may take as an example the distribution of scores made by the pupils of the eighth grade at Butte, Montana, in May, 1914.

No. of papers	1	9	32	39	43	22	6	2		
Rated at	0	1	2	3	4	5	6	7	8	9

All together there were 154 papers from the eighth grade, so that if they were arranged in order according to their merit we might begin at the poorest and count through 77 of them (n/2 = 154/2 = 77) to find the median point, which would lie between the 77th and the 78th in quality. If we begin with the 1 composition rated at 0 and count up through the 9 rated at 1 and the 32 rated at 2 in the above distribution, we shall have counted 42. In order to count out 77 cases, then, it will be necessary to count out 35 of the 39 cases rated at 3.

Now we know (if the instructions given above have been followed) that the compositions rated at 3 were so rated by virtue of the fact that the judges considered them nearer in quality to the sample valued at 3.69 than to any other sample on the scale. We should expect, then, to find that some of those rated at 3 were only slightly nearer to the sample valued at 3.69 than they were to the sample valued at 2.60, while others were only slightly nearer to 3.69 than they were to 4.74. Just how the 39 compositions rated on 3 were distributed between these two extremes we do not know, but the best single assumption to make is that they are distributed at equal intervals on step 3. Assuming, then, that the papers rated at 3 are distributed evenly over that step, we shall have covered .90 (35/39 = .897 = .90) of the entire step 3 by the time we have counted out 35 of the 39 papers falling on this step.

It now becomes necessary to examine more closely just what are the limits of step 3. It is evident from what has been said above that 3.69 is the middle step 3 and that step 3 extends downward from 3.69 halfway to 2.60, and upward from 3.69 halfway to 4.74. The table given below shows the range and the length of each step in the Hillegas Scale for English Composition.

The Hillegas Scale for English Composition

Step No.	Value or Sample	Range of Step	Length of Step
0. ...	0	0 – .91[32]	.91
1. ...	1.83	.92 – 2.21	1.30
2. ...	2.60	2.22 – 3.14	.93
3. ...	3.69	3.15 – 4.21	1.07
4. ...	4.74	4.22 – 5.29	1.08
5. ...	5.85	5.30 – 6.30	1.00
6. ...	6.75	6.30 – 7.23	.93
7. ...	7.72	7.24 – 8.05	.81
8. ...	8.38	8.05 – 8.87	.82
9. ...	9.37	8.88 –	

From the above table we find that step 3 has a length of 1.07 units. If we count out 35 of the 39 papers, or, in other words, if we pass upward into the step .90 of the total distance (1.07 units), we shall arrive at a point .96 units (.90 × 1.07 = .96) above the lower limit of step

32. The third decimal place is omitted in this table.

3, which we find from the table is 3.15. Adding .96 to 3.15 gives 4.11 as the median point of this eighth grade distribution.

The median and the percentiles of any distribution of scores on the Hillegas scale may be determined in a manner similar to that illustrated above, if the scores are assigned to the individual papers according to the directions outlined above.

A similar method of calculation is employed in discovering the limits within which the middle fifty per cent of the cases fall. It often seems fairer to ask, after the upper twenty-five per cent of the children who would probably do successful work even without very adequate teaching have been eliminated, and the lower twenty-five per cent who are possibly so lacking in capacity that teaching may not be thought to affect them very largely have been left out of consideration, what is the achievement of the middle fifty per cent. To measure this achievement it is necessary to have the whole distribution and to count off twenty-five per cent, counting in from the upper end, and then twenty-five per cent, counting in from the lower end of the distribution. The points found can then be used in a statement in which the limits within which the middle fifty per cent of the cases fall. Using the same figures that are given above for scores in English composition, the lower limit is 2.64 and the limit which marks the point above which the upper twenty-five per cent of the cases are to be found is 5.08. The limits, therefore, within which the middle fifty per cent of the cases fall are from 2.64 to 5.08.

It is desirable to measure the relationship existing between the achievements (or other traits) of groups. In order to express such relationship in a single figure the coefficient or correlation is used. This measure appears frequently in the literature of education and will be briefly explained. The formula for finding the coefficient of correlation can be understood from examples of its application.

Let us suppose a group of seven individuals whose scores in terms of problems solved correctly and of words spelled correctly are as follows:[33]

Individuals Measured	No. of Problems	No. of Words Spelled Correctly
A	1	2
B	2	4
C	3	6
D	4	8
E	5	10
F	6	12
G	7	14

From such distributions it would appear that as individuals increase in achievement in one field they increase correspondingly in the other. If one is below or above the average in achievement in one field, he is below or above and in the same degree in the other field. This sort of positive relationship (going together) is expressed by a coefficient of +1. The formula is expressed as follows:

---

33. In order to discover the relationship which exists between two traits which we have measured we would use many more than seven cases. The illustrations given are made short in order to make it easy to follow through the application of the formula.

$$r = \frac{(\Sigma x \cdot y)\, r}{(\text{sqrt}(\Sigma x \char94 2))(\text{sqrt}(\Sigma y \char94 2))}$$

Here r = coefficient of correlation.

x = deviations from average score in arithmetic (or difference between score made and average score).

y = deviations from average score in spelling.

Σ = is the sign commonly used to indicate the algebraic sum (*i.e.* the difference between the sum of the minus quantities and the plus quantities).

$x \cdot y$ = products of deviation in one trait multiplied by deviation in the other trait with appropriate sign.

Applying the formula we find:

x	x^2	Spelling	y	y^2	x·y

A	1	-3	9	2	-6	36	+18
B	2	-2	4	4	-4	16	+8
C	3	-1	1	6	-2	4	+2
D	4	0	0	8	0		
E	5	+1	1	10	+2	4	+2
F	6	+2	4	12	+4	16	+8
G	7	+3	9	14	+6	36	+18
		—	—		—	—	—
	7	28	$\Sigma x^2 = 28$	7	56	$\Sigma y^2 = 112$	$\Sigma x \cdot y = +56$

Av. $=4$ Av. $=8$

$$r = \frac{\Sigma x \cdot y}{\left(\text{sqrt}\left(\Sigma x \char`\^ 2\right)\right)\left(\text{sqrt}\left(\Sigma y \char`\^ 2\right)\right)} = \frac{+56}{\left(\text{sqrt}\left(28\right)\right)\left(\text{sqrt}\left(112\right)\right)} = \frac{+56}{56} = +1$$

If instead of achievement in one field being positively related (going together) in the highest possible degree, these individuals show the opposite type of relationship, *i.e.*, the maximum negative relationship (this might be expressed as opposition--a place above the average in one achievement going with a correspondingly great deviation below the average in the other achievement), then our coefficient becomes -1. Applying the formula:

	Arithmetic	x	x^2	Spelling	y	y^2	$x \cdot y$
A	1	-3	9	14	+6	36	-18
B	2	-2	4	12	+4	16	-8
C	3	-1	2	10	+2	4	-2
D	4	0		8	0		
E	5	+1	2	6	-2	4	-2
F	6	+2	4	4	-4	16	-8
G	7	+3	9	2	-6	36	-18
	7	28		$\Sigma x^2 = 28$	7	56	$\Sigma y^2 = 112$ $\Sigma x \cdot y = -56$
	Av. $= 4$			Av. $= 8$			

It will be observed that in this case each plus deviation in one achievement is accompanied by a minus deviation for the other trait; hence, all of the products of x and y are minus quantities. (A plus quantity multiplied by a plus quantity or a minus quantity multiplied by a minus quantity gives us a plus quantity as the product, while a plus quantity multiplied by a minus quantity gives us a minus quantity as the product.)

$$r = \frac{\Sigma x \cdot y}{\left(\sqrt{\Sigma x^2}\right)\left(\sqrt{\Sigma y^2}\right)} = \frac{-56}{\left(\sqrt{28}\right)\left(\sqrt{112}\right)} = \frac{+56}{56} = -1$$

If there is no relationship indicated by the measures of achievements which we have found, then the coefficient of correlation becomes 0. A distribution of scores which suggests no relationship is as follows:

	Arithmetic	x	x^2	Spelling	y	y^2	x.y + -
A	2	-2	4	12	+4	16	-8 +6
B	1	-3	9	8	0		0 +4
C	4	0		2	-6	36	0 +4
D	5	+1	1	14	+6	36	-6
E	3	-1	1	4	-4	16	-14 +14
F	7	+3	9	6	-2	4	
G	6	+2	4	10	+2	4	
	28		Σx^2=28		7	56	Σy^2=112 x·y=0
	AV.=4			AV.=8			

Arithmetic	x	x^2	Spelling	y	y^2	
A	1	-3	9	4	-4	16	+ 12
B	2	-2	4	2	-6	36	+12
C	3	-1	1	8	0		+4
D	4	0		6	-2	4	+4
E	5	+1	1	12	+4	16	+18
F	6	+2	4	10	+2	4	Sx·y=50
G	7	+3	9	14	+6	36	
Av. =4		$\Sigma x^2 = 28$	Av. = 8		$\Sigma y^2 = 112$	

In a similar manner, when the relationship is large-ly positive as would be indicated by a displacement of each score in the series by one step from the arrange-ment which gives a +1 coefficient, the coefficient will approach unity in value.

$$r = \frac{\Sigma x \cdot y}{\left(\text{sqrt}\left(\Sigma x ^ 2\right)\right)\left(\text{sqrt}\left(\Sigma y ^ 2\right)\right)} = \frac{+50}{56} = +.89$$

Other illustrations might be given to show how the coefficient varies from + 1, the measure of the highest positive relationship (going together) through 0 to -1, the measure of the largest negative relationship (oppo-sition). A relationship between traits which we measure as high as +.50 is to be thought of as quite significant. It is seldom that we get a positive relationship as large as +.50 when we correlate the achievements of children in school work. A relationship measured by a coefficient of ±.15 may *not* be considered to indicate any consider-able positive or negative relationship. The fact that rela-tionships among the achievements of children in school subjects vary from +.20 to +.60 is a clear indication of the fact that abilities of children are variable, or, in other words, achievement in one subject does not carry with it an *exactly corresponding* great or little achievement in another subject. That there is some positive relation-ship, *i.e.,* that able pupils tend on the whole to show all-round ability and the less able or weak in one sub-ject *tend* to show similar lack of strength in other sub-jects, is also indicated by these positive coefficients.

QUESTIONS

1. Calculate the median point in the following distribution of eighth-grade composition scores on the Hillegas scale.

Quality	0	18	26	37	47	58	67
Frequency			2	68	73	3	

2. Calculate the median point in the following distribution of third-grade scores on the Woody subtraction scale.

No. problems	Frequency
0	
1	
2	2
3	2
4	2
5	
6	3
7	3
8	5
9	4
10	5
11	8
12	16
13	16
14	16
15	23
16	20

No. problems	Frequency
17	21
18	11
19	22
20	11
21	2
22	1
23	
24	
+	

3. Compare statistically the achievements of the children in two eighth-grade classes whose scores on the Courtis addition tests were as follows:

Class A--6 , 5, 8, 9, 7, 10, 13, 4, 8, 7, 8, 7, 6, 8, 15, 6, 7, 0, 6, 9, 5, 8, 7, 10, 8, 4, 7, 8, 6, 9, 5, 7, 2, 6, 8, 5, 7, 8, 7, 8, 5, 8, 10, 6, 3, 6, 8, 17, 5, 7.

Class B--10, 4, 8, 13, 11, 9, 8, 10, 7, 9, 11, 10, 18, 7, 12, 9, 10, 8, 11, 10, 12, 9, 2, 11, 8, 10, 9, 14, 11, 7, 10, 12, 10, 6, 11, 8, 10, 9, 10, 17, 8, 11, 9, 7, 9, 11, 8, 12, 9, 13.

4. If the marks received in algebra and in geometry by a group of high school pupils were as given below, what relationship is indicated by the coefficient of correlation?

	Geometry Marks	Algebra Marks
1.	80	60
2.	68	73
3.	65	80

	Geometry Marks	Algebra Marks
4.	96	80
5.	59	62
6.	75	65
7.	90	75
8.	86	90
9.	52	63
10.	70	55
11.	63	54
12.	85	95
13.	93	90
14.	87	70
15.	82	68
16.	79	75
17.	78	86
18.	79	75
19.	82	60
20.	70	82
21.	52	86
22.	94	85
23.	72	73
24.	53	62
25.	94	85

5. Compare the abilities of the 10-year-old pupils in the sixth grade with the abilities of the 14-year-old pupils in the same grade, in so far as these abilities are measured by the completion of incomplete sentences.

(Note: 5 = 5.0-5.999.)

No. Sentences Completed	10-Year-Olds	14-Year-Olds
24	--	--
23	--	--
22	--	--
21	1	--
20	--	--
19	--	--
18	--	--
17	--	1
16	3	--
15	--	2
14	7	4
13	10	3
12	18	7
11	9	10
10	7	9
9	8	10
8	2	10
7	3	10
6	--	2
5	2	3
4	--	2
3	--	--
2	--	1
1	--	--
0	--	--

6.   From the scores given here, calculate the relationship between ability to spell and ability to multiply. Use the average as the central tendency.

Pupil	Spelling	Multiplication
A	9	22
B	10	16
C	2	19
D	6	14
E	13	24
F	8	22
G	10	17
H	7	20
I	3	21
J	2	21
K	14	20
L	8	18
M	7	23
N	11	25
O	8	25
P	17	24
Q	10	21
R	4	16
S	9	15
T	6	19
U	12	22
V	14	19
W	8	17
X	3	20
Y	11	18